Unmasking Academia

Unmasking Academia

Institutional
Inequities
Laid Bare
During
COVID-19

Edited by
Irene Shankar and
Corinne L. Mason

UNIVERSITY of ALBERTA PRESS

Published by

University of Alberta Press
1-16 Rutherford Library South
11204 89 Avenue NW
Edmonton, Alberta, Canada T6G 2J4
amiskwaciwâskahikan | Treaty 6 | Métis Territory
ualbertapress.ca | uapress@ualberta.ca

Copyright © 2025 University of Alberta Press

LIBRARY AND ARCHIVES CANADA
CATALOGUING IN PUBLICATION

Title: Unmasking academia : institutional inequities laid bare during COVID-19 / edited by Irene Shankar and Corinne L. Mason.
Names: Shankar, Irene, editor. | Mason, Corinne L., editor
Description: Includes bibliographical references and index.
Identifiers: Canadiana (print) 20250161214 | Canadiana (ebook) 20250161222 | ISBN 9781772128307 (softcover) | ISBN 9781772128505 (PDF) | ISBN 9781772128499 (EPUB)
Subjects: LCSH: Minorities in higher education. | LCSH: Discrimination in higher education. | LCSH: Racism in higher education. | LCSH: Diversity in the workplace. | LCSH: Education, Higher—Social aspects. | LCSH: COVID-19 Pandemic, 2020-2023—Social aspects.
Classification: LCC LC212.4 .U56 2025 | DDC 378.008—dc23

First edition, first printing, 2025.
First printed and bound in Canada by Houghton Boston Printers, Saskatoon, Saskatchewan.
Copyediting by Rachel Taylor.
Proofreading by Meaghan Craven.

All rights reserved. No part of this publication may be reproduced, stored in a retrieval system, or transmitted in any form or by any means (electronic, mechanical, photocopying, recording, generative artificial intelligence [AI] training, or otherwise) without prior written consent. Contact University of Alberta Press for further details.

University of Alberta Press supports copyright. Copyright fuels creativity, encourages diverse voices, promotes free speech, and creates a vibrant culture. Thank you for buying an authorized edition of this book and for complying with the copyright laws by not reproducing, scanning, or distributing any part of it in any form without permission. You are supporting writers and allowing University of Alberta Press to continue to publish books for every reader.

GPSR: Easy Access System Europe | Mustamäe tee 50, 10621 Tallinn, Estonia | gpsr.requests@easproject.com

This book has been published with the help of a grant from the Federation for the Humanities and Social Sciences, through the Awards to Scholarly Publications Program, using funds provided by the Social Sciences and Humanities Research Council of Canada.

University of Alberta Press gratefully acknowledges the support received for its publishing program from the Government of Canada, the Canada Council for the Arts, and the Government of Alberta through the Alberta Media Fund.

Contents

Introduction 1
CORINNE L. MASON and IRENE SHANKAR

I **Space Invaders**

1 / **Critical Reflections on Workload and Labour** 29
Navigating Graduate School as a Racialized Muslim Mother During the COVID-19 Pandemic
AYESHA MIAN AKRAM

2 / **Struggles of International Graduate Students During the COVID-19 Pandemic** 49
The Spectre of Equity, Diversity, and Inclusion Policies at a University
SEPIDEH BORZOO, ISABEL FANDINO, and PALLAVI BANERJEE

3 / **"We Missed Out on a Lot"** 71
The Pandemic, Schooling, and Black Youth
CARL E. JAMES

II **Communities of Care**

4 / **"Nobody's Gonna Talk to You About That"** 93
Methodological Considerations in Research with Undocumented Caribbean Care Workers During COVID-19
CARIETA THOMAS

5 / Community-Engaged Research with Refugee Communities During COVID-19 119
FAWZIAH RABIAH-MOHAMMED and LEAH K. HAMILTON

6 / Institutionalized Feminist Loneliness 133
An Exchange on Pandemic Disruptions to Research
CORINNE L. MASON and IRENE SHANKAR

7 / "Dissident Friendships" During COVID Times 161
ETHEL TUNGOHAN

III A Future Otherwise

8 / Resisting Racism Through a Pedagogy of Blackfoot Resilience 185
GABRIELLE ELLEN WEASEL HEAD

9 / Abolishing Grades 205
"Ungrading" to Foster Freedom, Creativity, and Autonomy in the Pandemic Classroom
HEE-JUNG S. JOO, ERIN KEATING, and NARDOS OMER

Exposed and Exacerbated 229
The Social and Institutional Conditions Underlying the Years of the Pandemic
ENAKSHI DUA

Contributors 255

Introduction

CORINNE L. MASON
and IRENE SHANKAR

The COVID-19 Context

In March 2020, with infection cases surging nationwide, public health policies were introduced across Canada to curb the spread of COVID-19. The novel coronavirus, which causes the disease COVID-19, began to spread in Wuhan, China, in January 2020 through air droplets and physical contact. Symptoms including fever, cough, and runny nose characterize the original variant of the virus, which made it difficult to differentiate from the common cold or influenza. According to the Johns Hopkins Coronavirus Resource Center, three months after it first emerged in China, there were almost 500,000 cases worldwide and 17,000 people died (Johns Hopkins University of Medicine, 2020). At the peak of the crisis in Italy, almost 800 people died from COVID-19 complications, including pneumonia, in a single day (Axelrod, 2020). In Australia, beachgoers were removed from the iconic Bondi Beach in Sydney after they ignored calls to social distance—to hold two metres of space between two people who were not living in the same household ("Coronavirus: Australian beach," 2020). In the United Kingdom, a lockdown was issued when it became clear that the slow response to the crisis meant the hospitals would be overloaded with patients requiring oxygen support and ventilators (Morales et al., 2020). India introduced a twenty-one-day lockdown for 1.3 billion people ("Coronavirus: India," 2020). In what is colonially known as Canada, provincial governments began to shut the doors of non-essential services, closed schools and daycares, and sent some employees home to work remotely (Rutty, 2022). As stay-at-home orders were enacted, Canadian universities largely closed their doors to faculty and students (Laucius, 2020).

Despite early claims of the COVID-19 pandemic being a "great equalizer," the pandemic further entrenched existing inequities within the post-secondary education sector (Górska et al., 2021; Oleschuk, 2020). University administrators sent emails across campuses expressing the now ubiquitous slogan "we are all in this together" and professed concerns about the impact of the pandemic on the campus community. However, institutional expectations to teach, research, and serve the university remained intact. The pressures associated with the ticking clock of tenure and thresholds for promotion were largely untouched, and for graduate students, the job market became even more competitive as universities cut budgets and froze their hiring plans (Friga, 2020). Early findings on academic research demonstrate a COVID-19 gender gap: women's publications and research have deteriorated while men have increased their publications (Bohanon, 2020; Davis et al., 2022; Flaherty, 2020). The gap is facilitated by the patriarchal family structure that downloads housework and child care onto women. The gendered household work was compounded by an additional mental workload, whereby women were expected to tend to their children's online schooling in addition to their own work as faculty members (Pettigrew, 2021). Of course, the feminization of domestic labour was a preexisting barrier to productivity and career advancement for women in the academy, and it was further exacerbated by the pandemic.

As early analyses of the pandemic's effects on women in the academy began to roll out, we wondered what an intersectional analysis might reveal about the impacts on Black, Indigenous, racially minoritized, 2SLGBTQIA+, disabled, neurodivergent, and/or precariously employed faculty and students. Partially, our curiosity was motivated by the lack of representation of our own experiences in these early studies. Irene, a racially minoritized tenured professor, similarly to many others all over the world, found herself immensely anxious about her elderly immuno-compromised parents residing in a different city and her heightened child-care and homeschooling responsibilities. At the same time, she felt an impetus to respond publicly to the racialized discourse of COVID-19 being propagated by the provincial government. For instance, Alberta's premier at that time, Jason Kenney, blamed communities in northeast Calgary, communities that have a higher proportion of racially minoritized and/or low-income residents, for spreading the virus through their lack of adherence to health protocols (Hamilton et al., 2020). In addition, Irene felt despondent that the growing escalation of racism during the pandemic—especially against Asian Canadians—resulted in scant public concern from governing bodies (Newbold et al., 2022). While academic journals were readily discussing the decreased publication by women, there was almost no attention paid to the fear and panic that many racially minoritized people were feeling due to the escalation of racist violence and racial scapegoating by those in power.

    Corinne, a white settler and non-binary tenured professor, also experienced the juggling of child care with ongoing work expectations and was seeing first-hand the specific impacts on 2SLGBTQIA+ communities. From increased mental-health distress and isolation (Egale and Innovative Research Group, 2020), to being stuck at home with unsafe and non-affirming family members (Trevor Project, 2020), "non-essential" gender-affirming surgeries being cancelled or deferred ("COVID-19 Delaying," 2021; Somos, 2021), and misgendering and deadnaming experienced by trans and gender non-conforming people at large-scale vaccination sites (Azucar et al., 2022; Bergen, 2021), 2SLGBTQIA+ communities were experiencing specific, and largely ignored, outcomes of COVID-19 and subsequent public mitigation efforts. At the same time, queer- and disability-justice responses to the social and economic impacts of the pandemic on 2SLGBTQIA+ were bubbling up across Turtle Island. Mutual aid, in particular, was harnessed as a means to ensure communities had what they needed to survive and as a way to chart new pathways to collective resistance (Spade, 2022). Corinne was both concerned about how 2SLGBTQIA+ faculty and students were navigating the pandemic and curious about the queer navigation techniques that may be happening in the community to ensure vulnerable people received care.

    Accordingly, as part of our ongoing feminist collaboration (and friendship), we began this project as a means to better understand the intersectional impacts of white supremacy, colonialism, xenophobia, homo- and transphobia, sexism and misogyny, classism, ableism, and saneism on marginalized faculty and students. In our earliest exploration, we found that long-standing issues facing marginalized faculty and students in university contexts were compounded by the COVID-19 pandemic. For example, international students faced new and more intensive pressures when universities closed their doors and pivoted to online learning. When universities closed their residence buildings on campus in Spring 2020, many international students could not return to their home countries due to the overwhelming travel cost or because of border restrictions. Often dependent on on-campus employment and other resources to meet essential needs, international students were made particularly vulnerable by policies that restricted access to campuses (Coulton, 2022; Varughese & Schwartz, 2022). During the pandemic, the Canadian Federation of Students (n.d.) called on provincial governments to extend Medicare to all international students upon arrival in Canada. Despite the ongoing COVID-19 pandemic, many international students found themselves uncovered by provincial health plans and could not afford private health coverage. Furthermore, international students faced a myriad of barriers to returning to campus when access was granted, including backlogs in visa and passport processing, lack of access to vaccinations in countries of origin before travelling to Canada, quarantine restrictions, and limited availability of flights ("International Students," 2021). As Sepideh Borzoo, Isabel Fandino, and Pallavi Banerjee demonstrate in this collection, equity, diversity, and inclusion (EDI) policies—which claim to support the most marginalized on campuses—did not adequately extend to international graduate students during the pandemic. While some of these challenges for international students were new, such as pandemic-imposed travel restrictions, many of the barriers to resources and support faced by international students did not emerge in the pandemic context. Instead, ongoing inequities within universities were revealed when it became clear how much universities were unwilling to support the most marginalized members of the campus community.

In the so-called post-pandemic context, a few collections on the impact of COVID-19 on higher education have been published. In the collection *Research and Teaching in a Pandemic World: The Challenges of Establishing Academic Identities During Times of Crisis*, edited by de Caux, Pretorius, and Macaulay (2020), the emotional and affective stories of faculty and student experiences during the pandemic are told as a mechanism for understanding and catharsis. Focusing on the identity of academics, the authors in the collection centre "the stories we tell about ourselves about who we are, who we are not, and who we would like to or should be in academia" (p. 7). For the authors in *Unmasking Academia*, not only did scholars' relationships to their research and teaching change, but the pandemic transformed their relationships with peers and colleagues. For the editors, our identities as scholars and academics shifted during the pandemic, especially through the pivot to online teaching and research, which augmented reality as the boundaries between work life and home life became more blurry.

In *Navigating Academia During COVID-19: Perspectives and Strategies from BIPOC Women*, edited by Njoku and Evans (2023), the voices and experiences of scholars, administrators, and students are highlighted to illustrate the resiliency and navigation tactics employed by BIPOC women to deal with the compounding effects of the pandemic at the intersection of "invisible burdens, discrimination, political turmoil, social unrest" (p. vi). *Navigating Academia* reveals how feminized and racially minoritized labour was invisibilized while simultaneously allowing for institutions—like K–12 schools and higher education—to continue to function. The experiences of marginalized faculty members during the pandemic are grounded in ongoing inequities within the academy, and they shine a light on how racially minoritized women were burdened by intensifying care work at home with care-taking the institution. More than a failure to address the lived realities of marginalized faculty and students during this crisis, our collection contends that universities failed to live up to their EDI commitments.

Equity, Diversity, and Inclusion During the Pandemic

Part of this project's commitment to unmasking academia is reckoning with the inadequacies of university commitments to EDI. During COVID-19, EDI labour for faculty and students intensified. Those who experience inequities and exclusions at the university—especially racialized, Indigenous, 2SLGBTQIA+, disabled, or neurodiverse faculty, staff, and students—faced intensification of EDI-based workloads while they simultaneously navigated compounding inequitable outcomes of coronavirus transmissions and public mitigation efforts. As demonstrated by authors in this collection, the COVID-19 pandemic (further) revealed the ineffectiveness of university EDI mandates and policies. The chapters illustrate how underserved, excluded, and/or ignored students and faculty were tasked with enacting EDI measures through labouring on committees and task forces, writing policies, and organizing events for their institutions. Using the COVID-19 pandemic as a case study, chapters in this collection demonstrate the inadequate frameworks of EDI policies and mandates at post-secondary institutions (PSIs), and their over-reliance on marginalized faculty and students to bring EDI measures to fruition, often within the context of under-resourced and understaffed EDI offices (Coen-Sanchez, 2023; Dhamoon, 2020; Dua & Bhanji, 2017a; Dua & Bhanji, 2017b). Against the backdrop of a crisis, such as a pandemic, the stakes of the EDI project in the academy are revealed, as are realities for those seeking equity and institutional transformation on the ground.

In many ways, this collection is in conversation with scholarship in what is sometimes called critical university studies (Williams, 2012). With a critical and interdisciplinary focus on how systems of colonization, white supremacy, misogyny, homo- and transphobia, classism, ableism, and sizeism structure the foundation and form of the university, critical studies of higher education focus on the contemporary outcomes of long and insidious histories of injustice. For us as editors, this book reflects our engagement with a rich literature of scholarship from Black people, Indigenous people, people of colour, women, queer people, and crip scholars investigating the systems of power that operate within the academy. Following Ahmed's (2017) call to make visible a genealogy of ideas, our work as editors here is informed by the feminist, critical race, decolonial, and queer scholarship of Chandra T. Mohanty, Patricia Hill Collins, Eve Tuck, Joyce Green, Angela Davis, Audre Lorde, bell hooks, Patricia Monture, Robert McRuer, Malinda Smith, Nirmal Puwar, Sherene Razack, Sunera Thobani, Rinaldo Walcott, and Sara Ahmed. For us both, the conferences and publishing by the Researchers and Academics of Colour for Equity (RACE) network in Canada were central to our earliest engagements with the critical studies of the university, and it was in these spaces where we learned to make sense of and articulate our experiences of being—what Irene later would come to think of as "the others within."[1] In fact, it was at Irene's 2017 symposium "Others Within: Racialized, Gendered, and Queer Bodies in Academic Spaces" held at Mount Royal University in Calgary, Alberta, that our friendship and eventual research collaboration emerged.

Canadian PSIs have made commitments to some form of equity, diversity, and inclusion since the 1980s, but the proliferation of EDI mandates, offices, and policies is more recent (Henry et al., 2017). Many of the PSI EDI mandates were developed to abide by federal policies such as the Tri-Agency EDI Action Plan for all universities receiving funding through the Canada Research Chairs Program, the Universities Canada Inclusive Excellence Principles, and through the Government of Canada's Dimensions (al Shaibah, 2014; Tamtik & Gueneter, 2019). Despite the resulting EDI mandates, a study by the Academic Women's Association (2019) at the University of Alberta found that PSI equity work has largely diversified whiteness, meaning that the representation of racially diverse faculty remains incredibly low. And yet, the labour expectations for marginalized scholars have skyrocketed (CAUT, 2018; Henry et al., 2017; Misra et al., 2021).

For Thobani (2021), EDI mandates and policies within the university should not be understood as transformational projects, rather they are tools to contain and control more radical, decolonial, and insurgent knowledge and activism on campuses. Relying on Ferguson's (2012) study of the contemporary university, Thobani maintains that radical and transformative movements, ideas, and those who embody difference, are caught in the "configurations of power" in the university where difference is "prefigured by courtship, invitation, and acknowledgement" by the university (2021, p. 4). In other words, differences based on race, gender, sexuality, class, disability, citizenship, and size are courted, invited, and (at times) acknowledged in the university. However, the recognition of differences within institutions is not in service of upending the ongoing operations of power or addressing injustice, instead, it serves to legitimize the institutional status quo.

Similarly, Patel and Nath (2022) explain that whiteness is the principle organizing logic of universities, including EDI work. Calling the university a "deep site of colonization," Nath states that our work in this context "can be confusing because institutions pretend not to be what they are" (Patel & Nath, p. 159). Asking what urgency drives universities' reconciliation mandates—and slows down practices of decolonization—she asks who feels the urgency *now* to reconcile, to what end, and at whose expense? Similarly, in this collection, many authors reflect on the manufactured urgencies within the crisis of the pandemic (Mason, 2017)—to pivot, to keep going, to react, to respond, to return to normal.

About the ramping up of EDI during the pandemic, specifically, we ask: Who felt this urgency most acutely? To what end? And, at whose expense?

The COVID-19 pandemic provides an interesting case study to better understand how the "equity/diversity/inclusion machinery" (Thobani, 2022), functions to obscure these everyday realities of injustices on campus. The chasm between the institutional rhetoric of EDI and the structural realities of academia was made especially clear following the critical and demanding work of Black Lives Matter activism, which resurged in the summer of 2020 (contemporaneous with the first year of the COVID-19 pandemic) following the murders of Black and Indigenous people by police, including Breonna Taylor and George Floyd in the United States and Regis Korchinski-Paquet in Canada (Diverlus et al., 2020). Faculty, staff, and students called for a "racial reckoning" of the university—specifically, for institutions of higher learning to address anti-Black racism and white supremacy.

According to Smith (2021), in the wake of Black Lives Matter organizing, university leaders embarked on "listening and learning" sessions with Black students, faculty, and staff, but, "in many instances, these initiatives are short-term and one-offs." Calling attention to under-resourced EDI advisors and EDI offices with limited power, Smith warned about the expected fading spotlight on racial injustice brought to the fore within universities in response to the activism of students and faculty. Meaningful responses, such as adopting the Scarborough Charter, were executed by some institutions, but many universities struck committees and task forces, the labour of which fell largely on racially minoritized women (Fossett, 2021; Simien & Wallace, 2022). As Ayesha Mian Akram writes in chapter 1 of this collection, the work of organizing, leading, and facilitating discussions about anti-racism fell on racially minoritized faculty and students, further exacerbating their excessive invisible workload of emotional, mental, and relational labour (Dhamoon, 2021; Melaku & Beeman, 2022). In this collection, Ethel Tungohan also demonstrates how the same demographic populations who were experiencing the harshest effects of COVID-19 were also tasked with managing simultaneous and increasing demands to serve on EDI committees in response to calls for racial justice at universities.

In the summer of 2021, the Tk'emlúps te Secwépemc First Nation announced the presence of approximately 200 unmarked burial sites of children who died at the Kamloops Indian Residential School (Dickson & Watson, 2021; Petruk, 2021). According to the organization Indigenous Watchdog (2023), 2,444 unmarked graves across colonial Canada have been confirmed. While statements of solidarity and collective grief were issued by university communications teams, these performative statements did not promise resources or concrete actions needed to transform campuses (Blell et al., 2023; Davis et al., 2022). As demonstrated by the mass exodus and public resignations of Indigenous faculty over the failures of universities to decolonize, Indigenize, and address anti-Indigenous racism (Warick, 2020), the university remains a hostile location for Indigenous faculty and students. In "Decolonizing Equity Praxis," Pete (2022, p. 47) reflects on the extensive (and often undocumented and invisible) expectations of Indigenous faculty to transform the university. Pete writes, "We are hired to be change agents, and our numbers are usually small, so we carry the unfair burden of responsibility to fulfill the needs of settlers" (p. 51). Questioning the relevance of EDI to the political project of decolonization—"What does the equitable distribution of stolen land look like?" (p. 47)—Pete reminds us that decolonization is not meant to be "swappable for other things we want to do" (Tuck & Yang, 2012, p. 3). As explored by Gabrielle Ellen Weasel Head in chapter 8 of this collection, Indigenous faculty and students experienced intensified hostilities and labour expectations during the COVID-19 pandemic and insufficient institutional support. Amid overwhelming and complex grief, faculty members like Weasel Head were simultaneously tasked by the university to push forward EDI and "wreckonciliation" agendas (Green, 2020), while experiencing unmitigated harassment and bullying by colleagues. Her experience, as outlined in this collection, is a stark and necessary reminder that EDI cannot mitigate colonial violence.

Publishing "Post" Pandemic

When curating this edited collection, we asked authors to respond to the following questions: "What impact has the pandemic had on scholars located within the intersections of race, Indigeneity, class, gender identity and expression, sexuality, immigration status, disability, and neurodiversity?"; "How do institutions' initial calls to 'pivot'—and more recently, to 'return to normal'—reflect and/or further entrench ongoing inequities in academia?"; "How are scholars who embody 'otherness' tasked with transforming their institutions through new or intensified EDI mandates while multiple and ongoing crises rage?"; "What is the impact of institutional cultures that demand the continued labour faculty and students constructed as 'others' during a global pandemic despite the deep and disproportionate impact of COVID-19, and the subsequent health measures, on historically and currently underrepresented communities?"

Grounded by anti-racist, feminist, and queer praxis, this collection exposes the reality of structural injustice laid bare by COVID-19. Employing autoethnography and feminist reflexivity, the authors in this collection represent marginalized and historically underrepresented faculty and students' experiences of teaching, research, publishing (or not), and service obligations during the COVID-19 pandemic. Specifically, in the context of faculty navigating multiple crises—including ongoing white supremacy and colonialism—this collection examines the experiences of Black, Indigenous, racially minoritized, 2SLGBTQIA+, disabled, neurodivergent and/or precariously employed faculty, and undergraduate and graduate students in what is colonially known as Canada. As the authors in this collection consider this global crisis as a moment of reckoning for academia, this collection offers insights into both the challenges of the pandemic and the survival mechanisms, navigation tactics, and resistances employed by faculty and students. Some of the scholars we approached to contribute to this collection were overextended and extremely fatigued by the demands of the multiple and simultaneous crises we describe here, and as such, were unable to submit their work to this collection. Our own "pressing on" with publishing this collection without their insights, in turn, facilitates the perpetual invisibility and erasure of certain experiences. As we move this collection out of our offices and into the world of publishing, we remain accountable for our complicity in the systems we critique. In other words, the voices that are missing from this collection are the ones that would further reveal system and structural injustices and are also the voices that should be at the forefront of any call for institutional transformation. We, like many others, have been encouraged to move on from the pandemic context—as if it is over and as if it has not radically shaped our experiences of the world and our place in it—and we returned to an academic culture where imperatives to "publish or perish" are considered normal and neutral. Such cultures, necessarily, leave people behind.

Returning to normal, including returning to the "normal" timelines of academic publishing, has further exacerbated inequities in the academy where those who are most impacted by coronavirus—including those who are now suffering from long COVID (O'Mahoney et al., 2022) and those who continue to be most at risk of severe outcomes (CDC, 2023)—and for whom public mitigation efforts had the most negative effects ("Experiences," 2020; "Impacts," 2020; Prokopenko & Kevins, 2020). Without the time (and often without access to rituals) to mourn those who died from COVID-19, and without space to grieve social and political disruptions in our lives during the pandemic, the "return to normal" has been extremely challenging. In our own experience of returning to the university in what is imagined to be a "post-pandemic" context, we have felt the pressures to not just return but to ramp up our productivity, and to make up for lost time. We have also returned to an academy where some threats and challenges are even more formidable and present.

In the Canadian context, the rise of right-wing extremist organizations during lockdowns has created pressing challenges on our campuses and in our classrooms. As anti-hate researchers explain, there was a drastic uptick in conspiratorial theories and thinking during the COVID-19 pandemic, fuelled by misinformation about the origins of coronavirus, disinformation about vaccines, and right-wing extremists recruiting new followers who are against public-health orders like masking (Public Safety Canada, 2022). During the pandemic, more people moved into virtual spaces to connect, thereby increasing their exposure to information that facilitated online radicalization (Davey et al., 2020). The Freedom Convoy of 2022 began as a response to vaccination mandates for cross-border truckers and ultimately saw thousands of protestors descend on Parliament Hill in Ottawa in January and February, where transportation trucks blocked roadways and took over downtown neighbourhoods for three weeks (Public Order Emergency Commission, 2023). In other provinces, truckers organized blockades at border crossings aimed at shutting down trade routes between Canada and the United States ("Convoy Blockades," 2022). Loosely bound by anti-COVID sentiments, "Freedom Convoy" protests and blockades did not represent a singular group or singular event. The pandemic, and other political factors, brought people who felt disenfranchised together with right-wing extremists, including the People's Party of Canada, and white supremacist groups like Canada First and the Diagonal network, under the guise of freedom. On campuses, students and faculty reckoned with their colleagues' connections to the movement. For example, a website called Distributed Denial of Secrets published a list of donors obtained from a GoFundMe database that included twelve members of the University of Toronto community, including three professors (Shi, 2022).

In the so-called post-COVID-19 context, the "freedom" movement has mutated from anti-vaccine and anti-masking organizing into groups focusing on book bans in schools and challenging inclusive curriculum, specifically critical race theory and 2SLGBTQIA+ content. For example, movements against masking mandates for children in schools gave rise to the self-styled "parental rights movement," inspired by the anti-government extremist organization Moms for Liberty in the United States (Southern Poverty Law Center, 2022). In Canada, movements to ban 2SLGBTQIA+ books in schools overlap with violent protests against drag story hours at public libraries and culminated in the homo- and transphobic "One Million March for Children," which used slogans and rhetoric depicting 2SLGBTQIA+ people as "groomers" and pedophiles (Egale, 2023; Mason & Hamilton, 2023). In the summer of 2023, Geovanny Villalba-Aleman entered a gender studies classroom at the University of Waterloo and stabbed the course instructor and two students. This "hate-motivated" attack was inspired by "anti-gender ideology"—that posits 2SLGBTQIA+ people are both pedophiles and the cause of the decline of Western civilization (Bueckert, 2023; Butler, 2024).

Questions remain about how and whether PSI measures and EDI offices have sufficient resources and mandate to respond meaningfully to the rising hate movements on our campuses. For example, in the Alberta context, the United Conservative Party introduced an academic freedom "report card" for publicly funded post-secondary institutions aimed at "strengthening free speech on campus" (Aldrich, 2023). Advanced Education Minister Demetrios Nicolaides announced that this new report card would be part of the province's 2019 mandate to require post-secondary schools to adhere to the Chicago Principles on free expression. The Chicago Principles purportedly protect freedom of speech on campuses and yet have been used to quell collective responses to hate-motivated speech on campuses. At the same time, the United Conservative Party passed a resolution at its 2023 annual meeting to "eliminate all Diversity, Equity, and Inclusion (DEI) offices at all public universities" to ensure "they are not places for indoctrination of identity politics, reverse racism, or radicalization" (United Conservatives, 2023).[2]

As critical as we, the editors and some of the authors herein, may be of EDI mandates in the post-secondary landscape, this resolution to remove EDI offices is an affront to the (limited) progress made on campuses and is a threat to the scholars and scholarship dedicated to creating a more just academia. As we have seen play out in the United States and other global contexts, it is not just EDI offices that are under threat, but also scholars researching and teaching critical race theory and areas pertaining to social justice (Bernstein, 2023; Butler, 2021). Even with functioning EDI offices and administrators appointed to positions of anti-racism and equity at Canadian universities, students and faculty, especially Palestinian and Jewish scholars and students, have lost their jobs and/or faced backlash for taking a stand against the genocide in Gaza (Nestel & Gaudet, 2022). At York University, for example, the administration issued a warning to three student unions following their joint statement expressing support for Palestinians' fight against settler colonialism, apartheid, and genocide. Arguing that "freedom of speech" on campus was "not absolute," the administrative leaders of York demanded that the unions retract their statement, make a statement to make clear that the unions did not "support anti-Semitism," and have all executives resign from their positions. York University is not a lone actor in its response to on-campus activism against genocide in Gaza ("York University," 2023). Calls for a ceasefire have placed faculty and student leaders at risk of losing their positions and have intensified the chilly climate for Palestinian, Jewish, and other critical scholars (MacIntosh, 2023; Nestel & Gaudet, 2022; Zandbergen, 2024).

It is within this larger context that we are now publishing this collection. The nine chapters in this volume explore the impacts of university responses to COVID-19 on the authors' work and lives during the first two years of the COVID-19 pandemic (2020–22) and show how faculty and students worked on charting new and resistant practices against the ongoing pressure of universities to press on during a global pandemic. These nine chapters explore obstacles to teaching, research, service, or learning with specific attention to the author's subject position, research program, or pedagogy. Each author interrogates their experiences of the structural impacts of the COVID-19 pandemic beyond the question of career success or productivity in order to reveal inequities and injustices in the university that are compounded, made complex, and at times made more obvious, during the pandemic. Although our experiences of return to the university are not archived here, the chapters in this collection flesh out enduring conversations about belonging, care, and futurity in the university that can help us better understand and contend with these more recent and intensifying challenges.

Outline of This Book

In part I, "Space Invaders," the authors explore racially minoritized and international students' experiences of the university during the pandemic. As Ahmed (2002) articulates, universities are institutional spaces where some are more at home than "others." In other words, academia is established around the somatic norm of privileged body-minds that renders all others "space invaders" (Mohamed & Beagan, 2019; Puwar, 2004). Accordingly, authors in part I wrestle with the question of belonging and otherness, as exemplified during the pandemic. In her autoethnographic chapter "Critical Reflections on Workload and Labour: Navigating Graduate School as a Racialized Muslim Mother During the COVID-19 Pandemic," Ayesha Mian Akram reflects on her complex challenges of being a racially minoritized and visibly Muslim graduate student, instructor, and parent. Calling attention to the silencing and erasure of Muslim women in the academy and pointing to the entrenched structural racism and sexism of the institution revealed by COVID-19, Mian Akram offers both personal reflections and theoretical insights into the increasing unpaid emotional and intellectual EDI labour that university demands from racially minoritized women.

In chapter 2, "Struggles of International Graduate Students During the COVID-19 Pandemic: The Spectre of Equity, Diversity, and Inclusion (EDI) Policies at the University," Sepideh Borzoo, Isabel Fandino, and Pallavi Banerjee interrogate the inability of EDI offices to adequately support the most marginalized during the COVID-19 pandemic. Using qualitative data from fifteen interviews with international graduate students at a large research university in Alberta, Canada, the authors illustrate the limitations of EDI policies that materially exclude international students and discuss the ways in which citizenship status within the larger conceptualization of Canadian nationhood remains a structural obstacle to equity and social justice. Borzoo, Fandino, and Banerjee, like Mian Akram, call for universities to adopt more robust and radical EDI measures.

Chapter 3, Carl E. James's "'We Missed Out on a Lot': The Pandemic, Schooling, and Black Youth," explores the pandemic's effects on the educational experiences of Black K–12 students in the Greater Toronto Area. Based on qualitative data from Spring 2021, James shows how Black students experienced online schooling, and especially how their relationships with teachers and their aspirations about the future were challenged by COVID-19. Pointing to an ongoing "sorting process" that places Black students at the lowest level of the educational hierarchy, James focuses on how pandemic learning intensified the structural obstacles of anti-Black racism within educational contexts and offers insight into how prepared—or not—Black students will be for post-secondary studies. James makes clear that COVID-19 will have long-term effects on the university and should not be treated as a historical and concluded event. Instead, universities need to prepare for the ongoing impacts of learning disruption during the pandemic and to understand the realities of inequity faced by future Black students. James's chapter points readers in the direction of thinking about the future capacity of universities to support students most impacted by the pandemic. Like the other authors in part I, using the COVID-19 pandemic as a case study, James considers who the university is set up to serve and who is excluded from the frames of belonging.

The chapters that make up part II of this collection, "Communities of Care," grapple with the hurdles of maintaining relationships with collaborators, friends, and research communities during the pandemic. In *Care Work: Dreaming Disability Justice*, Peipzna-Samarasinha (2018) explains how marginalized communities build care webs instead of solely relying on institutionalized care that is precarious and often abusive, or that takes control out of the hands of those who require care. Care work is not only a means of relationality but is, for Peipzna-Samarasinha, a movement for social justice. In part II, the authors focus on how they built care webs, which sustained them during the height of the COVID-19 pandemic. Specifically, the authors explore how their research collaborations and community connections were disrupted and reimagined during the pandemic. Often in opposition to the pressure from institutions to prioritize productivity, deadlines, and outcomes, scholars in part II demonstrate how they navigated their personal, ethical, and political commitments to care by prioritizing virtual connections, friendship networks, and research collaborations as relational, rather than transactional. Scholars also reflect on how they used frameworks of care to engage with research participants who were experiencing compounded impacts of COVID-19 and public-health mitigation efforts.

In chapter 4, "'Nobody's Gonna Talk to You About That': Methodological Considerations in Research with Undocumented Caribbean Care Workers During COVID-19," Carieta Thomas outlines the challenges of working with hidden and vulnerable communities within university ethics protocols. Focusing on how the university's COVID-19 policies produced barriers to participant recruitment and enacted new forms of surveillance to mitigate institutional risk, Thomas offers recommendations for ethics boards in their approach to research on undocumented immigrants. Thomas demonstrates a social-justice framework of care in her own research with vulnerable populations in a way that resists institutionalized conditions of compounded vulnerability.

Chapter 5, Fawziah Rabiah-Mohammed and Leah K. Hamilton's "Community-Engaged Research with Refugee Communities During COVID-19: Overcoming University Inaction," continues with the theme of care in research practices. Reflecting on their research with Syrian refugees about housing precarity in the Canadian context, Rabiah-Mohammed and Hamilton describe how the failure of universities to assist community-based research negatively impacted not only their work but the communities with whom they partner. Asking critical questions about the responsibility of universities to care for the communities they rely upon for data, Rabiah-Mohammed and Hamilton explain how they worked to sustain relationships with community partners. Like Thomas, they offer a series of recommendations for universities to better support community-engaged research through a caring approach.

In our own chapter, we explore one of the major outcomes of public-health mitigation efforts: isolation. In order to lower the risk of transmission, many of us moved toward models of living that created proximal loneliness. In other words, we found ourselves living and working away from our loved ones as a way to care for them. In "Institutionalized Feminist Loneliness: An Exchange on Pandemic Disruptions to

Research," we interrogate how academia creates the conditions for loneliness that were intensified during COVID-19. Expanding Magnet and Orr's (2021) term of "feminist loneliness," chapter 6 is a transcribed exchange in which we reflect on our friendship and collaboration, and discuss how our experiences of isolation during COVID-19 have offered us a new language to explain our desire to build care webs through our research practices. We also explore how time away from the university has provided us with a new perspective on our relationship with the institution. Like other chapters in part II, this chapter foregrounds care work in research practices, specifically research collaborations, as a framework for navigating the impacts of the COVID-19 pandemic.

Continuing the discussion on friendship and care in the academy, chapter 7, Ethel Tungohan's "'Dissident Friendships' During COVID Times," uses an intersectional ethnographic approach to interrogate the interlocking crises of COVID-19, anti-Black and anti-Asian racism, ongoing colonialism and genocide targeting Indigenous people, and Islamophobia alongside institutional failure to address the needs of racially minoritized and gendered faculty and students. Offering excerpts of articles, emails, and texts that Tungohan has written for friends experiencing similar academic and family struggles, she explores the possibilities of what Chowdhury and Philipose (2016) call "dissident friendships" to fight back against structural erasure. Calling attention to how "the university will never love you back," Tungohan explains how communities of care have helped her survive toxic cultures in academia.

Many of the authors in part II discuss the ways in which they paused or reimagined their research in the context of the pandemic because of a concern for research participants and critical self-reflections that led to deprioritizing research outcomes in favour of connection and care. In part III of this collection, "A Future Otherwise," scholars reflect on how they defied institutional expectations to simply carry on during the COVID-19 pandemic and how, in doing so, they reimagined research, teaching, and community engagement. As the chapters in part III demonstrate, faculty and students found ways to slow down, support communities most impacted, and refuse performances of resiliency to transform the harmful systems of the academy. As brown (2019) writes about social-justice organizing, employing our radical imagination is the work of "science fiction." She writes that when we collectivize, imagine, and enact strategies that foreground justice, we "are shaping the future" (p. 8). Accordingly, the authors in part III reflect on their strategies to enact the future now within the context of the institution.

In chapter 8, "Resisting Racism Through a Pedagogy of Blackfoot Resilience," Gabrielle Ellen Weasel Head writes about her compounding experiences of harm during the pandemic. Reflecting on her experiences as an Indigenous woman on campus and navigating institutional failures to address racism, Weasel Head offers a way to resist the colonial deficit model that too often informs conceptualizations of resiliency. Weasel Head shares her experiences of navigating the pandemic as a way to reflect on how stories of marginalized communities in academic contexts are too often framed through challenges, issues, and deficits. Stories of resilience, for Weasel Head, are couched in the trauma of colonization where Indigenous experiences are tied to the colonizer. This resistance to and reframing of resilience emerges for Weasel Head in the context of the pandemic in which the crises of ongoing colonization and institutionalized racism intersect with the horrific realities of an uncontained virus. Offering insights from her project "Mokakit Iyikakimaat," Weasel Head resists this Eurocentric and deficit-based understanding of resilience in favour of a future led by Blackfoot-embodied laws of truth, humility, kindness, and compassion.

In the final chapter of this collection, "Abolishing Grades: 'Ungrading' to Foster Freedom, Creativity, and Autonomy in the Pandemic Classroom," authors Hee-Jung S. Joo, Erin Keating, and Nardos Omer maintain that there is "no going back to normal." Noting how "normal" has always been harmful and never a solution to ongoing injustices, they posit ungrading as a resistant practice to colonial institutional demands for assessment and the facade of meritocracy. Suggesting that COVID-19 was a portal, the authors show how their experimentation with ungrading during online teaching and learning can be understood as a small blueprint toward the larger project of abolishing the colonial institution of the university. As Weasel Head uses the pandemic context to reflect on her aim to radically transform the frameworks within which research on marginalized communities is conducted, this chapter offers the practice of ungrading as a transformational teaching practice. Authors in part III make clear that there is no "returning to normal" and offer a way of imagining academia otherwise.

A Portal and a Mirror

Coining what is now a ubiquitous phrase, in 2020 Arundhati Roy first called the COVID-19 pandemic "a portal." Reflecting on India's experience with the initial onset of the pandemic, Roy wrote:

> Whatever it is, coronavirus has made the mighty kneel and brought the world to a halt like nothing else could. Our minds are still racing back and forth, longing for a return to "normality," trying to stitch our future to our past and refusing to acknowledge the rupture. But the rupture exists. And in the midst of this terrible despair, it offers us a chance to rethink the doomsday machine we have built for ourselves. Nothing could be worse than a return to normality.
>
> Historically, pandemics have forced humans to break with the past and imagine their world anew. This one is no different. It is a portal, a gateway between one world and the next. (section 4, final paras)

As Joo, Keating, and Omer illustrate in chapter 9, COVID-19 may be a portal, but it has also served as a mirror. In it, we have seen ongoing global and insidious injustices reflected to us. From high rates of transmission in poor and racially minoritized communities in the early days of the pandemic to the continued and utter disconcert for those most at risk of severe outcomes, and those currently suffering with the effects of long COVID, the pandemic has revealed the stark and disturbing way in which societal "normal" practices, and the race to return to them, create the conditions in which presently and historically marginalized communities are marked as disposable.

By asking who belongs in the university, insisting on and providing care work despite institutional demands to "press on," and illustrating how faculty and students are refusing to reproduce institutionalized inequities, this collection archives the impacts of the pandemic as a means to interrogate injustices of the university more broadly. From demands to "pivot" to teaching online in early 2020 to the institutional rhetoric that conceptualized the return to campus as "returning to normal," the authors in this collection reflect upon often chaotic institutional responses to the pandemic. Significantly, they reveal systemic failures to redress barriers and inequities that have been laid bare by the COVID-19 pandemic. In this way, our collection offers both a portal and a mirror with which to view the university; chapters here reflect the impact of the pandemic on those most marginalized, and they offer new and emergent pathways that resist institutional calls to return to what came before.

Notes

1. Irene started using this term to describe her positionality within academia after reading Ahmed's (2002) article "This other and other others" in *Economy and Society* 31(2) and Smith's (2010) chapter "Gender, whiteness and 'other Others' in the academy" in *States of Race: Critical Race Feminism for the 21st Century*. The term "others within" has been used extensively within feminist and critical race theoretical frameworks and it did not originate with Irene.
2. In 2025, the University of Alberta announced that it was moving away from EDI to "Access, Community and Belonging." In an Op-Ed, President Bill Flanagan explained the decision by stating that "the language of EDI has become polarizing, focusing more on what divides us rather than our shared humanity. Some perceive an ideological bias at odds with merit." Whether this move is a branding exercise or a substantive shift remains unclear.

References

Academic Women's Association. (2019). *U15 leadership remains largely white and male despite 33 years of equity initiatives.* University of Alberta. https://uofaawa.wordpress.com/2019/06/20/u15-leadership-remains-largely-white-and-male-despite-33-years-of-equity-initiatives/

al Shaibah, A. (2014). *Educational equity in Canadian academe: Implications of neoliberal discourse and ideology* [Doctoral dissertation, Queen's University]. Qspace. Retrieved from https://qspace.library.queensu.ca/items/39f72a72-a87d-420f-9949-0467db6aafaa/full

Aldrich, J. (2023, February 23). Province demands free speech "report cards" from colleges and universities after lecture cancelled. *Calgary Herald.* https://calgaryherald.com/news/alberta-requiring-universities-colleges-to-report-free-speech-efforts-after-cancellation-of-controversial-lecture

Ahmed, S. (2002). This other and other others. *Economy and Society*, 31(4), 558–572. https://doi.org/10.1080/03085140022000020689

Ahmed, S. (2017). *Living a feminist life.* Duke University Press.

Axelrod, T. (2020, March 21). Italy death toll from coronavirus again hits biggest one-day high. *The Hill.* https://thehill.com/policy/international/europe/488814-italy-death-toll-from-coronavirus-again-hit-biggest-one-day-high/

Azucar, D., Slay, L., Valerio, D.G., & Kipke, M.D. (2022). Barriers to COVID-19 vaccine uptake in the LGBTQIA community. *American Journal of Public Health*, 112(3), 405–407. https://doi.org/10.2105/AJPH.2021.306599

Bergen, R. (2021, May 13). *Vaccine consent form invalidating for non-binary and trans people, Manitoban says.* CBC News. https://www.cbc.ca/news/canada/manitoba/covid-19-vaccines-manitoba-transgender-1.6023988

Bernstein, S. (2023, February 24). Florida bill would ban gender studies majors, diversity programs at universities. *Reuters.* https://www.reuters.com/world/us/florida-bill-would-ban-gender-studies-majors-diversity-programs-universities-2023-02-25/

Blell, M., Liu, S.S., & Verma, A. (2023). Working in unprecedented times: Intersectionality and women of color in UK higher education in and beyond the pandemic. *Gender, Work & Organization, 30*(2), 353–372. https://doi.org/10.1111/gwao.12907

Bohanon, M. (2020). Colleges and universities must make marginalized students a priority during the pandemic. INSIGHT into Diversity. https://www.insightintodiversity.com/colleges-and-universities-must-make-marginalized-students-a-priority-during-the-pandemic/

brown, a.m. (2019). *Pleasure activism: The politics of feeling good.* AK Press.

Bueckert, K. (2023, July 11). *Accused in University of Waterloo triple stabbings to return to court July 25.* CBC News. https://www.cbc.ca/news/canada/kitchener-waterloo/university-waterloo-stabbing-accused-court-case-july-25-1.6903241

Butler, J. (2024). *Who's afraid of gender?* Penguin Random House Canada.

Butler, J. (2021, October 23). Why is the idea of "gender" provoking backlash the world over? *The Guardian.* https://www.theguardian.com/us-news/commentisfree/2021/oct/23/judith-butler-gender-ideology-backlash

Canadian Association of University Teachers (CAUT). (2018). *Underrepresented & underpaid: Diversity & equity among Canada's post-secondary education teachers.* https://www.caut.ca/sites/default/files/caut_equity_report_2018-04final.pdf

Canadian Federation of Students. (2022). *Students call on provincial governments to extend medicare to international students on arrival in Canada.* https://www.cfs-fcee.ca/blog/students-call-on-provincial-governments-to-extend-medicare-to-international-students-on-arrival-in-canada

Centre for Disease Control and Prevention. (2023, February 9). *Underlying medical conditions associated with higher risk for severe COVID-19: Information for healthcare professionals.* https://www.cdc.gov/coronavirus/2019-ncov/hcp/clinical-care/underlyingconditions.html

Chowdhury, E.H., & Philipose, L. (2016). *Dissident friendships: Feminism, imperialism, and transnational solidarity.* University of Illinois Press.

Convoy blockades halted almost $4B in trade, inquiry hears. (2022, November 16). CBC News. https://www.cbc.ca/news/politics/convoy-economics-1.6653986

Coronavirus: Australian beach closed after hundreds gather in defiance of "social distancing" rules. (2020, March 22). Sky News. https://news.sky.com/story/coronavirus-australian-beach-closed-after-hundreds-gather-in-defiance-of-social-distancing-rules-11961269

Coronavirus: India enters "total lockdown" after spike in cases. (2020, March 5). BBC News. https://www.bbc.com/news/world-asia-india-52024239

COVID-19 delaying life-saving transgender surgeries, doctor warns. (2021, October 9). CBC News. https://www.cbc.ca/news/canada/edmonton/covid-19-delaying-life-saving-transgender-surgeries-doctor-warns-1.6199069

Coulton, M. (2022, November 15). How the pandemic has disrupted the lives of international students in Canada. *Maclean's*. https://education.macleans.ca/feature/how-the-pandemic-has-disrupted-the-lives-of-international-students-in-canada/

Coen-Sanchez, K. (2023, January 24). How EDI policies are failing international students. *University Affairs*. https://universityaffairs.ca/career-advice/global-campus/how-edi-policies-are-failing-international-students/

Davey, J., Hart, M., & Guerin, C. (2020). *An online environmental scan of right-wing extremism in Canada: Interim report*. Institute for Strategic Dialogue. https://www.isdglobal.org/wp-content/uploads/2020/06/An-Online-Environmental-Scan-of-Right-wing-Extremism-in-Canada-ISD.pdf

Davis, J.C., Li, E.P.H., Butterfield, M.S., DiLabio, G.A., Sangunthanam, N., & Marcolin, B. (2022). Are we failing female and racialized academics? A Canadian national survey examining the impacts of the COVID-19 pandemic on tenure and tenure-track faculty. *Gender, Work & Organization*, 29(3), 703–722. https://doi.org/10.1111/gwao.12811

de Caux, B.C., Pretorius, L., & Macaulay, L., eds. (2022). *Research and teaching in a pandemic world: The challenges of establishing academic identities during times of crisis*. Springer Link.

Dhamoon, R.K. (2020). Racism as a workload and bargaining issue. *Socialist Studies*, 14(1), article 2. https://socialiststudies.com/index.php/sss/article/view/27273/20188

Dhamoon, R.K. (2021). Relational othering: Critiquing dominance, critiquing the margins. *Politics, Groups, and Identities*, 9(5), 873–892.

Dickson, C., & Watson, B. (2021, May 27). *Remains of 215 children found buried at former B.C. residential school, First Nation says*. CBC News. https://www.cbc.ca/news/canada/british-columbia/tk-emlúps-te-secwépemc-215-children-former-kamloops-indian-residential-school-1.6043778

Diverlus, R., Hudson, S., & Ware, S.M. (2020). *Until we are free: Reflections on Black Lives Matter in Canada*. University of Regina Press.

Dua, E., & Bhanji, N. (2017a). Shifting terrains: A picture of the institutionalization of equity in Canadian universities. In F. Henry, E. Dua, C.E. James, A. Kobayashi, P. Li, H. Ramos, & M.S. Smith (Eds.), *The equity myth: Racialization and indigeneity at Canadian universities* (pp. 171–205). UBC Press.

Dua, E., & Bhanji, N. (2017b). Mechanisms to address inequities in Canadian universities: The performativity of ineffectiveness. In F. Henry, E. Dua, C.E. James, A. Kobayashi, P. Li, H. Ramos, & M.S. Smith (Eds.), *The equity myth: Racialization and indigeneity at Canadian universities* (pp. 206–238). UBC Press.

Egale. (2023, December 18). *Court decision finds use of "groomer" slur against drag performers to be rhetoric based on hurtful, and hateful myths and stereotypes*. https://egale.ca/wp-content/uploads/2023/12/Egale-Canada-News-Release-Dec-18-2023.pdf

Egale and Innovative Research Group. (2020, April 6). *Impact of COVID-19: Canada's LGBTQI2S community in focus*. https://egale.ca/wp-content/uploads/2020/04/Impact-of-COVID-19-Canada's-LGBTQI2S-Community-in-Focus-2020-04-06.pdf

Experiences of discrimination during the COVID-19 pandemic. (2020, September 17). *The Daily*. Statistics Canada. https://www150.statcan.gc.ca/n1/daily-quotidien/200917/dq200917a-eng.htm

Ferguson, R.A. (2012). *The reorder of things: The university and its pedagogies of minority difference*. University of Minnesota Press.

Flaherty, C. (2020). Women are falling behind. *Inside Higher Ed*. https://www.insidehighered.com/news/2020/10/20/large-scale-study-backs-other-research-showing-relative-declines-womens-research

Flanagan, Bill. (2025, January 2). Why the U of A is moving from EDI to access, community and belonging. *Edmonton Journal*. https://edmontonjournal.com/opinion/columnists/bill-flanagan-why-the-u-of-a-is-moving-from-edi-to-access-community-and-belonging

Friga, P.N. (2020, April 20). Under COVID-19, university budgets like we've never seen before. *Chronicle of Higher Education*. https://www.chronicle.com/article/under-covid-19-university-budgets-like-weve-never-seen-before/

Fossett, K. (2021, April 9). Burnout, racism and extra diversity-related work: Black women in academia share their experiences. *Politico*. https://www.politico.com/newsletters/women-rule/2021/07/09/nikole-hannah-jones-black-women-academia-493523

Green, J. (2020, February 18). Opinion: Wreckonciliation for Wet'suwet'en. *Saskatoon StarPhoenix*. https://thestarphoenix.com/opinion/letters/opinion-wreckonciliation-for-wetsuweten

Górska, A.M., Kulicka, K., Staniszewska, Z., & Dobija, Z. (2021). Deepening inequalities: What did COVID-19 reveal about the gendered nature of academic work? *Gender, Work & Organization, 28*(4), 1546–1561. https://doi.org/10.1111/gwao.12696

Henry, F., Dua, E., James, C.E., Kobayashi, A., Li, P., Ramos, H., & Smith, M. (2017). *The equity myth: Racialization and indigeneity at Canadian universities*. UBC Press.

Hamilton, L., Shankar, I., & M. Hazzouri. (2020, December 2). NE Calgary needs elimination of structural racism, not a "wake up call." *Calgary Herald*. https://calgaryherald.com/opinion/columnists/opinion-northeast-calgary-needs-structural-racism-to-end-not-a-wake-up-call

Impacts of COVID-19 on persons with disabilities. (2020, August 27). *The Daily*. Statistics Canada. https://www150.statcan.gc.ca/n1/daily-quotidien/200827/dq200827c-eng.htm

Indigenous Watchdog. (2023). *Missing Children and Burial Information (71–76)* [Table: Residential Schools that have discovered "potential" unmarked graves]. https://www.indigenouswatchdog.org/subcategory/missing-children-and-burial-information/

International students coming to Canada navigate numerous barriers as they look to begin fall classes. (2021, June 21). CBC News. https://www.cbc.ca/news/canada/british-columbia/international-students-barriers-return-to-class-fall-2021-1.6082287

Johns Hopkins University of Medicine. (2020, March 15). *Coronavirus Resource Center*. https://coronavirus.jhu.edu/map.html

Laucius, J. (2020, March 10). Laurentian University suspends classes because of COVID-19. *Ottawa Citizen*. https://ottawacitizen.com/news/local-news/as-universities-close-in-the-u-s-their-canadian-counterparts-watch-and-wait

MacIntosh, M. (2023, November 30). U of M nursing student suspended, accused of antisemitic posts. *Winnipeg Free Press*. https://www.winnipegfreepress.com/featured/2023/11/30/u-of-m-nursing-student-suspended-accused-of-antisemitic-posts

Mason, C.L. (2017). *Manufacturing urgency: The development industry and violence against women*. University of Regina Press.

Mason, C.L., & Hamilton, L. (2023, September 30). How the "parental rights" movement gave rise to the 1 Million March 4 Children. *The Conversation*. https://theconversation.com/how-the-parental-rights-movement-gave-rise-to-the-1-million-march-4-children-213842

Magnet, S., & Orr, C.E. (2022). Feminist loneliness studies: An introduction. *Feminist Theory*, 23(1), 3–22, https://doi.org/10.1177/14647001211062734

Melaku, T.M., & Beeman, A. (2023). Navigating white academe during crisis: The impact of COVID-19 and racial violence on women of color professionals. *Gender, Work & Organization*, 30(2), 673–691. https://doi.org/10.1111/gwao.12823

Misra, J., Kuveava, A., O'Meara, K., Kiyoe Culpepper, D., & Jaeger, A. (2021). Gendered and racialized perceptions of faculty workloads. *Gender & Society*, 35(3): 358–394, https://doi.org/10.1177/08912432211001387

Mohamed, T., & Beagan, B.L. (2019). "Strange faces" in the academy: Experiences of racialized and Indigenous faculty in Canadian universities. *Race Ethnicity and Education*, 22(3), 338–354. https://doi.org/10.1080/13613324.2018.1511532

Morales, A., Ring, S., Hutton, R., & Paton, J. (2020, April 23). How the alarm went off too late in Britain's virus response. *Bloomberg*. https://www.bloomberg.com/news/features/2020-04-24/coronavirus-uk-how-boris-johnson-s-government-let-virus-get-away

Nestel, S., & Gaudet, R. (2022). Unveiling the chilly climate: The suppression of speech on Palestine in Canada. *Independent Jewish Voices*. https://www.ijvcanada.org/wp-content/uploads/2022/10/Unveiling-the-Chilly-Climate_Final-compressed.pdf

Newbold, K.B., Vrabic, K., Wayland, S., Wahoush, O., & Weerakoon, Y. (2022). "Strange eyes": Immigrant perceptions of racism during the COVID-19 pandemic. *Population, Space and Place*, 28(7), https://doi.org/10.1002/psp.2603

Njoku, A., & Evans, M., eds. (2023). *Navigating academia during COVID-19: Perspectives and strategies from BIPOC women*. Springer International. https://doi.org/10.1007/978-3-031-35613-1.

Oleschuk, M. (2020). Gender equity considerations for tenure and promotion during COVID-19. *Canadian Review of Sociology*, 57(3), 502–515.

O'Mahoney, L.L., Routen, A., Gillies, C., Ekezie, W., Welford, A., Zhang, A., Karamchandani, U., Simms-Williams, N., Cassambai, S., Ardavani, A., Wilkinson, T.J., Hawthorne, G., Curtis, F., Kingsnorth, A.P., Almaqhawi, A., Ward, T., Ayoubkhani, D., Banerjee, A., Calvert, M.... Khunti, K. (2022). The prevalence and long-term health effects of Long Covid among hospitalised and non-hospitalised populations: A systematic review and meta-analysis. *eClinicalMedicine*, 55:101762. https://doi.org/10.1016/j.eclinm.2022.101762

Patel, S., & Nath, N. (2022). What can "settler of colour" teach us? A conversation of the complexities of decolonization in white universities. In A. Gebhard, S. McLean, & V. St.

Denis (Eds), *White benevolence: Racism and colonial violence in the helping professions* (pp. 146–162). Fernwood Publishing.

Pete, S. (2022). Decolonizing equity praxis. In B. Allen & R. Hackett (Eds), *Decolonizing equity* (pp. 40–54). Fernwood Press.

Petruk, T. (2021, June 5). *Casimir says Tk'emlups find is series of unmarked graves, not a mass burial.* The Squamish Chief. https://www.squamishchief.com/bc-news/casimir-says-tkemlups-find-is-series-of-unmarked-graves-not-a-mass-burial-3848382

Pettigrew, R.N. (2021). An untenable workload: Covid-19 and the disproportionate impact on women's work-family demands. *Journal of Family & Consumer Sciences, 113*(4), 8–15. https://doi.org/10.14307/jfcs113.4.8

Piepzna-Samarasinha, L.L. (2018). *Care work: Dreaming disability justice.* Arsenal Pulp Press.

Prokopenko, E., & Kevins, C. (2020, December 15; revised 2022, September 9). Vulnerabilities related to COVID-19 among LGBTQ2+ Canadians. *StatCan COVID-19: Data to insights for a better Canada* [Catalogue no. CS45-28/1-2020-88E-PDF]. Statistics Canada. publications.gc.ca/pub?id=9.894690&sl=0

Public Order Emergency Commission. (2023). *Report of the public inquiry into the 2022 public order emergency.* https://publicorderemergencycommission.ca/final-report/

Public Safety Canada. (2022, April 29). *Parliamentary committee notes: Ideologically motivated violent extremism (IMVE) and terrorist listings.* Government of Canada. https://www.publicsafety.gc.ca/cnt/trnsprnc/brfng-mtrls/prlmntry-bndrs/20220914/21-en.aspx

Puwar, N. (2004). *Space invaders: Race, gender and bodies out of place.* Berg.

Roy, A. (2020, April 3). The pandemic is a portal. *Financial Times.* https://www.ft.com/content/10d8f5e8-74eb-11ea-95fe-fcd274e920ca

Rutty, C. (2022, March 2). COVID-19 pandemic in Canada. *Canadian Encyclopedia.* https://www.thecanadianencyclopedia.ca/en/article/covid-19-pandemic

Simien, E., & Wallace, S. (2022). Disproportionate service: Considering the impacts of George Floyd's death and the coronavirus pandemic for women academics and faculty of color. *PS: Political Science & Politics, 55*(4), 799–803. https://doi.org/10.1017/S1049096522000580

Shi, R. (2022, March 15). The freedom convoy at the University of Toronto. *The Strand, 64*(11), https://thestrand.ca/the-freedom-convoy-at-the-university-of-toronto/

Smith, M. (2021, February 25). Racial equity leadership in COVID times. *University Affairs.* https://www.universityaffairs.ca/opinion/from-the-admin-chair/racial-equity-leadership-in-covid-times/

Smith, M. (2010). Gender, whiteness and "other Others" in the academy. In S. Razack, M. Smith, & S. Thobani (Eds.), *States of race: Critical race feminism for the 21st century* (pp. 37–58). Between the Lines.

Smith, P. (2023, January 31). *What everyone still gets wrong about the freedom convoy.* Canadian Anti-Hate Network. https://www.antihate.ca/what_everyone_still_gets_wrong_about_the_freedom_convoy

Somos, C. (2021, November 30). *"It's life saving": Addressing pandemic backlog in gender-affirming surgeries crucial for trans community, expert says.* CTV News. https://www.ctvnews.ca/health/it-s-life-saving-addressing-pandemic-backlog-in-gender-affirming-surgeries-crucial-for-trans-community-expert-says-1.5687050

Southern Poverty Law Center. 2022. "The Year in Hate & Extremism." https://www.splcenter.org/resources/guides/year-hate-extremism-2022/

Spade, D. (2022). *Mutual aid: Building solidarity during this crisis (and the next)*. Penguin Random House Canada.

Tamtik, M., & Guenter, M. (2019). Policy analysis of equity, diversity and inclusion strategies in Canadian universities—How far have we come? *Canadian Journal of Higher Education, 49*(3), 41–56.

Trevor Project. (2020). *How COVID-19 is impacting LGBTQ youth: Polling presentation.* https://www.thetrevorproject.org/wp-content/uploads/2020/10/Trevor-Poll_COVID19.pdf

Thobani, S (Ed). (2021). *Coloniality and racial (in)justice in the university: Counting for nothing?* University of Toronto Press.

Tuck, E., & Yang, K.W. (2012). Decolonization is not a metaphor. *Decolonization: Indigeneity, Education & Society, 1*(1), 1–40. https://jps.library.utoronto.ca/index.php/des/article/view/18630

United Conservatives. (2023). *AGM resolutions 2023.* https://www.unitedconservative.ca/wp-content/uploads/Resolutions2023.pdf

Varughese, A., & Schwartz, S. (2022, January 24). The pandemic exposed the vulnerability of international students in Canada. *The Conversation.* https://theconversation.com/the-pandemic-exposed-the-vulnerability-of-international-students-in-canada-174105

Warick, J. (2020, August 30). *Indigenous professors cite racism, lack of reform in University of Saskatchewan exodus.* CBC News. https://www.cbc.ca/news/canada/saskatoon/indigenous-professors-cite-racism-lack-of-reform-in-university-of-saskatchewan-exodus-1.5703554

Williams, J.J. (2012, February 19). Deconstructing academe: The birth of critical university studies. *Chronicle of Higher Education.* https://www.chronicle.com/article/deconstructing-academe/

York University threatens recognition of 3 student unions following statement on Israel-Hamas war. (2023, October 21). CBC News. https://www.cbc.ca/news/canada/toronto/york-university-israel-hamas-statement-update-1.7004246

Zandbergen, R. (2024, January 20). *U of O doctor suspended for pro-Palestinian posts says he's been reinstated, won't go back.* CBC News. https://www.cbc.ca/news/canada/ottawa/u-of-o-doctor-suspended-for-pro-palestinian-posts-says-he-s-been-reinstated-won-t-go-back-1.7088887

Space Invaders

/1
Critical Reflections on Workload and Labour

Navigating Graduate School as a Racialized Muslim Mother During the COVID-19 Pandemic

AYESHA MIAN AKRAM

Introduction

Canadian critical race scholarship about the university theorizes how institutions reproduce the racial, gendered, and colonial hierarchies and inequities of society at large (Hampton, 2020; Henry et al., 2017; James, 2021; Thobani, 2021). These structural inequities marginalize Indigenous, Black, and racialized students, faculty, and staff through practices of exclusion and discrimination.[1] Academics belonging to equity-deserving groups (i.e., women and gender-diverse individuals, Indigenous peoples, Black and racialized peoples, persons with disabilities, and LGBTQ2S+ people) are often required to assume the labour of resisting and advocating for structural equity. For example, Dhamoon (2020) argues that expectations of labour and workload are compounded for academics who are Indigenous, Black, and racialized as additional demands, including expectations from administration, colleagues, and students to engage in labour based on their expertise and knowledge of the inequities faced by their communities, leads to intensified labour that is not explicitly stipulated in employment contracts or can be articulated into tenure, renewal, and promotion applications. Some examples include being tasked with preparing new courses that "conceptually and pedagogically interrupt white hetero-patriarchy," being "the token equity representative on multiple department, faculty, university committees," or taking on the arduous labour of debriefing, supporting, and educating colleagues and students in response to or in anticipation of racist, sexist, homophobic, or transphobic encounters in the university space (p. 8).

In this chapter, I contribute to and extend the body of critical race scholarship on the university that exposes how racialized and gendered scholars' experiences and presence in the academy are simultaneously complicated, contradictory, and remarkable (Ahmed, 2012; Dhamoon, 2020; Puwar, 2004; Thobani, 2021). This chapter also contributes to emerging research, including chapters published within this collection, which demonstrate how pre-pandemic racialized and gendered inequities were exacerbated and amplified during the COVID-19 pandemic, particularly against the backdrop of global anti-racist organizing and awareness, leading to ontological insecurities for racialized and gendered academics, particularly in relation to "whose knowledge and what knowledge is being impacted at this juncture" (Wright et al., 2020, p. 3). For example, Canadian faculty reported a "negative impact on mental health, work satisfaction, work productivity, and overall quality of life" due to the COVID-19 pandemic, with academic mothers experiencing a more significant caregiver burden than academic fathers (Gordon & Presseau, 2022, p. 5). Women academics paid "the pandemic penalty," referring to the growing disparity in scholarly productivity suffered by women academics during the pandemic (King & Frederickson, 2021, p. 1). Moreover, within academia, doctoral students experienced "the highest level of stress and pessimism" due to the pressure to publish (Suart et al., 2022, p. 1). Racialized and gendered Canadian faculty reported lower levels of well-being with increased rates of stress and isolation (Davis et al., 2022). Further, racialized academics experienced additional emotional stress related to the inability to distinguish personal and professional boundaries between the COVID-19 pandemic, global racist events, and anti-racism organizing (Belikov et al., 2021).

In this chapter, I engage in critical researcher reflexivity (Mao et al., 2016) to critically reflect on the compounding impacts of the COVID-19 pandemic on navigating graduate school as a racialized Muslim mother involved in equity, diversity, and inclusion (EDI) work on campus. I reflect on how my personal experiences, reflective of narratives that are typically silenced and invisibilized in the academy, shed light on problematic structural and systemic issues. Specifically, I draw attention to the unrealistic institutional expectations required of students who are parents to continue to progress in degree programs at the same pace as other students and pay tuition for unfunded additional semesters, all the while surviving a pandemic, engaging in unpaid emotional and intellectual labour to challenge ongoing and systemic injustices around racism, and producing a CV reflective of sufficient teaching, research, and service expertise to compete within the challenging job market.

During the COVID-19 pandemic, the challenges facing caregiver academics became even more pronounced, particularly for graduate-student parents who were already facing a lack of time, support, and space to manage their simultaneous and institutionally mandated responsibilities. Research on the experiences of Indigenous, Black, and racialized graduate students in doctoral programs reflect similar structural inequities to those faced by faculty, particularly in terms of

> experienc[ing] the classroom as a space of alterity, where they are made to feel alien and are pushed to represent their entire group; as a space of hostility where they encounter stereotypes and microaggressions; and, as a space in which they are burdened with emotionally-taxing pedagogical labour to educate peers and faculty on issues of race and colonialism. (Park & Bahia, 2022, p. 138)

I apply and extend Dhamoon's (2020) framework to explore the labour demanded from racialized graduate students such as me during the specific conjunctural moment of the COVID-19 pandemic. Although graduate students are not financially compensated in the way many faculty are in terms of salary, benefits, and permanent positions, they are expected to take on service work (committee membership at various levels, informal mentorship, conference organizing, etc.) as a means of contributing to the university community and their CVs.

Here, I explore how balancing the intertwining demands of caregiving, academia, and sociopolitical responsibility became unwieldy and arduous—all while trying to complete my doctoral program in a timely manner. Like Ethel Tungohan (chapter 7 in this collection), I argue that EDI work within the institution derails anti-racist organizing on campuses. Faculty and students are overburdened, overwhelmed, and exhausted with EDI work and are left without the required time, space, and capacity to do anti-racist organizing. It is the subsequent ontological insecurities and precarities that I explore here, which though experienced since the start of my doctoral program, were acutely compounded by the onset of the COVID-19 pandemic. After providing the context of the COVID-19 pandemic, I in turn reflect on the various components of graduate school—as a mother, as a Muslim, as an instructor, and as someone engaged in EDI-related service.

The COVID-19 Pandemic

Since the World Health Organization declared the coronavirus outbreak to be a global pandemic on March 11, 2020, the world witnessed fatalities in the millions, overburdened health-care systems, the subsuming of small businesses by multinational corporations, and the physical, mental, and emotional health effects of enduring months of social isolation, illness, loss of loved ones, and economic stress. Research demonstrated how Indigenous and racialized populations were more susceptible to the impacts of the COVID-19 pandemic due to the burden of intergenerational systemic racism with additional risk factors such as housing constraints, overrepresentation in low-wage and precarious employment situations, and limited access to adequate health care (Chief Public Health Officer of Canada, 2020). Women were further disproportionately impacted, not only in terms of their overrepresentation as essential and frontline workers (and therefore increased exposure to the virus), but also in terms of added domestic and child-care responsibilities due to the closures of schools and child-care facilities (Whiley et al., 2021).

The COVID-19 pandemic intersected with heightened sociopolitical awareness arising from a series of tragic events that mobilized public conversations and actions around racism and settler colonialism in Canada. This included the Black Lives Matter protests of the police murder of George Floyd in the United States and, closer to home, the wrongful death of Regis Korchinski-Paquet while in the presence of Toronto Police ("Regis," 2022), as well as the confirmation of unmarked burial sites for hundreds of Indigenous children at the Kamloops Indian Residential School. Subsequently, societal pressure to demonstrate accountability for protecting the safety and well-being of Indigenous,

Black, and racialized individuals led to an explosion of institutional EDI initiatives, task forces, committees, and events across the nation. The intensity of this moment, along with the impacts of the pandemic, enabled the conditions for political mobilization and led to administrative zeal to accomplish lofty EDI goals, which relied on the labour and expertise of structurally marginalized groups, especially racialized and Indigenous women in the academy, who were most impacted and least supported by both ongoing racism and colonialism and the COVID-19 pandemic.

Graduate School and Motherhood
On April 10, 2020, the provincial Ontario government ordered the closure of schools and child-care centres to curb the spread of COVID-19. Many women, once again overburdened with domestic and child-care responsibilities at the intersections of domestic and care work, experienced "the guilt thing," the patriarchal discourse of judgement of mothers for their decisions around child care, resulting in continual anguish and uncertainty (Whiley et al., 2021, p. 4). With few options, women who were mothers and caregivers negotiated a new normal involving little time and space for their non-domestic or "non-work" responsibilities as many continued to work from home while also parenting full time.

The COVID-19 pandemic hit while I was on my second parental leave from my PHD program. Like other families, as parents to two children under the age of five, my spouse and I had many difficult decisions to make, all related to the fears and anxieties of potentially catching and spreading the virus while keeping up with our work, school, and domestic responsibilities. In January 2021, I returned to my program from parental leave amidst ongoing lockdowns, school closures, and fluctuating public-health guidelines. Though we were privileged to have the option to work from home, my spouse and I had some difficult decisions to make about how to *effectively* work from home. Playing parenting tag ("it's your turn now"), hyper-scheduling, and figuring out who would work from which room in order to keep the background noise at a minimum while lecturing or in a meeting were our everyday considerations. Since we did not have any family in the city where we lived, it was just the two of us all day, every day—work, kids, home, repeat. Work, kids, home, repeat. Seeing online videos of how some people's lives had slowed down during the early days of the COVID-19 pandemic (which provided them with more time to bake bread and learn new TikTok dances) made me anxious and jealous.

As a doctoral candidate nearing the end of my program, I found myself on a tight institutional timeline for completion. Conscious of the compounding institutional barriers facing racialized and gendered academics (Kowlessar & Thomas, 2021; Wijesingha & Robson, 2021), which were amplified during the COVID-19 pandemic (Davis et al., 2022; Douglas et al., 2022), I endeavoured to continue to build my CV through unpaid "extra" service opportunities while completing my doctoral research. Upon reflection, the standardized and linear doctoral journey, which remains rooted in heteronormative constructions of whiteness, necessitates undivided focus and rigidity—tenuous characteristics for racialized caregiver students during the COVID-19 pandemic. Instead of focus and a rigid schedule, I experienced extreme unpredictability of my time, the uncertainty of my children's health (and therefore their need to stay home from school and child care every other week), and lack of space (physical, mental, and emotional) to prioritize my work commitments. I learned to function around the clock, all to remain a "good" student and a "good" mother. Scholarship on intensive mothering demonstrates that being a "good" mother equates to "great energy, time, financial, and emotional investments in child-rearing," and yet it is at odds with academia's neoliberal culture of nonstop productivity and quantifiable output, "which also requests scholar's total engagement, foregrounding the prominence of faculty mothers' bodies in the academic space as out of place" (França et al., 2022, p. 38). At the same time, I felt an ethical and political obligation to be present in the spaces where I could demonstrate solidarity and speak out as a racialized Muslim woman—whether through joining an institution-adjacent group comprised of Black, Indigenous, and racialized faculty, students, and staff committed to anti-colonialism and anti-racism or accepting all institutional requests to join equity-based committees. I wanted to support the push for meaningful and sustained change at our university, and this led to a shift in my own practices as a mother, student, instructor, and academic, as I describe below.

At a session I co-organized at the Canadian Sociological Association's annual conference in 2021 about the experiences of graduate-student parents, mothers on the panel reported not talking about the details of their day-to-day experiences of motherhood with their colleagues and professors for fear of developing a reputation as unprofessional or unable to meet deadlines. Many practiced self-policing in terms of what they disclosed, not wanting the stress of managing child-care and domestic responsibilities to be perceived as hindering their productivity or reputation. Most continued to say "yes" and stay involved in unpaid commitments for fear of missing out on opportunities for career advancement, and others were advised by mentors not to put parental leaves on their CVs to not draw attention to their caregiver responsibilities. Panelists spoke about not wanting to appear unprofessional by using their children as an excuse for not being able to attend a meeting or hesitating to request an extension on a publication deadline because children were home sick that week from school or child care. This is an ontological challenge to many parents whose identity as parents was silenced, hidden, or compromised in order to navigate the neoliberalist and misogynist rules, spoken or unspoken, of the institution. Facing additional responsibilities with stay-at-home orders during COVID-19, graduate-student mothers in particular faced the pressures of navigating these misogynist rules in the academy compounded by parenting under white supremacy.

Muslim Motherhood and Anti-Muslim Racism
The impact of global anti-Muslim racism (Razack, 2022) and its violent manifestations became debilitating at times, especially as a Muslim parent navigating whiteness and anti-Muslim racism in the diaspora (Abdalla & Chen, 2021; Özdemir, 2022). On June 6, 2021, while taking an evening walk in their neighbourhood, the Afzaal family was murdered in London, Ontario. A white man deliberately drove his car into the six family members while they were waiting at an intersection (Dubinski, 2023). This act of violence was enacted by sheer hatred for Islam and Muslims, and immediately Muslims across Canada mobilized and united around their grief and fears (Jiwani, 2022). The next day, I was scheduled for a day surgery in London, Ontario, and recall the simultaneous grief and dread, not wanting to leave my house much less travel to that same city where this horrific Islamophobic violence had just occurred.

As a racialized hijabi Muslim woman, I am visible. As a racialized and visibly Muslim woman who is both a graduate student and sessional instructor, I am a minority in the academy and therefore hyper-visible. During the COVID-19 pandemic, twenty years post-9/11, amidst the backdrop of growing racial violence and anti-racist organizing, I embodied a very particular type of simultaneous invisibility and visibility (Puwar, 2004) in academia. My hijab, both in a seat and at the front of the classroom, remains politicized, rooted in neo-Orientalist racial logic that frames Muslim women as submissive, homogenous, and fundamentalist. Law professor Nadia Ahmad (2021) wittily describes this as "the trope of the anti-intellectual illiterate Islamist terrorist hijabi" (p. 31). Thus, counter-narratives of Muslim women's hijabs as feminist resistance to the male gaze and challenges to state-led restrictions on the practice remain contested by the everyday racism that shapes our understandings of our identities (Mian Akram, 2018). To this point, Puwar (2004) writes that those who are hyper-visible and hyper-marked as "other" through their bodies come under question, implicitly and sometimes explicitly, for their lack of rationality and mind (read: mechanized rigour, quantifiable hours, and numerical output) with little consideration for context, personal circumstance, or humanity. The academy remains steeped in the notion of the "universal," defined as:

> The capacity to be unmarked by one's body, in terms of race, gender or for that matter any other social feature…It is a "privileged position" that is "reserved" for those who are not bedraggled by the humble shackles of nature, emotion and, in effect, the bodily, allowing them to escape into the higher realms of rationality and mind. (p. 57)

The body that is raced and gendered and thus simultaneously visible and invisible experiences a series of complicated dynamics in the institution (Puwar, 2004), an institution that expects and rewards objectivity, maleness, and whiteness.

As a Muslim mother, I am tasked with working and studying in a general climate of hostility toward Islam and raising my children in an environment that generally does not understand nor embrace who they are. There is a growing body of scholarship that unpacks how Muslim parents navigate whiteness and anti-Muslim racism in the diaspora (Abdalla & Chen, 2021; Özdemir, 2022; Saleh, 2019), which reflects the growing research that contributes to a more nuanced understanding of how global sociopolitical contexts related to colonial-racial logics shape the everyday decision-making and experiences of Muslim parents with their children, such as ongoing conversations that affirm their identities and provide strategies for navigating their own lives in anti-Muslim contexts. On a backdrop of growing anti-Muslim violence and targeting, the fears of a parent exacerbate, and it becomes overwhelming and exhausting—another way in which the labour and workload of racialized academics is compounded.

Compounded Workload as a Sessional Instructor

The Workload of Representation
Being perceived as a representative of all hijabi Muslim women added compounded labour to my work as a sessional instructor. For example, I experienced a moment of affirmation while teaching an undergraduate course as a sessional instructor in the humanities when a Muslim student approached me at the end of the first class to tell me that I was the reason they chose to stay in the course as they were so proud to see a Muslim woman professor in hijab, which they had never seen before, and felt like it was possible for them to one day also teach in higher education. Nervous for the first day of a new course, this comment affirmed my commitment to a career in academia. This student's experience is consistent with the study by Henry et al. (2017), which reports that Indigenous and racialized students rarely see themselves reflected within the faculty composition or university leadership positions, especially in social-science and humanities departments.

Embodying an academic position, however, also comes with a particular kind of responsibility, part of which is having to take on the labour of responding to questions of credibility. A few weeks later, this same student visited my office hours to discuss the topic for their final project. After a lengthy discussion, they asked, "How do you keep your personal beliefs and opinions as a Muslim out of your lessons, especially when you teach about more controversial topics such as same-sex marriage or cisnormativity?" I was surprised. The same student who commended me for paving the way for Muslim students like them was questioning me on how I keep my personal beliefs out of the class material—never mind that I spent countless hours every week curating material for my lectures to encourage critical thinking; amplify Indigenous, Black, and racialized voices, women's voices, and queer and trans voices; use a range of sources from around the world to challenge Eurocentric normativity, and so on. This student assumed that because I was Muslim, my classes would be rooted in Islamic scripture, or I would not be comfortable teaching about gender and sexual diversity. Academia's whiteness and Christianness are so often invisible and ubiquitous, even to this Muslim student. The privilege extended to white male Christian professors—that of objectivity and rationality—was not extended to me. At a time of heightened sociopolitical awareness during the COVID-19 pandemic, this student chose to critique my objectivity rather than think through how to direct that critique toward the institution. Puwar's (2004) work is useful here for contextualizing this conversation, as my credibility and professionalism, my ability to teach the material and not my personal beliefs, was easily called into question by this student. Puwar (2004) writes that the circumstances of those who are simultaneously invisible and visible in the institution are complicated by four aspects: "a burden of doubt, infantilization, super-surveillance and a burden of representation" (p. 58). They are simultaneously conspicuous and selected for representing a certain category, as well as invisible in their abilities as capable—this makes for a complicated ontological existence in the academy.

Student Over-Disclosure and Precarious Work
At the height of the COVID-19 pandemic in Fall 2021, I secured my first opportunity to teach an undergraduate course on social justice as a sessional instructor. As a younger-presenting, racialized hijabi Muslim woman professor, I knew that I would face obstacles. Teaching an entirely online, first-year course with 150 students—many of whom had just completed high school remotely—during the ongoing COVID-19 pandemic presented a whole new set of challenges. As an instructor, I tried to be empathetic but fair with the students, and scholarly yet creative with the material. We studied settler colonialism and the legacies of residential schools, anti-Black racism and other racism, hetero- and cisnormativities, and other challenging and important social-justice topics. I pushed students to become critical social-justice scholars, which also involved interrogating their own privileges and socialization.

About halfway through the course, a student asked to speak to me after class. During that meeting, she spoke about how she, as a white woman, was enjoying the course and was grateful for the course material and my teaching style because it encouraged self-reflection. Through this introspective process, however, she realized that she was "disgusted by Black men." I was shocked to hear these words. I was not expecting this disclosure. I spoke at length with the student, trying to remain composed and yet challenging her on the racist core of her statements. Trying to err on the side of educating, and not reprimanding, as she had taken the steps to recognize these racial ideologies, I could not stop my insides from churning. I provided supplemental reading material and asked her to come regularly to my office hours to continue our conversations. She did not come again to discuss this matter. This one interaction weighed heavy on me for weeks and months after, as I laboured through my insecurities about how I had handled the situation. Talking with colleagues and friends, I questioned: What should I have said differently? What should I have done differently? This conversation and the racist disclosure took an emotional toll on me and consumed my thoughts for weeks: How could this student vocalize these hateful sentiments? And why did she share them with me? Would she have shared this with my white counterparts? As a new instructor, was this the type of labour I would be engaging in throughout my career?

Racialized instructors are expected to engage with the additional workload of managing this type of disclosure (Dhamoon, 2020), as students may feel more comfortable opening up to them or expect a more comprehensive response as compared to white instructors. This was amplified during the COVID-19 pandemic in the heightened racial awakening of many who were just developing awareness of their responsibilities toward challenging racial and colonial inequities. However, this is not without consequences. In addition to the added emotional labour, Daniel (2019) argues, "As academics, if we work to support or promote the critical thinking skills of students and staff, the styles that we employ can negatively affect our ratings" (p. 26). Racial and gender biases in student evaluations of teaching (SETs), which students complete at the end of every course (although in many universities, these shifted to the virtual and as such the completion rate has decreased significantly), are well documented. For example, Mowatt (2019) argues that SETs "truly only gauge the students' satisfaction and experience within the course, not the faculty's abilities or teaching philosophy" (p. 110). As student evaluations are an important component of my teaching dossier, reviewed by hiring committees to assess my teaching capabilities, I wondered, am I jeopardizing career prospects by engaging in these methods of teaching? And if students are disclosing racist sentiments to me, what does that mean about how they are experiencing my teaching? What happens to faculty who engage students in unlearning systems? Teaching while still a graduate student and looking for permanent employment meant that I was multiply-precarious and must maintain a stellar application to even be considered for competitive positions. These surreptitious ways in which workload increases for racialized instructors teaching in the areas of social justice are not accounted for in a CV.

EDI-Related Service Work

University Governance and Fear of "Muslim Invasion"
In 2010, during my master's program, I was elected as president of our department's graduate-student group. I took this role seriously as I was excited to build the infrastructure for a group that had until then operated at a more informal level. When I was first elected, I was asked by a white male student in the department how being a Muslim woman would affect my presidency. I hesitated, unsure how to respond. At the moment, I did not think to ask, "How does being a white man affect your presidency?" My otherness had emboldened him to question my bias and lack of objectivity as if my hypervisibility as other would overwhelmingly and problematically affect the direction of the department's governance.

All these years later, I reflect back on this questioning, realizing now that this was my first experience in academia of encountering this explicit questioning of my embodiment in relation to my eligibility to assume a position of authority. I thought, why did he ask that? Did he think I wasn't going to do a good job in that leadership position? Or that I wouldn't know what to do? Or was it a fear of bringing in Muslim practices or Islamic teachings into our department? It is hard to know, but as I still find myself reflecting on this question over a decade later, I realize that even in representation in leadership positions in the academy, my credibility and capability will continue to be called into question in a way that white colleagues will not, and I will be expected to assume the labour required to respond, challenge, or resist it. This sustained racial logic will continue to govern racialized people as we strive to challenge its very nature.

Creating New Spaces of Knowledge, Support, and Resistance
In the Spring of 2020, at the start of the COVID-19 pandemic, I was invited to join a group of faculty, staff, and students at my institution to challenge anti-Black racism on our campus. This was a grassroots group that began to meet and organize adjacent to the university. We rallied around the case of a Black student who faced institutional repercussions when charged with a crime he did not commit. This group knew that pressure needed to be put on the university to make tangible changes to make our campus safer and more equitable for Black, Indigenous, and racialized students. And yet, the responsibility primarily fell on Black, Indigenous, and racialized people to push for that change. Meeting virtually against the backdrop of global anti-racism organizing and calls for universities to challenge their colonial and racist structures and policies, sociopolitical upheaval and uprising felt like a tangible and radical way to challenge and address issues of racism on our campus. Knowing that racialized students put themselves in more precarious positions by pursuing activist endeavours on campus (Mbakogu et al., 2021), I went through moments of intense involvement to moments of stepping back, unable to commit the sustained additional labour (mental and emotional) required to maintain this sort of grassroots organizing, primarily due to competition for my time during the COVID-19 pandemic. What do I prioritize—my dissertation research, my children, or anti-racism organizing? Of course, I knew this work was important because writing about anti-racism in my dissertation meant very little if I were not doing what I could in terms of tangible action. Eventually, our group organized an academic conference and started our own academic journal—our own way of creating new knowledge dedicated to anti-colonialism and anti-racism on our campus. This pooling of knowledge is so key to being able to make the invisible visible by identifying and naming racism as such.

This group was unique in its function and meaning, unlike other service committees I had experienced, particularly those that originated from within the institution. Equity work expanded significantly during the COVID-19 pandemic as universities could no longer ignore the calls for comprehensive and radical change. However, much of this labour was pushed onto racialized communities, which were already experiencing higher transmission rates and death by COVID-19 than white individuals (Chief Public Health Officer of Canada, 2020). How problematic that academic institutions were asking those same communities to deal with ongoing and systemic inequities! Being critical of typically performative EDI work, I was hesitant but also knew that this was an opportunity to grow my CV and be further involved in, hopefully, making the institution more equitable. I spent hours of unpaid service work every week at the department, institution, and national levels—doing committee work, organizing conferences and events, supporting mentorship programs, and in doing so, met and worked with some radical racialized faculty and students from whom I learned how to work within the system to change it. Being the token Muslim representative at the table, even while it takes time away from completing my dissertation, is necessary even if calls for accountability tend to become the responsibility of the racialized. The labour of transforming the institution is passed down to the most marginalized, and Muslims, like me, make diversity visible through our presence on committees. What does the image and presence of my racialized, visibly Muslim woman body represent? Am I being invited simply to check a box? Here, I am reminded of how a racialized professor during my master's degree warned me: "Be careful about how the image of you as a brown Muslim woman in hijab is used by others at the university—for their benefit and to your detriment." This has stayed with me since he shared this wisdom with me over a decade ago.

Workload and Labour of Racialized and Gendered Graduate Students During a Pandemic

As a racialized woman in academia, my experiences are part of broader structural and systemic issues that reflect white heteropatriarchal Christian colonial foundations and governance in the academy (Hampton, 2020; Henry et al., 2017; Thobani, 2021), which results in the discriminatory ways in which Black, Indigenous, racialized, and gendered bodies are read, categorized, and treated. For example, racialized and Indigenous professors earn lower wages than their white counterparts and are underrepresented in positions of leadership (Henry et al., 2017). Racialized faculty face specific challenges related to hiring, promotion, student evaluations, and colleague perceptions (James, 2012). They must play the game to outperform their white colleagues when it comes to publishing and securing research funding. Additionally, Black and racialized faculty face attacks on their credibility and questioning of their competence (Daniel, 2019) from students, colleagues, and administration. Daniel (2019) concludes, "The academy is not a safe space for Black or racialized faculty members" (p. 34). Finally, racialized graduate students report three primary areas in which they face additional challenges: lack of representation, lack of support from faculty and staff, and microaggressions on campus (Kowlessar & Thomas, 2021).

In the face of this persistent discrimination, EDI is invoked as an institutional solution to the colonial and racist foundation and continued impacts on students, faculty, and staff. Sara Ahmed's work is particularly useful for unpacking the problems with diversity work in the institution. Ahmed (2012) cautions, "Diversity becomes about *changing perceptions of whiteness rather than changing the whiteness of organizations*" (p. 34, emphasis in original). This dangerous surface-level approach to anti-racism and anti-colonialism is about appearances, reputations, and reporting about—instead of critiquing and dismantling—the coloniality and racism upon which these institutions are built. Even the work of diversity or equity becomes institutionalized, routinized, and numerical, becoming a study of those who look different and have different traditions, and the goal becomes to superimpose an image of a vibrant mosaic to cover up the foundation of a "white, elite, male, old-fashioned" institution (Ahmed, 2012, p. 34). Diversity work, similar to that undertaken in some of the spaces to which I was invited, then becomes my busywork for the benefit of institutional optics and reporting.

For racialized women academics, gendered embodiment adds a list of additional challenges. Ahmed (2012) argues that one of the most significant challenges faced by women of colour faculty is the ontological questioning of their intellect and identities, as her identity is presumed under the colonial and racial logic of "the woman of colour," which is read as "angry," "motivated by ideology," and an "origin of terror" (p. 162). This is reflected in my experience with the Muslim student questioning my biases and motivations, concerned about how I would keep what they assumed to be my personal beliefs and ideologies out of the course curriculum.

Amidst institutional responses to racial reckonings, the increased attention to EDI work must be problematized, particularly in terms of the whitewashing of radical movements against heteropatriarchal colonial-racial structures. The 2021 collection *Coloniality and Racial (In)Justice in the University: Counting for Nothing?*, edited by Sunera Thobani, is particularly useful for exploring the complexities of the university for Indigenous and racialized academics in the context of ongoing white-supremacist politics. In her introduction, Thobani (2021) argues that the current "equity/diversity" regime functions as "a containment zone" in which the demands of radical insurgent scholars, women/queers of colour, and Indigenous women are converted into EDI portfolios to "advance inclusion" (p. 6). Ultimately, Thobani (2021) argues that energies are diverted away from the struggle for racial justice and transformative potential and redirected to a mechanical, institutionalized "zone embodied and peopled by bodies of colour" (p. 18). These scholars must then be attuned to this diversion and redirection and keep the focus on the radical anti-colonial politics needed to address generational discrimination—again, the labour of speaking out falls on those who are most intimately affected.

Despite EDI work being management for institutions, the labour of EDI is downloaded onto racialized faculty. In this regard, Dhamoon's (2020) work is important for explaining the ways in which racism shapes the distribution of labour for racialized and Indigenous faculty in the academy. All of this requires immense time and labour to be redirected away from research, teaching, and service commitments for which those faculty are hired, but it is something that is expected as the double-edged nature of representation. The university expects that "you know why you were hired—to represent 'your' communities and take care of marginalized students" (Henry et al., 2017, p. 312). And so, overwhelmingly racialized faculty are overtasked with meeting institutional expectations, supporting racialized students, and labouring for countless additional hours each week through time, stress, and emotional investment.

On the Changing Academy

In this chapter, I have unpacked my experiences as a Muslim mother, graduate student, sessional instructor, and EDI worker during a pandemic to highlight specific equity-based issues within the academy, all to problematize and challenge standardized normative conceptions of the universal academic. Most significantly, my experiences demonstrate the larger struggle of academic mothers and how the burden of care they disproportionately took on during the pandemic was minimized in academia, primarily through the expectation to continue their academic responsibilities with the same rigour as prior to the pandemic (França at al., 2022). During the pandemic, mothers resisted this through naturalization of children in workspaces (i.e., foregrounding their presence in online classes or taking breaks to attend to children's mealtimes) or refusal to take on tasks that were impossible based on competing time demands (França et al., 2022). Even in the midst of resistance, the impacts on graduate-student mothers, such as me, were enormous. The intensity of parenting during the pandemic without support serves as a deterrent for those thinking about graduate school and working in academia, particularly those students with families or thinking about starting a family. The paradox is, however, that one of the primary EDI goals for racialized students is for them to see themselves reflected in positions of higher education and administration. That is why the creation of alternative spaces of equity-based organizing and support is so important, as it provides the care and attention that the university cannot.

My narratives as a doctoral student trying to finish the program while still paying tuition, with a family to support, not wanting to miss out on research, teaching, service, and publication opportunities to grow my CV, and attempting to engage in important equity work arising during the COVID-19 pandemic, meant that the commitments kept growing and growing, and my time, labour, and capacity kept diminishing. Telling my story is one way to resist the neoliberal academy so that our experiences, while unique to this pandemic moment, do not go unnoticed. I present this chapter as an offering to Muslim graduate-student mothers in coming generations—despite the exhaustion, I continue to advocate for the necessary changes to ensure they are cared for and embraced, every step of the way.

Note

1. It is necessary that I highlight how in this critical reflection, I am not critiquing my incredible doctoral supervisor nor the other racialized and non-racialized faculty at various institutions who have been ardent mentors and advocates. If not for my

supervisor's unwavering support and dedication to her students, I would not have survived this program.

References

Abdalla, M.I., & Chen, Y. (2021). "So, it's like you're swimming against the tide": Didactic avowals and parenting as intersectional Muslim women in the United States. *Journal of International and Intercultural Communication, 15*(3), 1–22. https://doi.org/10.1080/17513057.2021.1896768

Ahmad, N.B. (2021). "Blood, sweat, tears:" Muslim woman law professor's view on degenerative racism, misogyny, and (internal) Islamophobia from preeclampsia and presumed incompetent to pandemic tenure. *FIU Law Review, 16*(1), 13–74.

Ahmed, S. (2012). *On being included: Racism and diversity in institutional life.* Duke University Press.

Belikov, O., VanLeeuwen, C.A., Veletsianos, G., Johnson, N., & Prusko, P.T. (2021). Professional and personal impacts experienced by faculty stemming from the intersection of the COVID-19 pandemic and racial tensions. *Journal of Interactive Media in Education, 1,* 1–15. https://doi.org/10.5334/jime.647

Chief Public Health Officer of Canada (CPHO). (2020). *The Chief Public Health Officer of Canada's report on the state of public health in Canada.* Public Health Agency of Canada. https://www.canada.ca/en/public-health/corporate/publications/chief-public-health-officer-reports-state-public-health-canada/from-risk-resilience-equity-approach-covid-19.html

Daniel, B. (2019). Teaching while Black: Racial dynamics, evaluations, and the role of White females in the Canadian academy in carrying the racism torch. *Race Ethnicity and Education, 22*(1), 21–37. https://doi.org/10.1080/13613324.2018.1468745

Davis, J.C., Li, E.P.H., Butterfield, M.S., DiLabio, G.A., Sangunthanam, N., & Marcolin, B. (2022). Are we failing female and racialized academics? A Canadian national survey examining the impacts of the COVID-19 pandemic on tenure and tenure-track faculty. *Gender, Work & Organization, 29,* 1–22. https://doi.org/10.1111/gwao.12811

Dhamoon, R.K. (2020). Racism as a workload and bargaining issue. *Socialist Studies, 14*(1), 1–22.

Douglas, H.M., Settles, I.H., Cech, E.A., Montgomery, G.M., Nadolsky, L.R., Hawkins, A.K., Ma, G., Davis, T.M., Elliott, K.C., & Cheruvelil, K.S. (2022). Disproportionate impacts of COVID-19 on marginalized and minoritized early-career academic scientists. *PLoS ONE 17*(9), e0274278. https://doi.org/10.1371/journal.pone.0274278

Dubinski, K. (2023, September 15). *Accused killer of Muslim family explains in post-arrest rant his rationale for truck attack in London, Ont.* CBC News. https://www.cbc.ca/news/canada/london/accused-killer-of-muslim-family-explains-in-post-arrest-rant-his-rationale-for-truck-attack-in-london-ont-1.6967808

França, T., Godinho, F., Padilla, B., Vicente, M., Amâncio, L., & Fernandes, A. (2022). "Having a family is the new normal": Parenting in neoliberal academia during the COVID-19 pandemic. *Gender, Work & Organization, 30*(1), 35–51. https://doi.org/10.1111/gwao.12895

Gordon, J.L., & Presseau, J. (2022). Effects of parenthood and gender on well-being and work productivity among Canadian academic research faculty amidst the COVID-19 pandemic. *Canadian Psychology, 64*(2), 144–153. https://doi.org/10.1037/cap0000327

Hampton, R. (2020). *Black racialization and resistance at an elite university.* University of Toronto Press.

Henry, F., Dua, E., Kobayashi, A., James, C., Li, P., Ramos, H., & Smith, M.S. (2017). Race, racialization and Indigeneity in Canadian universities. *Race Ethnicity and Education, 20*(3), 300–314. https://doi.org/10.1080/13613324.2016.1260226

James, C.E. (2012). Strategies of engagement: How racialized faculty negotiate the university system. *Canadian Ethnic Studies Journal, 44*(2), 1–13.

James, C.E. (2021). *Colour matters: Essays on the experiences, education, and pursuits of Black youth.* University of Toronto Press. https://doi.org/10.3138/9781487538781

Jiwani, Y. (2022). From the ground up: Tactical mobilization of grief in the case of the Afzaal-Salman family killings. *Conjunctions: Transdisciplinary Journal of Cultural Participation, 9*(1), 1–19. https://doi.org/10.2478/tjcp-2022-0002

King, M.K., & Frederickson, M.E. (2021). The pandemic penalty: The gendered effects of COVID-19 on scientific productivity. *Socius: Sociological Research for a Dynamic World, 7,* 1–24. https://doi.org/10.1177/23780231211006977

Kowlessar, K., & Thomas, C. (2021). "This space is not for me": BIPOC identities in academic spaces. *Canadian Review of Sociology, 58*(3), 447–449. https://doi.org/10.1111/cars.12353

Mao, L., Mian Akram, A., Chovanec, D., & Underwood, M.L. (2016). Embracing the spiral: Researcher reflexivity in diverse critical methodologies. *International Journal of Qualitative Methods, 15*(1), 1–8. https://doi.org/10.1177/1609406916681005

Mbakogu, I., Duhaney, P., Ferrer, I., & Lee, E.O.J. (2021). Confronting whiteness in social work education through racialized student activism. *Canadian Social Work Review, 38*(2), 113–140.

Mian Akram, A. (2018). I am not a problem, I am Canadian: Exploring Canadian Muslim women's experiences of "being Canadian." In S. Guo & L. Wong (Eds.), *Immigration, racial and ethnic studies in 150 years of Canada: Retrospects and prospects* (pp. 281–297). Brill Sense.

Mowatt, R.A. (2019). Twelve years a servant: Race and the student evaluation of teaching. *Schole: A Journal of Leisure Studies and Recreation Education, 34*(2), 109–119. https://doi.org/10.1080/13613324.2018.1468745

Özdemir, S. (2022). Remote schooling during a pandemic: Visibly Muslim mothering and the entanglement of personal and political. *Gender, Work & Organization, 29*(4), 1–11. https://doi.org/10.1111/gwao.12819

Park, A.S., & Bahia, J. (2022). Exploring the experiences of Black, Indigenous and racialized graduate students: The classroom as a space of alterity, hostility and pedagogical labour. *Canadian Review of Sociology, 59*(2), 138–155. https://doi.org/10.1111/cars.12373

Puwar, N. (2004). *Space invaders: Race, gender and bodies out of place.* Bloomsbury Academic.

Razack, S.H. (2022). *Nothing has to make sense: Upholding white supremacy through anti-Muslim racism.* University of Minnesota Press.

Regis Korchinski-Paquet's family files $10M civil lawsuit in connection with her death. (2022, June 29). CBC News. https://www.cbc.ca/news/canada/toronto/regis-korchinski-paquet-family-civil-lawsuit-1.6505802

Saleh, M. (2019). *Stories we live and grow by: (Re)telling our experiences as Muslim mothers and daughters*. Demeter Press.

Suart, C., Neuman, K., & Truant, R. (2022). The impact of the COVID-19 pandemic on perceived publication pressure among academic researchers in Canada. *PLoS ONE*, *17*(6), 1–23. https://doi.org/10.1371/journal.pone.0269743

Thobani, S. (2021). Present pasts: The anxieties of power. In S. Thobani (Ed.), *Coloniality and racial (in)justice in the university: Counting for nothing?* (pp. 3–46). University of Toronto Press.

Whiley, L.A., Sayer, H., & Juanchich, M. (2021). Motherhood and guilt in a pandemic: Navigating the "new" normal with a feminist identity. *Gender, Work & Organization*, *28*(S2), 612–619. https://doi.org/10.1111/gwao.12613

Wijesingha, R., & Robson, K. (2021). Glass ceiling or murky waters: The gendered and racialized pathway to full professorship in Canada. *Canadian Review of Sociology*, *59*, 23–42. https://doi.org/10.1111/cars.12365

Wright, K.A.M., Haastrup, T., & Guerrina, R. (2020). Equalities in freefall? Ontological insecurity and the long-term impact of COVID-19 in the academy. *Feminist Frontiers*, *28*(S1), 1–5. https://doi.org/10.1111/gwao.12518

2
Struggles of International Graduate Students During the COVID-19 Pandemic

The Spectre of Equity, Diversity, and Inclusion Policies at a University

SEPIDEH BORZOO, ISABEL FANDINO, and PALLAVI BANERJEE

Introduction

The COVID-19 pandemic exacerbated all existing social and economic inequities globally. Not surprisingly, the most marginalized and vulnerable in society have been the most impacted (Banerjee et al., 2022a; Nanda, 2020). Racially motivated violence intensified between 2020 and 2021 in North America with the murders of George Floyd and Breonna Taylor by the police in the United States; the mass shooting of Asian women in massage parlours in Atlanta, Georgia; the confirmation of the unmarked graves of Indigenous children on residential school grounds in Canada; and hate crimes against Asians—and so did the anger and protests against these majoritarian, colonial, and institutional violence and injustices. As more inequities showed their ugliest faces in the form of racial hate crimes, domestic violence, border restrictions, and poverty. As the pandemic was raging, institutions were called on to respond to these inequities. Many of them, including higher-education institutions, responded by bolstering their equity, diversity, and inclusion (EDI) initiatives and policies (Campbell, 2021).

Given this backdrop, our chapter explores if, and how, equity-oriented programs impacted the lives of International Graduate Students (IGSs) during the COVID-19 pandemic at a large research university in Alberta, Canada.[1] This university, like most universities during the summer of 2020 and 2021, made several public statements on the injustices brewing during the pandemic and also took significant steps to strengthen its EDI commitments by instituting EDI policies and equity-oriented programs. However, even in a regular non-pandemic context, EDI frameworks often discount the experiences of IGSs, as we demonstrate here through analysis of equity-oriented programs developed before and during the pandemic. International students in Canada are mostly people of colour from the Global South (Canadian Bureau for International Education, 2022; Crossman et al., 2022) who, after arriving in Canada, struggle with several barriers and challenges. The most intense of these are the financial challenges and mental health issues that take gendered forms—particularly when there are children—owing to the lack of familial and institutional support. For IGSs, these experiences add to their liminal position as students and temporary residents such that they have neither the rights that immigrants have nor the benefits and rights that domestic graduate students have in Canada (Brunner, 2022; Guo & Guo, 2017; Ramos Fandino, 2021). The COVID-19 pandemic made these vulnerabilities worse, the extreme spectrum of which was made visible through the unfortunate deaths of international students in Canada due to stress, suicide, contracting COVID-19, and racial hate crimes (Banerjee & Fandino, 2020; Bascaramurty et al., 2022), making them one of the most vulnerable groups within higher education. This led us, three immigrant women in Canada, to delve deeply into the issue of EDI inclusion of IGSs.

The authors of this chapter are: i) a former IGS on a temporary work permit, ii) a former international student (undergraduate and graduate) and currently a university staff member on a temporary work permit, who directly supports international students, and iii) an immigrant faculty member who started her life in North America as an IGS and has occupied many temporary legal statuses. Our research interests stem from both a personal and political investment in the topic as immigrants, temporary workers, women of colour, present and former IGSs, and employees within a university context, all of whom have been involved in EDI initiatives of their university in different ways. Given our positionalities, we find it imperative that we unpack if, and how, equity-oriented programs within universities during the COVID-19 pandemic addressed the concerns of IGSS—one of the most vulnerable of what universities like to term "equity-deserving groups." What follows is an exploration of this query and an analysis of the impact of equity-oriented programs of a university for IGSS, in the context of the COVID-19 pandemic. Specifically, we explore if, and how, the equity-oriented programs of the university applied to the experiences of IGSS during the COVID-19 pandemic.

EDI in Educational Institutions

To allay growing public concern about inequality and systemic oppression across lines of gender, race, sexuality, religion, nationality, and other categories of difference, many organizations, including post-secondary educational institutions, strive to commit to the principles of EDI. Equity-oriented programs and EDI initiatives have been introduced and operationalized to identify and remove systemic barriers to the inclusion of marginalized groups and their access to resources in the context of post-secondary education (Milanczak, 2022; Universities Canada, 2019). Responding to the growth of international students' enrollment alongside increasing concern about the rights of Indigenous and Black populations and other marginalized groups on campuses, many institutions adopted EDI policies and initiatives before the pandemic (Canada's International Education Strategy, 2014, 2017; Henry et al., 2017; Pidgeon, 2016; Tamtik & Guenter, 2019; Truth and Reconciliation Commission of Canada, 2015).

The increase in the number of international students has been driven largely by economic logic across various countries within the Global North and is ultimately driven by neoliberalism (Haapakoski & Pashby, 2017). Due to their othered status in terms of racial identity, immigration status, ethnicity, and language, international students experience unique forms of oppression ranging from being exposed to monolingual and monocultural views of curriculum, to the challenges of informing transcultural friendship, to experiences of racism, to carrying the double burden of graduate school and parenthood, and most recently to COVID-19 pandemic–driven hate-crime experiences (Guo & Guo, 2017; Lee & Rice, 2007; Park et al., 2017; Tavares, 2021).

Despite this, international students are not regularly categorized as an "equity-deserving group" in university EDI frameworks, even during a global crisis such as the COVID-19 pandemic. Most university initiatives that mention or speak to international students are recruitment policies highlighting how international students serve as economic and political assets for post-secondary institutions. Tamtik and Guenter (2019), in their analysis of EDI strategies and policies in Canadian universities, show that most universities developed internationalization strategies to support international student recruitment, which squarely leads to reinforcing international students as economic objects. There is limited evidence that universities enact policies or initiatives to address the unique needs of international students, and during unprecedented times such as the COVID-19 pandemic this gap in EDI initiatives was laid bare. In the absence of initiatives inclusive of international students, as Stein and de Andreotti (2016) argue, international students are reduced to the economic profit that they bring to the host country.

The othering that international students experience due to their position does not preclude them from having to navigate maintaining high scholarly output and working on campus in lieu of their stipends—in fact, the pressures of these demands compound their sense of marginalization. Critical race scholarship provides a meticulous analysis of diversity initiatives by exploring how systemic privilege and oppression are reproduced and reinforced at institutional and policy levels (Abu-Laban & Gabriel, 2002; Ahmed, 2007; Chatterjee et al., 2022; Puwar, 2004; Schwarz & Lindqvist, 2018; Yancy & Davidson, 2014). At the heart of critical race theory is the idea that whiteness is the organizing structure of institutions and the racialized society as a whole (Ahmed, 2007; Buckner et al., 2021; Hiraldo, 2010). At an institutional level, as this scholarship shows, diversity has been mobilized as a means for institutions to rearticulate a politically correct image (Ahmed, 2012, 2018; Buckner et al., 2021; Chatterjee et al., 2022). One of the main goals of critical race theories has been identifying the subtle norms of whiteness that maintain the structure of inequality in higher education (Ahmed, 2007; Foste & Irwin, 2020). Ahmed's (2006, 2007, 2009, 2012, 2018) substantial body of work in feminist, postcolonial, queer, and whiteness studies sheds light on the contradictions that form equity, inclusion, and diversity policies within educational institutions. In her research on the language of diversity in higher education,

Ahmed (2012, 2018) shows how institutions deploy diversity discourse as a shell to protect themselves from criticism. Deploying the language of EDI, arguably, becomes the indicator of non-performativity for universities as they serve to signal that any issues of racism and discrimination have already been dealt with (Ahmed 2012, 2018; Buckner et al., 2021). "Non-performativity," as Ahmed (2018) writes, is a dynamic based on which "something is named without coming into effect or when something is named in order not to bring something in effect" (p. 333). Universities' public statements about their commitments to diversity and inclusion serve to create an illusion of being transformed while the organizational structures remain intact. That is, diversity aims at reversing the image of institutions as steeped in whiteness and hence exclusionary rather than transforming the institution through structural changes and by increasing the representation of women and gender-diverse people of colour within the institution and supporting them to succeed (Ahmed, 2018; Buckner et al., 2021).

The commodification of international racialized students as the bearers of diversity to create an appearance of EDI has received sustained pushback from critical race scholarship about North American, and more specifically Canadian, universities (Buckner et al., 2021; Chatterjee et al., 2022; Yao et al., 2018). Chatterjee and colleagues (2022) deploy the term "internationalization" as a way to highlight how educational institutions deploy and commodify the racialized bodies of international students as a way to gain representational capital. Paying closer attention to the official international documentation, Buckner and colleagues (2021) highlight how the diversity initiatives and strategies promote the recruitment of international students as a part of the higher level diversity project across the Global North, while ignoring their racial identities, thereby normalizing whiteness in higher education institutions.

Our reflections on the experiences of IGSs in the context of university commitments to EDI are built on this critical race scholarship about diversity in higher education. In this chapter, building on the conceptualization of the non-performativity of diversity initiatives in higher education by Ahmed (2012), we highlight the gap between EDI policies and the fulfilment of policy commitment and the way international students serve as economic and political capital for post-secondary institutions. That is, universities' efforts toward enhancing their reputation through the representation of international students as a cipher of diversity and inclusion have the dual function of increasing the organization's profitability while redefining its representation as more diverse and inclusive. We show how, even as international students shore up university reputations for diversity, EDI initiatives do not adequately extend to international students.

COVID-19 Pandemic and International Students

While international students experienced social exclusion due to language and cultural barriers as well as racism prior to the pandemic (Belkhodja & Esses, 2013; Zhang & Zhou, 2010), lockdown and travel constraints were specifically daunting for international students' mental health (Firang & Mensah, 2022; Hari et al., 2023). Since the onset of the COVID-19 pandemic, a body of research has emerged on the impact of the pandemic on international students (Banerjee & Fandino, 2020; Brunner, 2022; Fandino & Banerjee, 2022; Ferdiansyah et al., 2020; Firang, 2020; Firang & Mensah, 2022; Guo, 2021; Hari et al., 2023; Lipura, 2021; Varughese & Schwartz, 2022). In their study on international students in Canada during the pandemic, Hari and colleagues (2023) highlight the heightened experiences of anxiety and distress among international students.

For international students, the psychological impact of the pandemic has been exacerbated due to financial burdens and rising unemployment (Firang & Mensah, 2022; Monteiro, 2020). While Canada provided financial programs to assist vulnerable populations, including the Canada Emergency Student Benefit (CESB) and Canada Emergency Response Fund (CERB), international students, while contributing to the Canadian economy by paying some of the highest tuition fees, were not eligible to apply for most of these programs due to their immigration status as temporary residents. During the pandemic, the rising rate of unemployment and layoffs had made finding a job more and more difficult for international students (Firang & Mensah, 2022).

Beyond financial difficulties, international students have been at risk of hate crimes, racial discrimination, and stereotyping due to politics and social rhetoric, which focused on China as "ground zero" of the pandemic. In 2020 in Canada, hate crimes targeting Asian people increased by 300 percent (Ozyomum & Zhang, 2021). Based on another national report, the number of hate crimes rose from 1,951 incidents in 2019 to more than 2,600 in 2020, with Ontario, British Columbia, and

Alberta experiencing the largest increase in hate crimes at 321, 196, and 106 incidents, respectively (Bensadoun, 2021). Focusing on international students, Zhai and Du (2020) spotlight the mental-health problems that Chinese students grappled with during the outbreak as a result of living in fear for their families in China, as well as facing discrimination in the host country due to being considered as the potential carriers of the virus. Several other studies have cast light on racial discrimination faced by Chinese or other Asian students (Fan, 2022; Koo, 2021; Koo et al., 2021). The pandemic therefore, unraveled the intersectional exploitation and othering of international students in Canada both within the university and outside.

Methodology

This chapter contrasts if, and how, the equity-oriented policies and programs of the university applied to the experiences of IGSs during the COVID-19 pandemic. Our methodology is divided into two parts. The first author of this chapter, Sepideh Borzoo, conducted a preliminary analysis of the equity-oriented programs introduced by the university in 2021. Since the EDI policies were just being implemented at the time, the research team analyzed both equity-oriented programs and policies that were initiated. These programs/policies were collected from the university website and were grouped into themes (see table 2.1). To protect the anonymity of the university and our research participants, we anonymized the university's name. Our analysis of the programs centred on appraising those programs for their potentiality to address inequities pertaining to race, gender, class, nationality, and immigration status.

University-Implemented Equity-Oriented Programs and Policies

To assess the lived experiences of IGSs vis-à-vis the university's equity-oriented programs and policies, we used data from in-depth interviews conducted by the second author, Isabel Fandino, with fifteen IGSs in Canada. We used semi-structured, in-depth interviews in order to capture the many nuanced experiences of IGSs during the COVID-19 pandemic. Complex experiences that lead to theorization are best captured through qualitative methods, particularly in-depth interviewing (Small, 2021). Interviews allow researchers to describe and explore participants' interpretations of their experiences (Crabtree & Miller, 1999; Kim, 2012). For

TABLE 2.1: Equity-oriented and diversity-related policies and programs introduced by the university, grouped by theme.

Policy	Description	Date Initiated
Mental health strategic plan	An initiative/program to support the mental health of the students and staff	2015
Financial support programs	Two financial support programs as a response to the war in Ukraine	2022
Workplace equity-related acts/programs	Multiple policies and programs aimed at advocating for and fostering an inclusive work and learning environment	2016
Sexual and gender-based initiatives	Policies aimed at providing support for students or staff impacted by sexual and gender-based violence	2017

the interviews, we used open-ended questions and an interview guide that allowed us to adapt questions based on what the participants shared. This also created an environment where participants could speak to topics and themes that they deemed important (Daly, 2007). Interview questions included general demographic questions, as well as questions surrounding participant's day-to-day lives in Canada, the process of applying and arriving in Canada during a pandemic, feelings toward legal status, resources on and off campus, finances, housing, family-related questions, and COVID-19–related support from the university or the government. The specific question we addressed in the chapter is: "How, and if, the EDI policies of the university during the pandemic alleviated inequities experienced by IGSS in that university?" Our analysis involved line-by-line coding of the policies and the transcribed interviews to identify emergent themes (Charmaz, 2014; Corbin & Strauss, 2008; Emerson et al., 1995).

Findings

Financial Resources and EDI Policies

The Government of Canada introduced financial-aid policies during the COVID-19 pandemic to address the urgent needs of vulnerable and low-income populations. International students, however, were not categorized as a vulnerable social group. Lucas[2], a Brazilian IGS, discussed the financial challenges that international students grappled with amid the pandemic. He shared:

> A lot of people lost their jobs. Internationals are pushed to the back of the line of being hired in the pandemic. Like my music student, he could not find a job not even at Walmart. At the end of my course, I was hoping I would be closer to getting a job. Thankfully we have family in Brazil we can stay with until we decide what to do next.

As a response to the crisis in Ukraine, the university introduced financial support to incoming Ukrainian students who were survivors of war and persecution. The Faculty of Graduate Studies dedicated more than $100,000 to this fund in 2022. In the same year, another financial support program was introduced, in which international students coming from nations experiencing war and conflict were eligible to receive between $50 and $5,000. These initiatives allow the university to sell itself as a place where students with different lived experiences based on their social locations are welcomed and cared for. Up until the creation of these policies—which mainly emerged as a response to the war in Ukraine, a predominantly white country—international students of colour from war-affected countries such as Afghanistan, Myanmar, Palestine, Sudan, and Ethiopia caught no institutional attention. These interview narratives allude to the exclusion of a huge group of international students of colour from these financial aids. Lucas's narrative shows the extent to which such initiatives are created as a reaction to certain growing public concerns without addressing oppressive structures that often "push international students to the back of the line," as Lucas said, during times of crisis. Underneath the university's financial-aid initiatives was the neoliberal logic that commodifies race as well as education, which is considered a driver of economic profit and benefit

(Haapakoski & Pashby, 2017), allowing a change in the institution's appearance rather than its structures.

Betul, an IGS who had to quit her job due to taking maternity leave, shared her experience:

> I was not able to work on projects, because they were in person. So [I was] not able to work and not able to get paid, not being able to get participants. My supervisor was trying to find me another [research assistantship] that was more doable online, but then I was about to give birth and had to stop. This has impacted my financials; my husband is working five to six days a week, so he is compensating the financials.

Canada has attracted a large share of international students since the mid-2000s, reaching 621,600 in 2021 (Crossman et al., 2022). The number of international students at this major research university reached more than 6,800 in 2020, mainly from Iran, China, Nigeria, Saudi Arabia, and the United States. The generous financial support offered by the university in this study is powerful evidence of its equity, diversity, and inclusion commitment. However, this amount for all international students is possibly not enough to address the needs of the ever-growing body of international students at the university.[3] For Betul, the bursaries available to her were not enough, nor did they take into account her needs as an international student and new mother, unable to work outside of the home and with a limited support network. The Graduate Student Association offered emergency bursaries for students at a maximum of $1,500 a year per student; an amount that would not cover one month of expenses for Betul and her child. It is likely that either Betul did not know about this funding or was not eligible for it. Regardless, this pot of money did not help her even in her intersectional position of being an international graduate student of colour, a new mother, and someone in need of financial support. Therefore, without clear guidelines for the allocation of this fund, what seemed like an equity measure—aiming at providing different groups with different resources depending on needs—functioned as an equality measure, not accounting for the needs of differential groups when allocating resources, since it provided different groups with similar resources regardless of need. Equality measures, like this initiative, have the risk of reinforcing the system of oppression.

It is only through equity measurement that the institution can address the concerns of international students with different intersecting axes of identities, given that the inequities are intersectional and not all international students have the same intersecting axes of marginalization (Purkayastha, 2012).

In perhaps the intentional ambiguity around the allocation of funds assigned to immigrant/refugee international students during the pandemic, what gets concealed is the inequity that even the more individualized/personalized initiatives, which aim at addressing trauma from war and persecution, cannot address. For instance, there are many international students of colour on campus who may have experienced the trauma of war and persecution in the past and needed support to cope during the lockdown as research on forced migrants during the pandemic has shown (Banerjee et al., 2022b), but the financial allocation was designed particularly for Ukrainian students escaping the current war. This demonstrates that racialized international students embody the figure of the stranger, as Ahmed (1999) describes, who is located at the boundary of the Canadian nation as the "space of belonging" (p. 330). The stranger, in a neoliberal multicultural society, is invited and welcomed to be a part of the host country but at a proximity that is deemed unthreatening (Banerjee, 2022; Ngai, 2014). While they are being invited to embody diversity and equity, and institutional commitments to inclusion, they do not get the same support as domestic students or white immigrants who are the primary target for the university's recent financial support.[4]

Betul's narrative also shows how the financial policies are gender-neutral and do not address the needs of those who carry the double burden of graduate school and motherhood. What is palpable in the financial and most of the EDI initiatives/policies is a lack of intersectional focus and an examination of social inequities that impact individuals located at the intersection of various marginalized social identities.

While they often struggle financially, universities treat IGSs as a source of profit. Gabriela, a PHD student from Mexico, highlighted how international students contribute to the Canadian gross domestic product (GDP) and the university's bottom line without being offered the necessary support to continue. She shared:

> They definitely see us…from an economic point of view. And I know that in Canada, one of the main incomes from the country is international students, so many international students know this and they expect more support. But even right now with the pandemic, the supports for students were given to Canadians, not international students, and international students still have to pay $5,000 each term. So [that's] just one of those things that it makes me down and [makes me feel] like this is not fair. Even the way the community, the university, communicated information—"At the moment, we're not kicking anyone out of residence." It's just—it's unacceptable.

Gabriela's narrative taps into the traditional construction of international students as economic units or assets (McCartney, 2020; Paltridge et al., 2014). In fact, international students have significantly contributed to the Canadian GDP over the past few years (Firang & Mensah, 2022). Immigration, Refugees and Citizenship Canada data shows that the Canadian GDP drastically increased up to $20 billion as a result of rapid growth in the number of international students in 2019 (Mendicino, 2020). In addition to the monetary benefits, international students of colour enhance the image of the diversity of universities.

Gender- and Race-Neutral Policies and Their Consequences
Over the past few years, the university in question has introduced initiatives to create an inclusive, diverse, and welcoming learning environment for students. Workplace-accommodation policies were introduced in 2016 to create a more diverse and inclusive workplace for all. These initiatives lack an intersectional lens to address the needs and concerns of international students. Participants highlight what Ahmed calls the "non-performativity" of these initiatives (2012, p. 117). For instance, Lucas's spouse Maria discussed the emotional and financial toll of graduate studies on her partner and herself. She noted the student work experience within her husband's department, and how he worked long hours with little pay and recognition. Maria stated she would not recommend international students pursue a PHD in Canada:

> I would not recommend [it] to people. We are lucky despite everything we were able to manage, but we are desperately exhausted, Lucas keeps questioning his decisions, and I think that is the opposite

of what higher education should do to you. It's not easy but we manage.

Maria's narrative shows the extent to which EDI and equity-oriented programs have failed to address the specific needs of racialized students, particularly students who have to juggle graduate school and providing for their families, and those living on temporary visas, which not only exclude them from financial aid available to domestic students but also does not allow them to find a job off campus. This usually has gendered consequences when the IGS or their spouse has maternal responsibilities. This means that IGSS are particularly intertwined with the university and experience financial instability that, unlike domestic students, only the university can fix. The statements "I wouldn't recommend it to anyone" and "We're desperately exhausted" reveal the non-performativity of EDI initiatives when it comes to those most vulnerable on campuses. Ahmed (2012, p. 117) describes non-performativity as a way to highlight the gap between commitment and its effects, such as the non-performativity of university EDI policies in bringing the changes that they are promising: creating a welcoming and inclusive working and learning environment for students.

Along the same line, Maria, Lucas's partner, discussed the dire consequences of racial and gender-neutral EDI policies for her family. She added:

> He is overworked, so at home, I have to deal with more things because he is often working. It gets imbalanced. As a couple, it's exhausting because we don't have free time together because it's 1:00 a.m., he's doing something, [and] then early in the morning he is working as well. We never have time.

Analysis of the interview narratives shows that married IGSS have a unique experience at the intersection of multiple identities as racialized women with temporary immigration status. Maria's statement shows work-life imbalance for IGSS and its consequences for their families. The graduate program, according to Maria's narrative, has changed the family dynamics and gendered division of labour, leading her to carry the greater domestic workload. This problem was exacerbated for IGSS with children during the pandemic as IGSS and some of their spouses struggled to balance virtual work and school life, as explored by Fandino and Banerjee (2022). IGS mothers with young children, like Betul, were the most impacted (Fandino & Banerjee, 2022).

Some IGSs offered a positive spin to their domestic situations during the pandemic. Nami, an Iranian man IGS with children, shared: "The pandemic, spending time together all day, it was our first experience with that, and it was quite good actually. I know some people struggled with that but for us, it was quite good. More time to spend with my daughter." Roya, his wife, said, "I am proud of the way we handled everything together, how we raised our daughter. We did it!" While the couple's positive experience of family is affirmative, their explanation hides multiple structural gendered inequities that should ideally be addressed by EDI policies. For instance, when Nami said that the pandemic, for the first time, offered him a chance to spend time with his family, it stood in sharp contrast to Betul, an IGS and a mother of colour who seemed to have struggled to balance motherhood with being an IGS with financial constraints. This shows how the pandemic exacerbated certain gendered inequities that were unaccounted for in EDI policies (LaBrenz et al., 2023). Achieving gender equity requires acknowledging that every program, as well as institutional policies and structures, affects not only women and men but also women at the axis of multiple identities differently. To achieve a equitable learning environment, policies need to address the differences in situations and needs between graduate students at the intersection of race, immigration status, gender, and marital status. While Roya's pride in how she and her husband "handled everything" should be honoured, it also becomes the trope for neoliberal diversity—what critical race and whiteness scholars assert is the labour taken on by employees of colour who then become the face of happy diversity (Ahmed, 2018; Buckner et al., 2021). In this case, unpaid reproductive labour is deflected to women, either when they are IGSs or when they are the dependent spouse of an IGS, while the institution reaps the benefit of their embodied and embedded diversity on campus.

Mental Health

Another equity-oriented program launched before the pandemic by the university aimed at fostering the well-being of the students and staff. Campus programs aimed at enhancing mental health on campus were initiated through raising awareness and promoting well-being, developing self-management, enhancing early response, and offering direct service to those in need. According to our interviews with IGSs, this mental-health policy was ineffective in enhancing their mental well-being, especially for students who are women.

Reflecting on the mental health struggles of IGSs, Lucas shared:

> I feel less of a person because I was not born in Canada. I was reading that four thousand [people die by] suicide in Canada per year, but no stats on international students, but in Toronto in November there were six suicides of international students. These things [are happening to] students who graduate and can't find a position.

The above statement reveals the emotional toll of being and feeling constantly out of place. The statement "I feel less of a person because I was not born in Canada" shows the participant's clear understanding of the oppressive structures that impact international students due to their marginalized racial identity and immigration status. "Not being able to find a job" and "feeling less of a person" as a means to refer to the subordinated social and economic status of immigrant people can have dreadful consequences, as Lucas mentioned, on their mental health.

Along similar lines, Carla, a Black woman IGS, discussed not receiving the mental-health support that she needed during the pandemic. She mentioned:

> The department was silent during COVID. I don't remember getting an email or them asking for a meeting about what we needed, about how we were doing. I suggested [it] to them, but they didn't think it was needed. My supervisor tries, we do meetings every other week, but that was just them, not other people. It was nice that they did that, but it was not that impactful. My family doesn't live here, so I could not see them, just me and my partner at home all the time. All the time. There was also a lot of things happening to the Black community at the time; it was really hard.

Carla's narrative not only unveils the ineffectuality of the mental-health strategy but more importantly, reveals the race, gender, and class neutrality of this policy. As a part of the Black community, she was experiencing traumatic events and stressors during the pandemic like the murder of George Floyd and its impact, which required race- and gender-pertinent mental-health support. She added:

> I want a Black woman [therapist], but it's Alberta. It's been a rough time with my mental health. I did a few sessions on campus—five sessions—[but] I did not find it helpful. They try to help you on how to cope with school, but that was not my issue. I was also trying to find [a] sliding scale [fee], but then my husband has me in his insurance, but then I still couldn't do it without sacrificing other aspects of my life, financially. And they do focus on schoolwork, but that is not my issue, I do get my stuff done. I don't feel the mental-health services are equipped.

The interview narratives indicate that international students struggle to access the most pivotal mental-health resources on campus, including finding a therapist who represents their racial and gender identity. Carla's narrative reveals the whiteness of the organizational structure, which has remained intact despite introducing various initiatives and pilot programs that aim to address obstacles faced by marginalized groups, including racialized and visible minority groups. As Ahmed (2009) writes, diversity policies are, at their core, about "changing perception of whiteness rather than changing the whiteness of organization" (p. 45). The experiences and struggles of IGSs to navigate their lives through graduate programs show the extent to which diversity policies have kept the unequal organizational structures intact.

Conclusion

This chapter illustrates the ineffectiveness of equity-oriented programs to substantially support IGSs, and it demonstrates the inequitable experiences of IGSs during the COVID-19 pandemic, which were left unaddressed despite the university's official commitments to EDI. We deploy critical race scholarship and its critique of diversity discourse in post-secondary educational institutions to analyze if, and how, EDI policies address the specific challenges of IGSs, paying attention to their intensified needs during the COVID-19 pandemic. We found that while EDI policies and initiatives technically covered issues of finance and mental health—two major concerns for IGSs—the impact of these policies and initiatives was negligible in the lives of IGSs as they struggled with challenges posed by the COVID-19 pandemic.

While EDI policies espoused protection for gendered and racialized students on campus, there was no acknowledgment in the policies that the pandemic made households of IGS, especially with children, more gender inequitable in terms of domestic labour, and IGSs who were mothers of colour experienced little support specific to their needs, making these policies gender- and race-neutral. Further, while the university made financial provisions for immigrant, refugee, and international students during the pandemic, we found that most IGSs with families struggled to make ends meet. The financial provisions created by the university functioned as equality measures—not equity measures—because there was no clear mechanism for the allocation of those funds based on the intersectional needs of international students. Finally, the emphasis of EDI policies on mental health and well-being of equity-seeking groups did not seem to help most IGSs during the pandemic, least of all Black women IGSs with no family support in Canada, who experienced the isolating effects of the pandemic lockdowns in addition to the traumatic events surrounding intensified police violence against Black communities in the summer of 2020.

We contend that EDI measures in the context of crisis sought to address structural inequity, but given that these policies were designed within a neoliberal, colonial institution, their impact was at best superficial for the IGSs we interviewed. As we highlight here, internationalization under neoliberal logic turns international students into economic capital, and while the diversity of international students is used to shore up the reputation of the university, EDI measures do not adequately address the needs of diverse students. The experiences of the IGSs in our study send a loud and clear message: if the university is serious about EDI, policies need to adopt a materially equitable framework and move beyond what Ahmed (2012) critiques as the "happy diversity" trope and non-performatives. Only then can we hope that the EDI discourse can move beyond being a cipher to affecting real change in the lives of those who are most harmed by the neoliberal, paternalistic, white-dominant, and colonial orientation of academic institutions.

Notes

1. In this chapter, we use "this/the university" to refer to a research-intensive university in Alberta, Canada, at the centre of this study.
2. The names of IGSs were changed to preserve their anonymity.
3. The financial support was introduced in 2020, and no further information is available about international students' access to this financial resource at the time.
4. International students pay twice as much as domestic students annually.

References

Abu-Laban, Y., & Gabriel, C. (2002). *Selling diversity: Immigration, multiculturalism, employment equity, and globalization*. Broadview Press.

Ahmed, S. (1999). Home and away: Narratives of migration and estrangement. *International Journal of Cultural Studies, 2*(3), 329–347. https://doi.org/10.1177/136787799900200303

Ahmed, S. (2006). Orientations: Toward a queer phenomenology. *GLQ: A Journal of Lesbian and Gay Studies, 12*(4), 543–574. https://doi.org/10.1215/10642684-2006-002

Ahmed, S. (2007). A phenomenology of whiteness. *Feminist Theory, 8*(2), 149–168. https://doi.org/10.1177/1464700107078139

Ahmed, S. (2009). Embodying diversity: Problems and paradoxes for Black feminists. *Race Ethnicity and Education, 12*(1), 41–52. https://doi.org/10.1080/13613320802650931

Ahmed, S. (2012). *On being included: Racism and diversity in institutional life*. Duke University Press. https://doi.org/10.2307/j.ctv1131d2g

Ahmed, S. (2018). Rocking the boat: Women of colour as diversity workers. In J. Arday & H.S. Mirza (Eds.), *Dismantling race in higher education* (pp. 331–348). Palgrave Macmillan. https://link.springer.com/content/pdf/10.1007/978-3-319-60261-5.pdf

Banerjee, P. (2022). *The opportunity trap: High-skilled workers, Indian families, and the failures of the dependent visa program*. New York University Press. https://doi.org/10.18574/nyu/9781479852918.001.0001

Banerjee, P., Khandelwal, C., & Sanyal, M. (2022a). Deep care: The COVID-19 pandemic and the work of marginal feminist organizing in India. *Gender, Work & Organization, 31*(4), 1479–1504. https://doi.org/10.1111/gwao.12857

Banerjee, P., Chacko, S., & Korsha, S. (2022b). Toll of the COVID-19 pandemic on the primary caregiver in Yazidi refugee families in Canada: A feminist refugee epistemological analysis. *Studies in Social Justice, 16*(1), 33–53. https://doi.org/10.26522/ssj.v16i1.2692

Banerjee, P., & Fandino, I. (2020, August 6). Canada's international graduate students and COVID-19: Beyond the rhetoric of welcome. *Canadian Dimension*. https://canadiandimension.com/articles/view/canadas-international-students-and-covid-19-beyond-the-rhetoric-of-welcome

Bascaramurty, D., Bhatt, N., & Rana, U. (2022, January 21). Canada's international student recruiting machine is broken. *The Globe and Mail*. https://www.theglobeandmail.com/canada/article-india-canada-international-student-recruitment/

Belkhodja, C., & Esses, V. (2013). Knowledge synthesis: Improving the assessment of international students' contribution to Canadian society. *Pathways to Prosperity: Canada*. http://p2pcanada.ca/wp-content/uploads/2014/02/International-Students-Contribution-to-Canadian-Society.pdf

Bensadoun, E. (2021, July 27). *Hate crimes rose "sharply" in 2020 despite police-reported crime drop, data shows*. Global News. https://globalnews.ca/news/8063163/hate-crimes-rise-canada-2020/

Britez, R., & Peters, M.A. (2010). Internationalization and the cosmopolitical university. *Policy Futures in Education, 8*(2), 201–216.

Brunner, L.R. (2022). Towards a more just Canadian education-migration system: International student mobility in crisis. *Studies in Social Justice, 16*(1), 78–102. https://doi.org/10.26522/ssj.v16i1.2685

Buckner, E., Lumb, P., Jafarova, Z., Kang, P., Marroquin, A., & Zhang, Y. (2021). Diversity without race: How university internationalization strategies discuss international students. *Journal of International Students, 11*(S1), 32–49.

Campbell, A. (2021). Equity education initiatives within Canadian universities: Promise and limits. *Perspectives: Policy and Practice in Higher Education, 25*(2), 51–61. https://doi.org/10.1080/13603108.2019.1631226

Canada's International Education Strategy: Harnessing our knowledge advantage to drive innovation and prosperity. (2014). Foreign Affairs, Trade and Development Canada [Catalogue no. FR5-86/2014E-PDF]. https://www.international.gc.ca/education/assets/pdfs/overview-apercu-eng.pdf

Canadian Bureau for International Education. (2022). *The student voice: National results of the 2021 CBIE international student survey*. https://cbie.ca/wp-content/uploads/2022/06/CBIE-2021-International-Student-Survey-National-Report-FINAL.pdf

Charmaz, K. (2014). *Constructing grounded theory* (2nd ed.). SAGE Publications.

Chatterjee, S., Shahrokni, S., Gomez, B., & Poojary, M. (2022). "Another university is possible?": A study of Indigenizing and internationalizing initiatives in two Canadian postsecondary institutions. *Comparative and International Education, 51*(1), 1–19. https://doi.org/10.5206/cieeci.v51i1.14829

Corbin, J., & Strauss, A. (2008). *Basics of qualitative research: Techniques and procedures for developing grounded theory* (3rd ed.). SAGE Publications.

Crabtree, B.F., & Miller, W.L. (1999). *Doing qualitative research* (2nd ed.). SAGE Publications.

Crossman, E., Choi, Y., Lu, Y., & Hou, F. (2022). International students as a source of labour supply: A summary of recent trends. *Economic and Social Reports 2*(3), article 1 [Catalogue no. CS36-28-0001/2022-3-1E-PDF]. Statistics Canada. publications.gc.ca/pub?id=9.909341&sl=0

Daly, K.J. (2007). *Qualitative methods for family studies & human development*. SAGE Publications. https://doi.org/10.4135/9781452224800

Emerson, R.M., Fretz, R.I., & Shaw, L.L. (1995). *Writing ethnographic fieldnotes* (2nd ed.). University of Chicago Press.

Fan, A. (2022). *During the pandemic: The response of North American university on discrimination against Chinese international students* [Master's thesis, McGill University]. https://escholarship.mcgill.ca/concern/theses/2801pn136

Fandino, I., & Banerjee, P. (2022). Temporary residents, lasting issues: International graduate students and Covid-19. *Canadian Ethnic Studies, 54*(3), 33–62. https://doi.org/10.1353/ces.2022.0024

Ferdiansyah, S., Supiastutik, & Angin, R. (2020). Thai students' experiences of online learning at Indonesian universities in the time of the COVID-19 pandemic. *Journal of International Students, 10*(S3), 58–74. https://doi.org/10.32674/jis.v10iS3.3199

Firang, D. (2020). The impact of the COVID-19 pandemic on international students in Canada. *International Social Work, 63*(6), 820–824. https://doi.org/10.1177/0020872820940030

Firang, D., & Mensah, J. (2022). Exploring the effects of the COVID-19 pandemic on international students and universities in Canada. *Journal of International Students, 12*(1), 1–18. https://doi.org/10.32674/jis.v12i1.2881

Foste, Z., & Irwin, L. (2020). Applying critical whiteness studies in college student development theory and research. *Journal of College Student Development, 61*(4), 439–455.

Guo, S. (2021). Multiculturalism at a crossroads: Towards pandemic anti-racism education in post-COVID-19 Canada. *Canadian Issues* (Fall 2020/Winter 2021), 81–85.

Guo, Y., & Guo, S. (2017). Internationalization of Canadian higher education: Discrepancies between policies and international student experiences. *Studies in Higher Education, 42*(5), 851–868. https://doi.org/10.1080/03075079.2017.1293874

Haapakoski, J., & Pashby, K. (2017). Implications for equity and diversity of increasing international student numbers in European universities: Policies and practice in four national contexts. *Policy Futures in Education, 15*(3), 360–379.

Hari, A., Nardon, L., & Zhang, H. (2023). A transnational lens into international student experiences of the COVID-19 pandemic. *Global Networks, 23*(1), 14–30. https://doi.org/10.1111/glob.12332

Henry, F., Dua, E., Kobayashi, A., James, C., Li, P., Ramos, H., & Smith, M.S. (2017). Race, racialization and Indigeneity in Canadian universities. *Race Ethnicity and Education, 20*(3), 300–314. https://doi.org/10.1080/13613324.2016.1260226

Hiraldo, P. (2010). The role of critical race theory in higher education. *The Vermont Connection, 31*(1), 7. https://scholarworks.uvm.edu/tvc/vol31/iss1/7

Kim, J. (2012). Acculturation phenomena experienced by the spouses of Korean international students in the United States. *Qualitative Health Research, 22*(6), 755–767. https://doi.org/10.1177/1049732311431442

Koo, K. (2021). Distressed in a foreign country: Mental health and well-being among international students in the United States during COVID-19. In K. Bista, R.M. Allen, & R.Y. Chan (Eds.), *Impacts of COVID-19 on international students and the future of student mobility: International perspectives and experiences* (pp. 28–41). Routledge.

Koo, K., Kim, Y.W., Lee, J., & Nyunt, G. (2021). "It's my fault": Exploring experiences and mental wellness among Korean international graduate students. *Journal of International Students, 11*(4), 790–811. https://doi.org/10.32674/jis.v11i4.2801

LaBrenz, C.A., Robinson, E.D., Chakravarty, S., Vasquez-Schut, G., Mitschke, D.B., & Oh, S. (2023). When "time is not your own": Experiences of mothering students during the COVID-19 pandemic. *Affilia, 38*(2), 263–277.

Lee, J.J., & Rice, C. (2007). Welcome to America? International student perceptions of discrimination. *Higher Education, 53*(3), 381–409. https://doi.org/10.1007/s10734-005-4508-3

Lipura, S.J. (2021). Adding an international student's voice to the pandemic discourse as thinkers, not subjects: Reflections on power, stillness and humanness. *Journal of International Students, 11*(1), 251–256. https://doi.org/10.32674/jis.v11i1.2564

McCartney, D.M. (2020). Border imperialism and exclusion in Canadian parliamentary talk about international students. *Canadian Journal of Higher Education, 50*(4), 37–51 https://doi.org/10.47678/cjhe.v50i4.188831

Mendicino, M.E.L. (2020, October 30). *2020 Annual Report to Parliament on Immigration*. Immigration, Refugees and Citizenship Canada. https://www.canada.ca/en/immigration-refugees-citizenship/corporate/publications-manuals/annual-report-parliament-immigration-2020.html

Milanczak, M. (2022, August 1). *EDI-D in Canadian universities* [Poster]. Undergraduate Student Research Internships Conferences. https://ir.lib.uwo.ca/cgi/viewcontent.cgi?article=1344&context=usri

Monteiro, S. (2020, May 15). *International students are vital to Canada's economic recovery after COVID-19*. Open Democracy. https://www.opendemocracy.net/en/pandemic-border/international-students-are-vital-to-canadas-economic-recovery-after-covid-19/

Nanda, S. (2020). Inequalities and COVID-19. In M.J. Ryan (Ed.), *COVID-19*, vol. 1, *Global Pandemic, Societal Responses, Ideological Solutions* (pp. 109–123). Routledge.

Ngai, M.M. (2014). *Impossible subjects: Illegal aliens and the making of modern America*. Princeton University Press.

Ozyomum, E., & Zhang, Q. (2021, December 22). Amid COVID-19 stressors, international students and their university communities should prioritize mental health supports. *The Conversation*. https://theconversation.com/amid-covid-19-stressors-international-students-and-their-university-communities-should-prioritize-mental-health-supports-173182

Paltridge, T., Mayson, S.E., & Schapper, J.M. (2014). Welcome and exclusion: An analysis of *The Australian* newspaper's coverage of international students. *Higher Education, 68*(1), 103–116. https://doi.org/10.1007/s10734-013-9689-6

Park, H., Lee, M.-J., Choi, G.-Y., & Zepernick, J.S. (2017). Challenges and coping strategies of East Asian graduate students in the United States. *International Social Work, 60*(3), 733–749. https://doi.org/10.1177/0020872816655864

Pidgeon, M. (2016). More than a checklist: Meaningful Indigenous inclusion in higher education. *Social Inclusion, 4*(1), 77–91. https://doi.org/10.17645/si.v4i1.436

Purkayastha, B. (2012). Intersectionality in a transnational world. *Gender & Society, 26*(1), 55–66.

Puwar, N. (2004). Thinking about making a difference. *British Journal of Politics and International Relations, 6*(1), 65–80. https://doi.org/10.1111/j.1467-856X.2004.00127.x

Ramos Fandino, I. (2021). *Lost in translation: The (unseen) experiences of international graduate students and families* [Master's thesis, University of Calgary]. http://hdl.handle.net/1880/114005

Schwarz, E., & Lindqvist, B. (2018). Exploring the phenomenology of whiteness in a Swedish preschool class. *International Journal of Early Childhood, 50*(1), 1–14. https://doi.org/10.1007/s13158-018-0210-3

Small, M.L. (2021). What is "qualitative" in qualitative research? Why the answer does not matter but the question is important. *Qualitative Sociology*, 44(4), 567–574. https://doi.org/10.1007/s11133-021-09501-3

Stein, S., & de Andreotti, V.O. (2016). Cash, competition, or charity: International students and the global imaginary. *Higher Education*, 72(2), 225–239. https://doi.org/10.1007/s10734-015-9949-8

Tamtik, M., & Guenter, M. (2019). Policy analysis of equity, diversity and inclusion strategies in Canadian universities—How far have we come? *Canadian Journal of Higher Education*, 49(3), 41–56. https://doi.org/10.47678/cjhe.v49i3.188529

Tavares, V. (2021). Feeling excluded: International students experience equity, diversity and inclusion. *International Journal of Inclusive Education*, 28(8), 1551–1568. https://doi.org/10.1080/13603116.2021.2008536

Truth and Reconciliation Commission of Canada. (2015). *Truth and Reconciliation Commission of Canada: Calls to Action*. https://www2.gov.bc.ca/assets/gov/british-columbians-our-governments/indigenous-people/aboriginal-peoples-documents/calls_to_action_english2.pdf

Universities Canada. (2019, November 4). *Equity, diversity and inclusion at Canadian universities: Report on the 2019 survey*. Universities Canada. https://www.univcan.ca/media-room/publications/equity-diversity-and-inclusion-at-canadian-universities-report-on-the-2019-survey/

Varughese, A., & Schwartz, S. (2022, January 24). The pandemic exposed the vulnerability of international students in Canada. *The Conversation*. http://theconversation.com/the-pandemic-exposed-the-vulnerability-of-international-students-in-canada-174105

Yancy, G., & Davidson, M. (2014). *Exploring race in predominantly White classrooms: Scholars of color reflect* (1st ed.). Routledge. https://doi.org/10.4324/9780203416716

Yao, C.W., George Mwangi, C.A., & Malaney Brown, V.K. (2018). Exploring the intersection of transnationalism and critical race theory: A critical race analysis of international student experiences in the United States. *Race Ethnicity and Education,* 22(1): 38–58, https://doi.org/10.1080/13613324.2018.1497968

Zhai, Y., & Du, X. (2020). Mental health care for international Chinese students affected by the COVID-19 outbreak. *The Lancet Psychiatry*, 7(4), e22. https://doi.org/10.1016/S2215-0366(20)30089-4

Zhang, Z., & Zhou, G. (2010). Understanding Chinese international students at a Canadian university: Perspectives, expectations, and experiences. *Comparative and International Education* [formerly *Canadian and International Education*], 39(3), 43–58. https://doi.org/10.5206/cie-eci.v39i3.9162

/3

"We Missed Out on a Lot"

The Pandemic, Schooling, and Black Youth

CARL E. JAMES

Introduction

Michael[1]: I was super excited to go to university. I was prepared. I had everything ready and we were supposed to have classes in person. Then, literally the day before or the day of—I don't remember exactly—they just shut everything down. Courses were all online, most tutorials were online, and by the end of COVID, I had one tutorial that wasn't online. Yeah. For my first year at university, it was all online and one tutorial was not. After that I basically dropped out because I was not feeling it anymore. I just felt like I wasn't really learning [as] much in those classes as I intended to because I already knew the core stuff that they were trying to teach. I wasn't looking forward to the following years as much. So I left, and I went to [college name removed for confidentiality] the next year, and that was easily a night and day difference. But then again, it was college. It's hands-on...and every single class I had was in person, and all my professors were way more—I don't want to say energetic, but they were more outgoing. It felt how the classroom was supposed to feel like, it's like what I was expecting.

Chris: I was excited to go to university because I was in a new city away from my family and stuff like that. I was hoping to meet people. Since everything's online, not seeing anyone in person...the classes were not being taught the same. I feel like I really struggled the first year because of those things. At high school, if I needed help, I would usually just go to the teacher after class and ask them. But I couldn't do the same thing at university because I just didn't feel the same doing it online. So really, if you're not on campus, you're not really meeting that many people because it's COVID—everything's locked down. If you needed help, there wasn't really too many people to go to besides just asking your professors. It's pretty much—if you did have an online class, you would get online and stay home, which was basically the experience for me.

Blessing: My college experience, well, half of it got cut short because of COVID. So that was, obviously, just the worst experience ever, because even when it came to graduation, we had our names rolling across the screen like movie credits, [but] we didn't get to walk across the stage. So, it was a very poor way for us to graduate. And for me, because of the fact that I didn't get to finish university, that was something that I was looking forward to so, so much. That was something that I wanted my parents and my grandparents to be able to experience. Okay, they have seen me through elementary, middle school, high school, and now getting to see me through college. It was my mom and I sitting at home one day on the laptop just watching things go across the screen. My courses were all online, so I never actually got to meet many professors in person. Mind you, the one Black professor that I did have for a business course, she was literally the sweetest human ever. She was so nice; she would see us all on Zoom and would call us by name from our first meeting.

For Michael, Chris, and Blessing, who entered university directly from high school, life as students during the COVID-19 pandemic was a "struggle." In a focus group interview in the spring of 2023, they shared that when "everything" shut down and classes shifted from in-person to online because of the pandemic, it caused them significant consternation. So, while Michael and Chris—who started university in the fall of 2019—were "excited to go to university," Michael found his educational situation to be untenable and, as a result, left university for college, which for him "was easily a night and day difference." On the other hand, Chris remained in university, resigned to the fact that he had to remain at home and not have opportunities to meet and interact with other students and his professors, as he hoped and would have done in high school. Blessing, who had also transferred from university to college, similarly missed in-person contact with her professors, but was relieved to have a Black professor whom she described as "literally the sweetest human ever." But a big regret for Blessing was not having her parents experience seeing her "walk across the stage at graduation."

Clearly, as it did with many of the focus group participants, COVID-19 had a substantial or life-changing effect on the lives of these three post-secondary education students. Also contributing to this effect was how their online classes made it difficult—if not impossible—for them to establish a personal connection or relationship with their professors. They would go and meet the professor after class for help with problems, something, as Chris indicates, they would have done with their high-school teacher. But was life any different for high-school students who were preparing for university? Did those in high school have opportunities to develop needed relationships with their teachers, to learn the skills and access the social capital that might serve them to effectively negotiate life in university?

Studies have shown that COVID-19 has had a disproportionate effect on the lives and well-being of racialized individuals (Tam, 2021; Thompson et al., 2021).[2] In fact, Canada's chief public health officer, Dr. Theresa Tam, writes:

> These disproportionate impacts among racialized and Indigenous communities are not due to biological differences between groups or populations. Rather, they reflect existing health inequities that are strongly influenced by a specific set of social and economic factors—things like income, education, employment and housing that shape an individual's place in society. (Tam, 2021)

Essentially, the COVID-19 virus—which triggered the pandemic—served to expose and exacerbate issues of inequity within Canadian society. In fact, combined with racism—sometimes referred to as "a permanent virus" or "an enduring pandemic"—the COVID-19 virus not only served to modify but also exacerbate the ways in which race (intersecting with gender, class, dis/ability, etc.) "operate[s] to maintain the existing oppressive systems and social hierarchy" (Gaynor & Wilson, 2020, p. 836), which significantly contribute to further struggles in the lived experiences of racialized individuals. This chapter explores the effects of COVID-19 on the schooling and educational experiences[3] of Black students who attended high school in the Greater Toronto Area (GTA) in the spring of 2021 during the time of online learning. In doing so, I explore what schooling was like for these students, their relationships with teachers, and how they grappled with their hopes and fears as they worked toward completion of high school and planned for university with the knowledge of the importance of credentials if they are to broaden their potential and realize their ambitions. Their schooling was in a context in which parents were not only concerned with the impact of racism but also that of the pandemic on their children's psychological well-being and capacity to fulfill their educational ambitions—especially at a time when, as parents, they were trying to cope with their own social and employment situations (Bhamani et al., 2020).

In what follows, I delineate the theoretical scaffolds that frame the exploration and then briefly discuss the schooling contexts and education circumstances of Black and other racialized students. I do this with an understanding that the experiences of K–12 schooling and educational circumstances will continue to impact Black and other racialized students' educational trajectories as they decide whether to pursue post-secondary education.

Theoretical Supports: Community-Reference, Categorical Inequality, and Social Reproduction

Scholars have reasoned that community is an important resource in the schooling and educational lives of students. And for marginalized and racialized students—for whom the Eurocentric and middle-class school context functions to alienate them—community provides important cultural reference and nourishing support (Collins, 2009; James, 2021; Shujaa, 1993; Yosso, 2005). Students acquire what Yosso (2005) calls community cultural wealth—a set of resources or assets consisting of aspirational, navigational, social, linguistic, familial, and resistance capital—which they bring to their schooling and education. Often unrecognized, unacknowledged, and under-utilized, these constructions of capital informed by familial, home, and community conditions, in which students grow up or reside, help to cultivate the sense they make of their schooling, and in turn, how they engage in their schooling processes.

Building on the notion that community plays an essential role in the social, schooling, and educational lives of students, I have previously discussed how taking a community-referenced approach when working with students in marginalized communities would enable them to experience a schooling context that is culturally relevant and responsive to their lived experiences (James, 2012). For the "selves" that students bring to their educational pursuits exist in relation to their identities and communities, and the relationships that educators build with students are influenced or enhanced by the knowledge (beyond what is obtained through media) that educators have of the communities in which students live.

Indeed, as Jack (2019) writes in his essay "I Was a Low-income College Student: Classes Weren't the Hard Part":

> Neighborhoods are more than a collection of homes and shops, more than uneven sidewalks or winding roads. Some communities protect us from hurt, harm and danger. Others provide no respite at all. This process is not random but the consequence of historical patterns of exclusion and racism. Life in privileged communities means that children traverse safer streets, have access to good schools, and interact with neighbours who can supply more than the proverbial cup of sugar. Life in distressed communities can mean learning to distinguish between firecrackers and gunshots. (para. 14)

The point is, that students' schooling and educational experiences are always culturally situated and informed by their communities, which carry meanings that operate as "major vehicles" that connect people to the institutions in which they are involved. And, as Collins (2009) asserts, community is much more than a "cognitive construct" or "a random collection of individuals," for it is "infused with emotions and value-laden meanings, which can move people to action" by stimulating feelings of connection (p. 28).

Being responsive to students' dynamic relationships with their communities also entails acknowledging the settler colonial context[4] in which schooling takes place, and how the ideology of neoliberalism, as shaped by "categorical inequality" drives the policies and practices of educational institutions. Categorical inequality, Domina and colleagues (2017) contend, takes as given the inequitable structure of society and the central role that schools—through their policies, programs, curriculum, courses, assessments, and disciplinary measures—play in maintaining the structure. Basically, as a major socializing institution of society, schools create categories into which individuals are sorted, and thereby generate, reinforce, and in effect, mirror the social inequities of society. Domina and colleagues (2017) write:

> Even if schools perfectly compensate for racial, ethnic, gender, or class inequalities among their students, they would still structure and legitimate social inequalities in schooled societies. One way in which schools structure inequality is by issuing a status-differentiated set of educational credentials that interact with labour markets and other social systems to influence individuals' placements in contemporary systems of social stratification. (p. 313–314)

If indeed the schooling system is not to reproduce the educational and social inequities within society[5]—that is the social-class divisions, power hierarchies, and marginalization created by the capitalist culture that serves to maintain the values and ideals of wealth (Serna, 2017, p. 4)—then, it must operate on the basis of equity rather than equality. Equity is the recognition of and respect for individuals' differences and social situations, while equality is to provide the same opportunities for and treatment to everyone regardless of their differences. Hence, if schooling is to provide students with equitable opportunities that will enable them to attain the education—including post-secondary education—and occupations to which they aspire, then the environment must be one in which *all* students are able to successfully participate and perform in ways that are consistent with their needs, interests, and expectations. In this regard, at a time when COVID-19 has caused much adjustment to the teaching and learning environments of students, it is crucial for all educators, including university educators and administrators, to take into account how racialization, and anti-Black racism in particular, might be operating to further disenfranchise Black students.

Enduring Inequalities in the Education of Black Students: What the Literature Says

A recent Statistics Canada report indicates that in 2021, "Japanese (31.7%) and Black (5%) populations were the only racialized groups where over 2% of the working-age population were in the third generation or more (born in Canada to Canadian-born parents)" ("A Portrait," 2023, p. 4). And while on average, Black Canadians (32.4%) were just as likely to hold a bachelor's degree as the national average (the national average being 32.9%), "46.3% of Black children of African immigrants had a bachelor's degree or higher, compared with 15.8% of Black children of Canadian-born parents" ("A Portrait," 2023, p. 3). The census data also shows that "in contrast to most other racialized groups…16% of Black workers with a bachelor's degree or higher from a Canadian institution worked in occupations that require a high school diploma or less. This was the highest overqualification rate of any Canadian-educated racialized group" ("A Portrait," 2023, p. 10). And Black men were among the group of racialized bachelor's degree graduates that "had the lowest employment incomes" ("Racialized," 2023, p. 3).

An earlier Statistics Canada report by Turcotte (2020) shows that "Black youth were less likely than other youth to attain a postsecondary qualification" (p. 2). About half of Black male youth aged 23 to 27 had a post-secondary certificate in 2016, compared to 62% for other youth (p. 2). Black female youth were more likely than Black male youth to have a post-secondary qualification, but they still compared unfavourably to other young women: "34% of Black girls aged 13 to 17 in 2006 had a university degree 10 years later, compared with 41% of other girls from the same cohort" (Turcotte, 2020, p. 3). Further, disaggregation of Statistics Canada data pertaining to recent immigrant and Canadian-born youth reveal that those who have lived in Canada the longest fare the worst. Specifically, among non-immigrant Black men, just 18% have a bachelor's diploma, compared to 29% of immigrant Black men, and about 32% of the general Canadian population. On the other hand, 31% of non-immigrant Black women (about the same as other Canadians) and 25% of immigrant Black women (significantly lower than other Canadians) have a university diploma (Turcotte, 2020). That Black immigrant men tend to have university diplomas is, in part, a reflection of the fact that such degrees enabled them to enter Canada. But once in Canada, Black immigrants experience worse educational outcomes over every generation, so third-generation Black Canadians are less likely than their parents and grandparents to graduate from university.

This picture of Black youth is not surprising, since many of them, especially young men, are more likely to be streamed into non-academic programs, are less likely to have teachers (as well as curriculum materials) with whom they can culturally relate and tend to be over-represented in the lowest level of educational programs—including special education. Logically, these experiences not only contribute to the higher rates of school drop-out for Black students, especially non-immigrant men but also negatively affect their emotional well-being and mental health. This means that Black youth are less likely to pursue post-secondary studies, and those who do most often choose to attend college (James, 2021; Patel, 2015; Szekely & Pessian, 2015).

In terms of the impact of COVID-19 on the schooling and education of Black and other racialized students, evidence suggests that they experience added obstacles due to the inequitable conditions they confront. *Globe and Mail* education reporters Bascaramurty and Alphonso (2020) best represent what students in the GTA have had to confront by saying:

> Before the pandemic forced a crisis in the education system, many school boards had committed to addressing systemic racism and inequity by re-evaluating programs, such as French immersion (which attracts a higher proportion of affluent, white students) and streaming (which routinely put Black children on a path to applied courses, which limit their options after graduation), that have disadvantaged students from low-income and racialized communities.

But with educators focused on the "basics" of schooling, this crisis remains, because, as the reporters state, "reimagining the system seems impractical, if not impossible" (Bascaramurty & Alphonso, 2020). And as *Toronto Star* columnist Elghawaby (2020) tells us, racialized parents have asked: "How do we best help our children, who are now going through two different types of stress and anxiety?"

American studies have shown that unprepared for, and unfamiliar with, the requirements for teaching in a schooling context brought about by the pandemic, teachers were working fewer hours (seven versus nine) per day and taught less new material to their students. In turn, students were increasingly disengaged from learning (and with online sessions—many of them did not log in, or if they did, they did not turn on their cameras or make contact with the teacher) (Bhamani et al., 2020; Herold & Kurtz, 2020). Also, deviation from usual classroom instruction practices has created "additional variance in test scores so the ability to compare the same student's test performance" over the years "will be problematic" (Middleton, 2020, p. 42). Understandably, students without the language, and the social and cultural capital of middle-class white-centric schooling—for instance, lower income, immigrant, and racialized students, and those with disabilities—have had to work harder to pick up on the cultural differences, subtleties, and nuances in order to be successful in school.

The following discussion is based on data collected during spring 2021 of eight Black high-school students—six young women and two young men: five in grade 12, two in grade 11, and one in grade 10—who resided in the GTA. They participated in one focus-group interview and shared their insights into how the pandemic was affecting their learning and educational performance as they coped with online (or virtual or hybrid) learning—something for which neither they nor their teachers were prepared. The resulting "crisis," as Bascaramurty and Alphonso (2020) observe, was a consequence of the living and working circumstances of these students' parents,[6] as well as the "virtual" schooling to which the students were subjected. In the schooling context of the pandemic, the lack of access to relevant learning materials, quiet study spaces (including home), computers, and reliable internet, as well as having teachers and administrators who are not culturally conversant with the lives of their students, particularly Black students, meant that students struggled to keep up with their learning and the additional stresses which in turn contributed to their poor educational outcomes. All these discriminatory factors will impact Black and other racialized students' decision and ability to pursue higher education and will have an overarching impact on their overall well-being and economic success for many years.

The High School Experiences of Black Students During the Pandemic: "It Wasn't Fun"

Most of the students who participated in the focus group expressed dissatisfaction with their schooling, noting that "it wasn't fun" and that their teachers "weren't there" for them. According to Ronald, a student in the focus group: "We missed out on a lot of stuff that we could have potentially received if we were in person—even though we were trying hard to participate." Ronald insisted that he and his peers demonstrated that they were committed to learning despite the virtual-classroom context. "We were really engaged," he said, "and everybody had their cameras on." For her part, another focus-group participant, Marcella, questioned the usefulness of the education that they were receiving, suggesting that their lessons "were really sped up and the curriculum was rearranged." In Marcella's view, "the condensed speed" at which rearranged curricular materials were delivered and replaced by "quick studying" was unhelpful to learning since the materials were very quickly forgotten. She concluded: "But to be honest, I don't think I can remember half the stuff I learned from any of my classes, because essentially all I did was race to get everything done correctly and how the teacher wanted it done."

Building on the idea that they were not "learning anything" in their classes during the pandemic, Ronald added, "You were taking it [educational material] in and regurgitating whatever you got from the teacher." As a consequence, these students felt, as Heather, another student, did, that many of their "teachers didn't really care, or it seems like they don't care about their job...they care more about giving us the work and having it submitted if that makes sense." As teachers shifted—at least from the perspective of these students—to simply getting through the required curriculum, the students lowered their grade expectations to simply "pass." Summing up her own experience, Heather observed, "As I said on multiple occasions, I was there to pass, not to learn. So, unfortunately, online school will not be for me." In a similar instrumental logic, student Karen added that she routinely attended classes "for my grades" so that they "didn't decrease," and she admitted that her class attendance did not mean she was engaged in any meaningful learning.

Another problem that participants consistently identified was a feeling of being "under-prepared" for the next grade or stage of their education—specifically, for grades 11 and 12 and university. Marcella explained: "But overall, I don't feel that prepared going into grade 11. I just feel like I'm going to constantly stress and struggle to catch up with things that come. I have to learn what I should have done in grade 10." Likewise, Rachel explained that her experiences with schooling during the pandemic have mostly been negative because learning from home did not require the same attention as would have been the case with in-person classes. She expanded on her experiences with being unprepared:

> I would say that I have a majority of negative experiences when it comes to schooling during the pandemic. Especially going into grade 12, I feel that with some of the courses…I'm severely under-prepared. I know that especially because we had to do school online. It kind of made it so that you can kind of do it anywhere, which means that you don't have to focus…I know that for me, [in] the classes that I enjoyed…I was very engaged. But courses that I didn't really enjoy, it was like, I'm doing it just because they told me that I had to.

Similarly, Alicia voiced reservations about being unprepared for university because of online learning—both with respect to classroom learning and missed opportunities for a social life:

> Personally, I would not want to do online again, especially since I'm about to start my first year of uni. I feel like it kind of sucks because they say your last year of high school and your first-year university are supposed to be the best years of your life and with me being online in September, that would mean that I'm missing out on those two years and basically spending them at home. So, I guess I would want to make up for my grade 12 year with my first year [of university].

From Alicia's perspective, there was a high cost to attaining an education during the pandemic. That cost included two years at home—the final year of high school and the first year of university—with limited access to needed educational materials, minimized in-person learning, lack of study spaces, and limited personal interactions with educators. Also, there were missed opportunities, as Alicia contended with reference to mythologized popular cultural norms, to socialize with peers during "the best years" of a young person's life. An additional cost was time; not having some of the foundational learnings or educational prerequisites that should have been completed during high school or in the early years of university, means that students will likely have to put effort, time (in terms of months or years), and finances into extra or supplementary educational requirements.

Not knowing what to expect in their first year of university—especially since they would be attending university during the pandemic, and at a time when these students did not know if university classes would be in-person or virtual—some students contemplated whether they should attend, while others put off entering university after their grade 12 year. These considerations also have to do with the students' feeling ill-prepared and/or believing that they would not be able to maximize their learning, and hence obtain the education required, and/or to which they were entitled, during their first year of university. The students' uncertainty about when they should enter university was likely informed by the fact that most of them would be first-generation university students with little to no knowledge of the institution, and no suitable or sufficient familial support in this regard (see James & Taylor, 2023).

For some participants, despite, and even because of, the limitations posed by the delivery of their education and lack of support from teachers, there were some benefits in terms of what they learnt about themselves. Obligated to navigate learning on their own, these participants discovered and developed new capacities and responsibilities. For instance, after admitting that online learning was not "really useful," Marcella went on to say: "But it did teach me a few things, like how to multitask and work effectively; because I had a lot of assignments in a short amount of time." Similarly, Alicia felt that, by necessity, she became more responsible for her own learning, saying "I guess being online taught me to be a lot more disciplined with myself and to be a lot more responsible because only you can take care of yourself online—like, it really is only you. So, I guess I could say that I've become a lot more independent." And commenting that she was forced to become a self-motivated learner, which she hoped would serve her in her university studies, Munjeera surmised:

> Personally, I think this online experience was essential for my development, like, when I used to go to school before, I just would go to school and that was it. But when online, I found that I had to push myself—like, if the teachers were just giving us the information. But if you wanted to learn, you had to go learn on your own; and I think that was the downfall of a lot of students this year. Teachers didn't realize that we're still young. We're still children, like, sometimes, you just don't know how to get these resources ourselves, but I think it was essential for my development. But would I do it again? No, I'm ready to go back to school, have face-to-face interactions, live my life and live out my senior year. But I think it was good preparation for university—for me to know how to study.

While most of the students who participated in this study pointed to their teachers' failures to be responsive to their educational needs as a major impediment to their learning, there were some exceptions. Ronald was one of two participants who shared that he had teachers who were "always there," "looking out for students," and "always communicating" with them. Specifically, referencing the efforts made by his biology teacher, Ronald said:

> Even though the class was virtual, she understood, and she made the class fun or interesting. And she tried to engage the students even though some cameras wouldn't be on all the time, and she would know that the students were there because she would engage them virtually. So, she would do like a jam board, or have slides, or there's this whiteboard that you can use to tell exactly who's there and who's doing what. She would check-in with you daily to make sure you're keeping up with stuff. That was actually a fun class.

This positive experience, made possible by the extraordinary efforts of the teacher to engage students in multiple ways—her daily check-ins to ensure students continued to be on top of their work, and her ability to make learning online "fun"—remained the exception. That the teacher whom Ronald mentioned cared enough about her students that "she would check-in with you daily" is not only relevant but also a signal of the role gender plays in the student-teacher relationship—and likely in science courses where the teacher is someone who knows or understands what it means to be a member of a minoritized group who needs the extra support, particularly in a subject area in which the group is underrepresented.

Conclusion: Fears, Hopes, Re-imaginations, and Desired Changes
In their article "The Longer-Term Impact of COVID-19 on K–12 Student Learning and Assessment," Middleton (2020) points out that "classroom assessment, teaching and learning, and measurement and interpretation of student growth…will require much thought in order to examine the impact of the significant deviation from the classroom norms (p. 41). For years, these high-school classroom norms—which are also to be found in college and university classrooms—have sustained schooling contexts of racial inequities that structure a sorting process in which racialized students—in this case, Black students—tend to be found in the lower level of the educational hierarchy. As such, students struggle to effectively engage in schooling so that they might become productive and successful citizens (James, 2021). Hence, any examination of the impact that COVID-19 has been having on students' learning, academic performance, and educational attainment must take note of their particular situation (see Elghawaby, 2020).

The schooling experiences of the students indicate that they worked at being focused and engaged, and despite the limits of online teaching, they put efforts into proving to their teachers and professors that they were committed to learning. In return, they wanted educators to care about teaching, and by extension about them, their learning, and their educational plans. Their reasoning suggests an understanding that learning involves not just regurgitating or reproducing what educators cover in class in order to "get a passing grade," but to be given education materials and enrolled in programs that are useful and meaningful to them and responsive to their needs and related interests, so that they can become the successful adults they aspire to be.

Many of the students who participated in our studies revealed that negotiating their transitions from high school to college and/or university had numerous challenges that contributed to stress, anxieties, and poor mental health resulting partially in academic difficulties. Their challenges—much of which stemmed from disruptions to their routines—included: lacking access to campus resources, feeling a sense of isolation from their peers, being unable to build relationships with their instructors, and having a low sense of belonging in their academic programs (see also Blaskovits et al., 2023; Jessup-Anger, 2023). As Jessup-Anger (2023) also contends, at their stage of early adulthood, young people are able to tackle their difficulties more effectively when they can establish a strong sense of community and support system outside of the family. Hence, institutions should be providing culturally relevant and responsive support to racialized students—in this case, Black students—to help them cope with the particular challenges they face.

This assertion applies to all students; so, what of those who were transitioning from high school and would have had at least three years in a familiar school setting? As the research shows, for the most part, these students also had unsatisfactory schooling experiences during the pandemic, which meant that tangible educational engagement was difficult to attain since "getting through" curriculum content tended to be mainly the focus of their teachers, who, as Munjeera observed, seemed to forget that "we're still young." Munjeera's contention—which was supported by another young woman in the group—that teachers should treat them in relation to their young age is a telling reminder of the adultification that educators tend to employ in teaching Black students. Such an approach has a negative impact on students' educational, social, and emotional well-being and outcomes, especially those of females[7] (Epstein et al., 2017; George, 2020). It is not that these students wanted their teachers to treat them like children, but instead, they wanted to be recognized as young people (in terms of their biological age) who entered school with knowledge, talents, and competencies cultivated and fostered by their families and communities (in other words, community cultural wealth) (Yosso, 2005), and on which educators should build. Further, participants did not want teachers to use a deficit approach with its related low expectations, but to provide them with an education that was relevant and responsive to their stage of development, their gendered selves (valuing the intersection of gender and race), and their social and residential conditions.

In some cases, it is assumed that reduced physical interactions between students and teachers because of online learning would be somewhat advantageous to the educational development and attainments of students—especially when, as some of these students have demonstrated, they are able to exercise agency, take responsibility, cultivate independence, and satisfy their learning needs, interests and aspirations. As such, students might be able to avoid many of the consequences of ableism[8], racism, and stereotyping experienced through alienations, suspensions, and expulsions that often account for their poor educational performance. In Los Angeles, where being at home enabled parents to witness the poor treatment of their children by their peers and teachers, some Black parents questioned "whether it is in their child's best interest to be physically in school." Consequently, they surmised that the educational system "did not benefit" their children because they "seemed to learn better and thrive emotionally away from school" (Newberry & Blume, 2021).[9]

Nevertheless, the high-school students who participated in our study consistently voiced a preference for in-person classes. So, despite the difficulties that they might have had with in-person schooling, the students were prepared to endure—if not accept—the cost of learning in a context more conducive to their needs and interests even though they would have to invest more time into their learning processes, efforts, finances, emotional energy, and other resources. These students' preference for in-person learning is supported by research findings which assert that "remote learning experienced over the past year is a poor substitute" for classroom learning, for related stress, isolation, and mental-health issues have contributed to the "heavy price in lost learning" that students have paid. And while "remote classes have improved as schools adopt best practices," things "remain difficult for students who struggle with issues such as learning challenges, isolation, or a lack of resources. The full impact of this unprecedented global shift to remote learning will likely play out for years to come" (Chen et al., 2021).

Further, recognizing the significance of credentials, and despite the difficulties they might have had in school—both before and during COVID-19—participants were very concerned with being unprepared for the world they would enter after high school—including post-secondary studies. Those planning to attend university were worried about their lack of preparedness for university, their inability to maximize their learning, and not getting the required education to which they are entitled. In fact, all of the students—high-school and post-secondary students—were well aware that as racialized Black individuals, they needed the additional post-secondary education credentials in order to access many of today's jobs and obtain the earnings that would provide them a comfortable and healthy life (see Frenette, 2019; Turcotte, 2020; Zeman & Frenette, 2021). Besides, given the support and expectations of their immigrant parents and grandparents, and their dream of social mobility, which is thought to be made possible by attending college and university, all of the participants indicated that they planned to pursue, or were pursuing, post-secondary education—an aspiration typical of first- and second-generation Black Canadians, many of whom were often the first in their families to do so (James, 2021; James & Taylor, 2023). So, limitations notwithstanding, this pandemic generation of Black students seemed to be reimagining their schooling during the pandemic with the hope that their robust confidence will make up for any lacunae in their education, or at least their perceptions of whatever they might be lacking as they transition to a post-pandemic world.

Notes

1. Pseudonyms have been used for confidentiality.
2. According to Thompson et al. (2021), "studies have shown that factors such as income, employment, education and housing differ vastly between racialized and non-racialized groups. In particular, racialized individuals are more likely to work in low paying jobs with limited access to paid sick leave, and live in poorly maintained, unstable or crowded housing"—all of which are associated with the impact of COVID-19 on the racialized population.
3. Echoing Richmond (1975), I take schooling to be "largely concerned with training on specific skills whereas 'education' is all pervasive in its influence" (p. 15). And, as Shujaa (1993) further delineates, schooling is "a process intended to perpetuate and maintain society's existing power relations and the institutional structures"; whereas education is "the process of transmitting from one generation to the next the knowledge, values, skills and traditions that will maintain its culture and ensure its survival" (pp. 330–351).
4. That colonialism is responsible for the living conditions and plight of Indigenous peoples, as well as the pattern of immigration and settlement of the various ethnic and racial group members, and the residential communities in which they reside.
5. With reference to "Reproduction Theory," Collins (2009) writes that "schools are institutions of equal opportunity but mechanisms for perpetuating social inequalities" (p. 35).
6. Parents who were essential workers often travelled by public transport and lived in small apartments with little to no extra space for privacy (Bascaramurty & Alphonso, 2020).
7. Research relating to the adultification of Black females in the United States context indicates that they tend to be "viewed as more adult [or biologically older] than their white peers at almost all stages of childhood, beginning most significantly at the age

8. of five, peaking during the ages of 10 to 14, and continuing during the ages of 15 to 19" (Epstein et al., 2017, p.1; see also Asare, 2021; and Meadows-Fernandez, 2020). And, as George (2020) suggests, the process of adultification is problematic because it takes for granted that Black girls are more knowledgeable, self-sufficient, resilient, and need less nurturing and support.
8. In some cases, students with disabilities are said to fare better with distance learning (Newberry & Blume, 2021).
9. Writing in the *Los Angeles Times* about the impact of distance learning on children, Newberry & Blume (2021) also note that "some parents of Black Los Angeles school students opted to keep their children in distance learning after schools reopened in April because they wanted to shield them from inequitable and sometimes harsh treatment on campus…"

References

A portrait of educational attainment and occupational outcomes among racialized populations in 2021. (2023, January 18). *Census in Brief* series [Catalogue no. CS98-200/2021-11E-PDF]. Statistics Canada. publications.gc.ca/pub?id=9.919008&sl=0

Asare, J.G. (2021, April 23). How the adultification bias contributes to Black trauma. *Forbes*. https://www.forbes.com/sites/janicegassam/2021/04/22/how-the-adultification-bias-contributes-to-black-trauma/

Bascaramurty, D., & Alphonso, C. (2020, September 5). How race, income and "opportunity hoarding" will shape Canada's back-to-school season. *The Globe and Mail*. https://www.theglobeandmail.com/canada/article-how-race-income-and-opportunity-hoarding-will-shape-canadas-back/

Bhamani, S., Zainab Makhdoom, A., Bharuchi, V., Ali, N., Kaleem, S., & Ahmed, D. (2020). Home learning in times of COVID: Experiences of parents. *Journal of Education and Educational Development*, 7(1), 9–26.

Blaskovits, F., Bayoumi, I., Davison, C.M., Watson, A., & Purkey, E. (2023). Impacts of the COVID-19 pandemic on life and learning experiences of Indigenous and non-Indigenous university and college students in Ontario, Canada: A qualitative study. *BMC Public Health*, 23(96). https://doi.org/10.1186/s12889-023-15010-5

Chen, L.-K., Dorn, E., Sarakatsannis, J., & Wiesinger, A. (2021, March 1). *Learning loss is global—and significant*. McKinsey & Company. https://www.mckinsey.com.br/industries/education/our-insights/teacher-survey-learning-loss-is-global-and-significant

Collins, J. (2009). Social reproduction in classrooms and schools. *Annual Review of Anthropology*, 38, 33–48. https://doi.org/10.1146/annurev.anthro.37.081407.085242

Domina, T., Penner, A., & Penner, E. (2017). Categorical inequality: Schools as sorting machines. *Annual Review of Sociology*, 43, 311–220. https://doi.org/10.1146/annurev-soc-060116-053354

Elghawaby, A. (2020, September 8). Anti-racism education must not take a back seat to pandemic this fall. *Toronto Star*. https://www.thestar.com/opinion/contributors/2020/09/08/anti-racism-education-must-not-take-a-back-seat-to-pandemic-this-fall.html

Epstein, R., Blake, J.J., & Gonzales, T. (2017). *Girlhood interrupted: The erasure of Black girls' childhood*. Center on Poverty and Inequality, Georgetown Law. https://genderjusticeandopportunity.georgetown.edu/wp-content/uploads/2020/06/girlhood-interrupted.pdf

Frenette, M. (2019, January 23). *Are the career prospects of postsecondary graduates improving?* Analytical Studies Branch research paper series, no. 415 [Catalogue no. CS11-0019/2019-3E-PDF]. Statistics Canada. publications.gc.ca/pub?id=9.866442&sl=0

Gaynor, T.S., & Wilson, M.E. (2020). Social vulnerability and equity: The disproportionate impact of COVID-19. *Public Administration Review, 80*(5), 832–838. https://doi.org/10.1111/puar.13264

George, R.C. (2020). Holding it down? The silencing of Black female students in the educational discourses of the greater Toronto area. *Canadian Journal of Education, 43*(1), 32–58. https://journals.sfu.ca/cje/index.php/cje-rce/article/view/3801

Henry, F., Dua, E., Kobayashi, A., James, C., Li, P., Ramos, H., & Smith, M.S. (2017). Race, racialization and Indigeneity in Canadian universities. *Race Ethnicity and Education, 20*(3), 300–314. https://doi.org/10.1080/13613324.2016.1260226

Herold, B., & Kurtz, H. (2020, May 11). Teachers work two hours less per day during COVID-19: 8 key EdWeek survey findings. *Education Week*. https://www.edweek.org/teaching-learning/teachers-work-two-hours-less-per-day-during-covid-19-8-key-edweek-survey-findings/2020/05

Jack, A.A. (2019, September 10). I was a low-income college student. Classes weren't the hard part. *The New York Times*. https://www.nytimes.com/interactive/2019/09/10/magazine/college-inequality.html

James, C.E. (2012). *Life at the intersection: Community, class and schooling*. Fernwood Publishing.

James, C.E. (2021). *Colour matters: Essays on the experiences, education and pursuits of Black youth*. University of Toronto Press. https://utorontopress.com/9781487526313/colour-matters/

James, C.E., & Taylor, L.E. (2023). *First generation students' experiences in higher education counterstories*. Routledge.

Jessup-Anger, J.E. (2023). The experience of adolescents who transitioned to college during the pandemic. *Current Opinion in Psychology, 54*, 101693. https://doi.org/10.1016/j.copsyc.2023.101693

Meadows-Fernandez, R.A. (2020, January 8). Why won't society let Black girls be children? *The New York Times*. https://www.nytimes.com/2020/04/17/parenting/adultification-black-girls.html

Middleton, K.V. (2020). The longer-term impact of COVID-19 on K–12 student learning and assessment. *Educational Measurement, Issues and Practice, 39*(3), 41–44. https://doi.org/10.1111/emip.12368

Newberry, L., & Blume, H. (2021, June 8). Black parents see less bullying, racism with online learning. *Los Angeles Times*. https://www.latimes.com/california/story/2021-06-08/black-parents-see-less-bullying-racism-with-online-learning

Patel, A. (2015, June 29). Stigma and silence: Black Canadians and the fight for mental health awareness. *Huffpost.* https://www.huffpost.com/archive/ca/entry/stigma-and-silence-black-canadians-and-the-fight-for-mental-hea_n_7345182

Racialized Canadians are less likely to find as good jobs as their non-racialized and non-Indigenous counterparts early in their careers. (2023, January 18). *The Daily.* Statistics Canada. https://www150.statcan.gc.ca/n1/en/daily-quotidien/230118/dq230118b-eng.pdf

Richmond, W.K. (1975). *Education and schooling.* Routledge. https://doi.org/10.4324/9780429440472

Serna, G.R. (2017). Social reproduction and college access: Current evidence, context and political alternatives. *Critical Questions in Education, 8*(1), 1–16. https://files.eric.ed.gov/fulltext/EJ1129434.pdf

Shujaa, M.J. (1993). Education and schooling: You can have one without the other. *Urban Education, 27*(4), 328–351. https://doi.org/10.1177/0042085993027004002

Szekely, R., & Pessian, P. (2015, August 6). Ontario Human Rights Tribunal finds there is a "racial disparity." *Durham Region.* https://www.durhamregion.com/news/ontario-human-rights-tribunal-finds-there-is-a-racial-disparity-in-durham/article_a3642be8-1304-5da6-8756-281cbfeffd71.html

Tam, T. (2021, February 21). The impact of COVID-19 on racialized communities. *CPHO Sunday Edition.* Public Health Agency of Canada. https://www.canada.ca/en/public-health/news/2021/02/cpho-sunday-edition-the-impact-of-covid-19-on-racialized-communities.html

Thompson, E., Edjoc, R., Atchessi, N., Striha, M., Gabrani-Juma, I., & Dawson, T. (2021). COVID-19: A case for the collection of race data in Canada and abroad. *Canada Communicable Disease Report, 47*(7/8), 300–304. https://doi.org/10.14745/ccdr.v47i78a02

Turcotte, M. (2020, February 25). Results from the 2016 Census: Education and labour market integration of Black youth in Canada. *Insights on Canadian Society* [Catalogue no. CS75-006/2020-2E-PDF]. Statistics Canada. publications.gc.ca/pub?id=9.885008&sl=0

Yosso, T.J. (2005). Whose culture has capital? A critical race theory discussion of community cultural wealth. *Race Ethnicity and Education, 8*(1), 69–91. https://doi.org/10.1080/1361332052000341006

Zeman, K., & Frenette, M. (2021, October 4). Youth and education in Canada. *Portrait of Youth in Canada: Data Report* [Catalogue no. CS42-28-0001/2021-3E-PDF]. Statistics Canada. publications.gc.ca/pub?id=9.903788&sl=0

II
Communities of Care

/ 4

"Nobody's Gonna Talk to You About That"

Methodological Considerations in Research with Undocumented Caribbean Care Workers During COVID-19

CARIETA THOMAS

Introduction

At the start of 2020, I was preparing to embark on my research on undocumented[1] Caribbean women care workers' employment experiences. The project was designed to open multiple lines of inquiry by including interviews that probe the micro-level vulnerabilities of undocumented care workers, meso-level interviews with care-work employers, and an interpretive policy analysis of the macro-level immigration and employment laws and regulations impacting the lives of undocumented care workers. In keeping with standpoint and intersectionality theory, the study was designed to reflect the interest of the most marginalized potential participants. The undocumented workers at the centre of this study are employed in precarious jobs, characterized by low status and low wages. The participants in my study navigate between spaces of visibility and invisibility. For them, the possibility of deportation is related to whether they are identifiable and visible to immigration enforcement. Unlike clandestine border crossers who enter the United States and Canada without inspection by immigration authorities, most of the participants in my study became undocumented after entering the US and Canada legally then falling out of status or violating the terms of their status. Thus, they often envisioned themselves as visible to the immigration regime and engage in avoidance behaviours to limit or decrease that visibility. As a researcher, I imagined challenges in working with a vulnerable and hidden population but could not have known that a global pandemic would make my research wholly dependent on the very technologies of surveillance[2] that my potential participants feared would make them detectable. In fact, when approached regarding recruitment or participation, countless potential participants, community members, and gatekeepers at organizations declared some iteration of "nobody's gonna talk to you about that."

While preparing my application to my university's research ethics board (REB) in October 2020, just months after a global pandemic was declared, I was informed that research requiring travel outside of Canada and face-to-face interactions would not be approved. This meant that to receive the required REB approval and begin my research, I had to redesign my study to use online or digital methods. In the context of ubiquitous and integrated systems of surveillance, voice calls, videoconferencing recordings, phone numbers, and signatures on consent forms could possibly provide identifying information that could result in detection and deportation. Furthermore, my methodological decisions required particular attention to the marginality of the care workers based on their immigration status; increased anti-immigrant sentiment; and the additional burden of gendered, unpaid, at-home care during the pandemic, as well as the reality that healthcare employment agents were scrambling to find care workers in a field where shortages were already a routine feature (Bahn et al., 2020; World Health Organization, 2017). In the end, the COVID-19 pandemic challenged me to explore a more ethical way of conducting this research through digital methods—allowing me to overcome the barriers of distance, space, time, and cost for more inclusive research. However, the use of digital methods with a vulnerable and hidden population also revealed the current structure of REBs as a barrier to conducting research with hidden populations.

In this chapter, I provide an account of conducting research with a hidden and vulnerable population living in Canada and the US during the COVID-19 pandemic. I present the methodological and ethical considerations of working with this population at each stage of the process, as well as the structural barriers posed by undergoing a university REB application process during the pandemic. Although research is an iterative and dynamic process that is not always linear, I have organized this chapter into three sections: before, during, and after fieldwork (McCracken, 2020). For the purposes of this chapter, these sections are a useful way of discussing the considerations and institutional interactions at different stages in my research process. I join others in arguing that REBs approach sociological research as a positivist endeavour, struggling to force them in line with medical and biomedical research methodologies (Dyer & Demeritt, 2009; McCracken, 2020; Sabati, 2019). Additionally, I argue that the standardization and legalization of the REB structure, as well as the power imbalance that exists between REBs and PHD candidates, threatens epistemic erasure by deterring work with marginalized groups and thus threatening to increase their marginalization. Other authors in part II of this collection, such as Ethel Tungohan (chapter 7) and Corinne L. Mason and Irene Shankar (chapter 6), similarly outline the ways institutional norms operate based on an ideal-type academic while marginalizing those researchers and community members considered "other." My experiences reflect those of others conducting community-engaged research during the COVID-19 pandemic, such as Fawziah Rabiah-Mohammed and Leah K. Hamilton (chapter 5), highlighting a lack of university guidelines for conducting community-engaged research. Furthermore, during a time of immense loss for many, the experiences of the academics included in part II of this collection and beyond demonstrate attempts to pause, pivot, and navigate institutional denial of the temporal realities in which we conduct research. However, my experiences also highlight that university REBs may not be the impenetrable institutions researchers imagine and cannot be solely held responsible for this chilling effect. Academic institutions also squeeze burgeoning student researchers into traditional areas of research with dominant groups based on a lack of support for scholars from underrepresented groups, limited access to funding, time constraints, and a difficult job market with dictates of publishing in "significant" journals (Gutierrez y Muhs et al., 2012; Henry et al., 2017). I recommend that researchers approach REBs as collaborators—rather than adversaries—and that REBs consider the positionality of researchers and attendant knowledge of participant communities. My experiences also illustrate the need for the development of best practices for research among undocumented immigrants that acknowledge these participants as actors with agency rather than objects for discovery.

Before the Fieldwork

Selecting a Research Topic and Design
When I first conceptualized and framed this project, I faced both the epistemic and ethical dilemma of whether the value of conducting policy-oriented research with a precarious immigrant group would outweigh the risks of harm to participants. I had been forewarned by many researchers that by simply endeavouring to conduct research with a population defined as undocumented and precarious, I was almost destined for full-board review, which would mean a designation of my research as "high risk." Had I allowed apprehension of full-board review to sway my commitment to working with this population, I would have fallen victim to the censorship that early critics of REBs have warned would result from the institutionalization of ethics that REBs represent (Bledsoe et al., 2007; Dingwall, 2008; Haggerty, 2004). These authors foresaw REB concerns about avoiding risk and harm as potentially stifling creativity and discouraging researchers from conducting critical research (Bledsoe et al., 2007; Dingwall, 2008). Within what Bledsoe et al. (2007) aptly—albeit dramatically—describe as the IRB[3] iron cage, researchers are seen as facing "a stark choice: to conduct innovative research in their fields or to meet the requirements of their institutions' IRB" (p. 594). As a student, my concerns around REB scrutiny in general, and full-board review more specifically, were based on limitations of time and funding. This is a concern that most graduate students must contend with and, understandably, it may deter some students from engaging in research with certain populations.

Relatedly, exploratory studies where little research has been done with the population, or where communities are allowed to define the parameters of research, are discouraged by REB regulation and disciplinary dictates of sample sizes masked as academic rigour (Bledsoe et al., 2007; Sabati, 2019; Whetung & Wakefield, 2018). In addition to being cautioned by the inquiries I would field from the REB, I also faced questions from senior scholars regarding working with a population they imagine to be statistically insignificant; the implication being that studies on marginalized populations with small sample sizes do not make important contributions to knowledge production. As a Black scholar working with a largely Black pool of participants, I bristled at these suggestions. Standpoint theory places importance on how knowledge is produced to include different experiences and acknowledge the way dominant groups silence the voices of "others" (Harding, 1992). Currently, there are an estimated 3.8 million Black immigrants from the Caribbean and Africa living in the US; of those, 16 percent are undocumented or out-of-status (Palmer, 2017). Yet, there is not enough research delineating the intersection of Black and immigrant in the US as discussions regarding immigrants remain centred on immigrants from Mexico and South America (Palmer, 2017). In Canada, there is an even greater paucity of information regarding undocumented people in general and Black undocumented populations specifically (Bernhard & Young, 2009; Brigham, 2015; Ellis, 2015; Maynard, 2019). Beyond my own positionality, this is why it is also epistemologically important that I have chosen to work with undocumented women care workers from the Caribbean as they are a group of mostly Black women immigrants. However, a consequence of the invisibility of this group within immigration research is that there is very little guidance on conducting research with Black immigrant populations. In my research, I relied on guidance from past research conducted with Latinx undocumented communities in the US and found opportunities to highlight the ways the experiences of the Black participants[4] differed materially and theoretically. Nonetheless, this experience reveals a positivist approach to research that exists within both REBs and the academy that when coupled can change the direction of research as early as the PHD stage and result in long-term epistemic erasure.

Another concern that many qualitative migration scholars and others working with marginalized communities must confront is the uncertainty around how the knowledge gained through their research will be taken up and used in policy (Jach et al., 2020; Lahman et al., 2011; Zapata-Barrero & Yalaz, 2020). Zapata-Barrero and Yalaz (2020) argue that because of the fluidity and mobility of migrants, risks and benefits must be weighed differently as migrants may not remain in the country long enough to benefit from any policy changes that may occur based on the research. The other danger they highlight is the misuse or abuse of information from the study by policymakers. For example, in my research, I explore the strategies undocumented care workers use to find work without authorization. Dissemination of my findings could potentially foreclose those options for the participants and other undocumented workers. However, this risk must be weighed against the important benefit of showing the ways these strategies increase the marginalization and exploitation of these workers in an effort to reduce inequality and exploitation.

Research Ethics Board Approval

Navigating REB approval is an institutional barrier to conducting research with undocumented immigrants in the academic setting (Bernhard & Young, 2009; Lahman et al., 2011). In Canada, the process of REB approval is guided by the Tri-Council Policy Statement on Ethical Conduct for Research Involving Humans, with three core principles for research practices: respect for persons, correlated with the requirement for informed consent; concern for welfare, associated with the requirement that researchers balance the benefits and risks of participation; and justice, correlated with requirements around recruitment and imbalances of power. Underpinning these overarching concerns is the protection of those made vulnerable by their "limited decision-making capacity, or limited access to social goods, such as rights, opportunities, and power" (Canadian Institutes of Health Research et al., 2018, p. 8).

These are admirable considerations and goals for guiding research. However, in practice, REB assessments of vulnerability and the attendant risks have the potential to further marginalize groups that are already vulnerable and underrepresented in research. Without adequate knowledge of the vulnerable populations, REBs approach the assessment of research studies based on an ideal-type participant against which potential participants from marginalized communities are compared. This is a form of standardization that researchers have criticized REBs for proliferating through increased regulation and rulemaking, where rules must sometimes be followed despite the particularity of your research participants and the chilling effect it may have on response rates (Dyer & Demeritt, 2009; Grayson & Myles, 2005). Some researchers argue the true mandate of REBs is to protect institutions rather than participants, arguing that REBs act outside and broaden their mandate of protecting participants to ensure limited legal risks for universities (Bledsoe et al., 2007; Haggerty, 2004; Hessler et al., 2011, p. 149). Beliefs such as this may contribute to the adversarial stance that many researchers take with REBs, citing their reluctance to try innovative research methods and to work with marginalized populations (Bledsoe et al., 2007; McCracken, 2020).

While I do not advocate for a more limited role for REBs, I do believe that it is important for REBs to interrogate how their practices contribute to the view of REBs as paternalistic gatekeepers and how this may impact the research that academics choose to conduct. Of specific importance is the way regulation through REBs frames ethics in legalistic terms. The emphasis on the risk-and-benefit analysis, conflicts of interest, and informed consent frame researcher interactions with REBs as a matter of compliance rather than an ethical consideration based on the vulnerabilities of participants. This framing may be a result of the history of REBs as a response to ethical breaches in medical research and their connection to sustaining funding from federal sources (Bledsoe et al., 2007; Dingwall, 2008; Dyer & Demeritt, 2009). This history is evident in some REB applications that describe participants as subjects—a problematic holdover from medical-research ethics—which connotes extraction on the part of researchers and inaction on the part of participants, who are not understood as contributors to the study. In fact, much of the opposition to REBs from social scientists stems from the idea that researchers in the social sciences are somehow immune from the biases that result in unethical medical research (Sabati, 2019), and claims that "the harms that are apt to result from social scientific research are rarely of the same magnitude as those produced by research in the medical sciences" (Haggerty, 2004, p. 399). However, social scientists need to be careful not to frame themselves as outside this history, particularly those seeking to work with marginalized, hidden, and/or vulnerable populations. Sabati (2019) argues that even researchers not working with these populations should "understand how our own disciplinary and institutional histories are connected to these processes" (p. 6).

Likewise, Whetung and Wakefield (2018) argue that instead of using positivist language based on risks and benefits, REBs should instead focus on researcher responsibility and accountability to communities.

REB applications are not designed to consider ethics in this way. They ask no questions about researcher positionality or how a person comes to the research they are conducting. The pandemic exacerbated the tendency not to embed research in this way. I found myself describing a disembodied community with no particular time, space, or place because interactions were to take place online or using other digital means. Whetung and Wakefield (2018) argue that changing this dynamic begins with embedding the research and research participants in a place and within social relations. I believe this can be institutionalized by REBs paying attention to the positionality of the researcher not only as potentially harmful but also as potentially beneficial to the participants and research.

In my study, I sought to address this issue through a theoretical framing grounded in Black feminism, standpoint feminism, and intersectionality. This calls for a reflexive methodology acknowledging that knowledge production is not a neutral act but a direct result of the producer's positionality (Collins, 2015; Harding, 1992). Understanding knowledge as situated and positional results in "a wider framing of relational and reflexive ethics, where partnership, commitment, accountability, epistemic responsibilities, and social justice are emphasized" (Goddard-Durant et al., 2021, p. 17). Framing my research in this way allowed me to engage in both the ethics of care dictated by feminist theory as well as the ethics of justice dictated by REB protocols. I understood the participants as agents with the potential to respond to their environment. These participants are "competent and capable yet vulnerable simultaneously" (Lahman et al., 2011, p. 305).

Guided by this conceptualization of participants and a nuanced understanding of the role of REBs, I approached the process as collaborative. This experience of the process may well be proof of the consensual censorship Bledsoe et al. (2007) predicted would become characteristic of researcher and REB relationships. They argued that creativity and innovation in research would only survive if researchers and REBs engage in forms of collusion, such as creating personal networks and reaching unspoken understandings that bypass forceful regulation. However, collusion suggests something far more sinister than what I experienced. In my view, it might be more aptly described as collaboration. The chair of the REB and reviewing members at my university were pivotal in not posing our interaction as adversarial.

Instead, they were available for consultation before I completed my application to address questions I had, and they provided information on what concerns the reviewers of my project may have so I could consider this in my application. They also offered a few important recommendations that are best practices for research with hidden and vulnerable populations. Nonetheless, I would be remiss if I did not point out that this collaboration did not occur on egalitarian terms. The REB, the university, and my supervisor are all parties in this nexus with more power than I hold in this process. As such, I still made methodological concessions to secure approval.

Positionality and Epistemology

At this juncture, it is important to discuss my positionality as the researcher in this study. Haraway (1988) and other feminist standpoint theorists argue that the idea of the objective researcher as unbiased and unaffected is not only problematic but also impossible to achieve. Instead, objectivity is a "situated knowledge" based on the researcher's position within the hierarchy of knowledge production (Haraway, 1988, p. 58). Challenging the intellectual hegemony of those in power through producing our own theories coming from our different positions is an integral part of fighting oppression. In planning this research and throughout conducting this research I viewed myself as an "outsider within" (Collins, 1986, p. 14) and sought to engage in reflexive methodology.

I am an immigrant woman from Guyana who has worked as a babysitter in the US and am currently in the precarious immigration status of an international student in Canada. This positions me as an insider in some regards, but I am otherwise an outsider because of my position as a researcher and no longer being engaged in care work. This positionality resulted in attendant benefits and challenges. The major benefit of being an insider/outsider was that I was able to access participants based on my kinship and friendship networks. Without these networks the research would have taken longer, been too costly to undertake, or required major modification of the study goals; this is especially true as recruitment was largely conducted during a global pandemic. My position as an outsider within was also helpful in determining the terminology to be used in recruitment and during interviews. The best example of this is in my decision not to use the term "undocumented" in recruitment. As a person from the Caribbean, I knew that the terminology most used among West Indians to describe the phenomenon of being undocumented or working without authorization is "without papers" or "without a work permit" (Robb, 2021). My recruitment materials use the phrase "without a work permit" and in discussions at association meetings or events, I used the phrase "without papers" to describe the inclusion criteria for the study. This was also helpful as many participants did not self-identify as ever having been undocumented based on their legal entry into the country.

However, challenges emerged as gatekeepers and potential participants grappled with having contradictory feelings about my insider status as a woman from the Caribbean whom they would like to help and their distrust of researchers. As part of the consent process, at several points during the interview, I reminded participants of the measures taken to protect their confidentiality. One participant was eager to help a fellow West Indian woman by participating, but she was also particularly worried about whether the information she was providing would be helpful and how much she should disclose. At several points in the interview, I reminded her that I was just interested in hearing about her experiences, that there were no "correct" answers, and that she should feel free to omit or share information based on her own discretion. I also often disclosed my own experience as an undocumented immigrant as a way of showing that I understood the potential consequences of disclosure. As a method, this was sometimes helpful in building trust with participants, but in some cases, the competing fear and distrust of researchers outweighed any ethnic affinity, and reluctance remained. I also reiterated the use of pseudonyms, the removal of identifying information during transcription, and the data-storage protocol. Maintaining a clear protocol for protecting confidentiality and continually reminding participants of this during times when their statements or affect revealed anxiety around this issue proved the most effective measure for ensuring the comfort and informed consent of the participants.

In terms of REB approval, my positionality was not necessarily seen as beneficial, and I did not always feel like a member of a community with situated knowledge that would be useful in making ethical decisions. Instead, the rigid REB approach that does not consider researcher positionality tends toward a paternalism that conceives of research participants as the subjects of research and strips groups designated as vulnerable of their agency (McCracken, 2020). This stems from assessments of vulnerability that are often based on generalizations and that dichotomize researchers and participants into the powerful and powerless respectively (McCracken, 2020; Peter & Friedland, 2017). These constraints became visible in our negotiation around honorariums and informed consent, two factors made particularly contentious because they had to be administered online due to the pandemic.

Honorarium

One of the first recommendations from the university's REB was that I offer an honorarium to the participants. Honorariums are often utilized for vulnerable populations to aid in recruitment and as a form of reciprocity (Biernacki & Waldorf, 1981; Liamputtong, 2007). For groups that are often excluded from knowledge production, honorariums may also help acknowledge the importance of their experiences and voices in research (Olukotun & Mkandawire-Valhmu, 2020). Accordingly, I provided an honorarium to undocumented care-worker participants in the form of e-gift cards of CAD$30 (USD$25). No honorarium was offered to key informant participants. I offered the honorariums as compensation for the participants' time and as an expression of appreciation rather than an incentive, and thus I did not advertise the honorarium on recruitment flyers.

However, as I engaged in the research, I found that the honorariums were problematic for anonymity and confidentiality in the context of COVID-19, and I should have pushed back on that recommendation. The REB instituted a stay on in-person research as a COVID-19 precaution and required honorariums be provided as e-gift cards rather than cash to meet public-health guidance at the time, thus making the honorariums a tool of surveillance. In order to offer electronic gift cards to participants, I had to ask participants to provide a phone number or email that they were comfortable using to receive the e-gift card. The fact that emails and phone numbers can be associated with specific names and identities possibly created another point of contact through which they could potentially be identified and detected as a participant in the study. While this risk was very low, some participants did decline receipt of the honorarium and others provided contact information for another person. I cannot be certain of all the reasons some participants declined the honorarium or provided the contact information for another person; I can surmise that this was a tactic to avoid providing more identifying information. A seemingly benign practice, honorariums are also rooted in a definition of vulnerable participants who are legally present in the country and have access to banking and forms of identification. In the context of COVID-19, where the use of cash was not possible, honorariums are more difficult to administer. Funding institutions also became involved because, as a graduate student, I had to use scholarship funds to finance the provision of the honorarium. An administrator for the scholarship providing this funding required that I provide an accounting of these e-gift cards through a log of interviews. Although I used the pseudonyms of participants in this log and never retained the names and contact information for participants, this unexpected inquisition into my use of these funds did cause me to keep receipts of the purchase of these cards out of fear that I would be audited and required to produce proof that I did not appropriate these funds for personal use. I redacted the contact information used to send the e-gift cards, but I still feel uncomfortable about this accounting because it reminded me that the contact information used may exist in a database somewhere. Given this experience, I suggest that (when feasible) cash honorariums should be used to compensate participants for their time, particularly when they help eliminate barriers to participation such as child-care and transportation costs. However, in this case, honorariums were a risk to anonymity and confidentiality because they had to be administered online. REBs should be more flexible about their dictates, even when well-meaning, and I should have devised more creative options for honouring the participants' time.

Oral Consent

In my initial meeting with members of the university's REB, oral consent was also suggested, and upon submitting my application it was approved. To avoid collecting names, signatures, and other identifying information, I asked for verbal consent before the interview began. Participants were also asked for oral consent to audio-recording the interviews, and all but one participant agreed to the audio recording. There was no video recording of interviews, interviews were audio-recorded on a separate device, including those conducted via Zoom. Relatedly, reviewers of my REB application required that I create informational sheets with support options accessible to undocumented immigrants such as counselling services and legal-aid services to mitigate the risk of emotional and psychological distress based on the sensitive topics discussed. I offered this option to all participants, but none requested the information. Much like the honorarium, providing this sheet may have proved problematic for anonymity and confidentiality as it may have required an email or phone number unless transmitted through dictation. Process consent, where the researcher checks for participant consent throughout the entire study, was only possible during the interviews because I was committed to deleting participant contact information after the interview.

However, one of the drawbacks of oral consent was its length. The oral consent that was prescribed through a template from the REB was rather lengthy and required a trivialization of the benefits of participation in the research. I observed participants becoming more anxious during this process, and continued reference to their rights signalled the process was a legal one, creating pause for some participants. Some researchers conducting surveys have argued that the legalization of consent through REB templates and regulated language has reduced response rates (Grayson & Myles, 2005). Black communities are aware of research that has reinforced stereotypes or been misappropriated by the government to their detriment. As such, they may be distrusting of researchers and not believe that the consent process provides all the information about the true goals of the study (Goddard-Durant et al., 2021). In the future, I would shorten the consent script and memorize it so that it could be conducted as more of a conversation. I also found the requirement to list the benefits of participation to be problematic because I could only list potential benefits that were not truly related to the improvement of their everyday lives now. Upon reading the oral-consent script, the main follow-up questions asked by participants were "What will you do with this?" and "What is this really for?" Participants were less concerned about a benefit to them than they were about where the information was going and what benefit I would receive by conducting this research. The section of the oral-consent script outlining the benefits to participants rang very hollow and disingenuous, as I could only make lofty promises of the potential policy change and contributing to knowledge production. This is an issue that many migration researchers face even when their goal is to affect policy change, because policy change can take a long time, and participants may either obtain permanent residence/citizenship or no longer reside in the host country when that change finally occurs (McCracken, 2020; Zapata-Barrero & Yalaz, 2020). Instead, most participants were cheered and encouraged by the prospect of helping someone they understood as part of their community attain a degree and create visibility for the issues faced by the community. I found the better approach was to allow participants to articulate what they would see as a benefit of participating in the study or a benefit resulting from the study by asking them questions about what would improve the hiring process and how they would shape policy to better respond to the needs of undocumented immigrants. As I mentioned earlier, academia and REBS are often too positivist and not flexible enough to recognize the agency of participants by allowing for more exploratory studies.

During the Fieldwork

The spectre of illegality and the threat of deportation, exacerbated by the dictates of COVID-19 precautions, made immigration-enforcement authorities an institutional barrier. The necessity of conducting the research online or over the phone created multiple issues and ethical dilemmas for consideration. My past research with the Liberian diaspora taught me the importance of meeting people in their everyday locations such as stores, churches, and restaurants as a way of embedding yourself as a member of the community and establishing rapport through sustained visibility (Goddard-Durant et al., 2021; Shedlin et al., 2011). However, COVID-19 foreclosed this as an option. Even though I attended community events, association meetings, and church services via Zoom, it did not allow for the organic interactions created when people linger after these meetings. I was also constrained by the structures of immigration (as an international student), funding institutions, and the academic job market. The academy did not provide enough support, such as extensions on funding, for students like me to suspend research and extend time in the program. As such, I had to proceed with the research using digital methodologies rather than wait to return to in-person interviewing.

Sampling and Recruitment

Recruitment was a slow and arduous process, which occurred mostly online because of COVID-19 precautions. One strategy for recruiting among hard-to-reach and hidden populations is to utilize gatekeepers to make initial contacts and gain access to participants, specifically through work with community organizations and associations (Adler & Adler, 2011). Based on other studies working with undocumented populations, I decided to try this strategy by approaching organizations and associations (Olukotun & Mkandawire-Valhmu, 2020). To limit the potential that participants would feel receiving services was conditioned on participating in the study, I only approached community associations and advocacy organizations rather than service providers. For the Caribbean population, community associations were promising as they are one of the primary means of organizing and maintaining networks within the Caribbean diaspora in Canada and the US (Branker, 2017). I also approached organizations involved in advocacy for care workers, domestic workers, and undocumented immigrants. To protect the confidentiality and anonymity of participants, a double-blind process was devised where the associations and fellow participants were instructed to provide members and potential participants with my contact information so that they could decide whether to participate without others being aware (Bernhard & Young, 2009). No contact information was stored for recruitment purposes. I did not collect the contact information of anyone suggested for participation by a gatekeeper or intermediary, instead directing them to provide the potential participant with my contact information (Bernhard & Young, 2009). Once initial contact was made by a participant, the contact information was stored only with a numerical marker, and no names were attached. This contact information was only stored until the completion of the interview; no follow-up interviews were conducted. Data collection, storage, and disposal are especially important when working with undocumented workers who are fearful of being identified by immigration authorities. In this regard, I believe REBs' strict adherence to protocol and requirements for clearly stating how to protect identifying data helps mitigate harm.

 Unfortunately, this strategy of recruiting through gatekeepers and associations was mostly unsuccessful and yielded very few care-worker participants. Some associations and organizations failed to respond to early inquiries regarding potential recruitment, while others responded that they lacked the capacity to help at that time due to the pandemic. Given the ongoing pandemic, it was understandable that organizations working with already vulnerable populations such as Black immigrants and care workers would lack the capacity at the time, especially considering they are often already short-staffed and not well-funded (Clement, 2024; Laforest, 2011). On the contrary, I thought associations and network-based organizations would be better positioned to support recruitment because, as mostly affinity groups, they are not necessarily direct service providers and advocates. I also suggested opportunities for collaboration and knowledge-sharing. The major roadblock in this strategy was the tendency for the gatekeepers to view themselves as responsible for protecting potential participants, making the moniker especially fitting (Liamputtong, 2007). Despite sharing a frequently asked questions (FAQ) sheet with information on the study and explicitly discussing the multiple strategies for protecting the confidentiality of participants, some gatekeepers were hesitant or refused to share information about the study for fear that participants would find the questions too invasive. One gatekeeper with access to several care workers responded that they would only pass along information if I did not ask any questions about immigration, and countless others declared some iteration of "nobody's gonna talk to you about that." This has been a documented issue among researchers hoping to utilize gatekeepers and organizations (Liamputtong, 2007; Olukotun & Mkandawire-Valhmu, 2020). It is an understandable reaction in communities where researchers and universities have been extractive (Goddard-Durant et al., 2021; Whetung & Wakefield, 2018) and could be mitigated by fostering relationships with these communities before approaching members for research purposes. In the context of COVID-19, I found it difficult to create and sustain relationships with organizations and individuals situated in other locations. Notwithstanding the harms that have been committed and are still being committed by researchers, it could be argued that this is a paternalistic protectionism that contributes to the framing of immigrants as deficient and lacking agency. Here, ethics of care and the duty to protect come into direct competition with the threat of epistemic erasure. To this end, REBs and academic institutions could be more supportive of students conducting community-based research projects where organizations are involved in all stages of the research process (McCracken, 2020). REBs and universities must also commit to protecting identifying information from prying governmental bodies rather than protecting the institution at the expense of researchers and participants (Bernhard & Young, 2009).

Aside from preliminary efforts to build relationships with organizations, recruitment for the study took place over a period of one year and three months beginning in February 2021. In the end, all care-worker participants in this study were recruited using snowball sampling through my own kinship-friendship networks. Snowball sampling has proven to be an effective strategy for research among hidden populations and with undocumented populations specifically (Biernacki & Waldorf, 1981; Olukotun & Mkandawire-Valhmu, 2020). Recruitment among my kinship-friendship groups started with asking family members and friends to share the study flyer and FAQ sheet on social media or with anyone they thought would be willing to participate. Due to the sensitive nature of the interviews and the probable fear of disclosure to even fellow undocumented immigrants and family, I did not specifically target family members or friends based on previous knowledge of their status and instructed those helping with recruitment that they were not to ask potential participants about their immigration status. Family members and friends were informed that they should not engage in screening participants for eligibility and were told to simply pass along my contact information. Unlike other studies using snowball sampling, where participant eligibility is not based on acts that are criminalized or illegalized, this was a necessary step in protecting sensitive participant information. In predominantly co-ethnic and immigrant communities, where immigrants are not considered a hidden population, this is sometimes even the case with undocumented immigrants where there is a large visible community supported by structural and institutional protections. However, because of the long history of immigration from the Caribbean to North America and the long-established communities, there is a perception that most Caribbean immigrants have received permanent status or that there is more opportunity for Caribbean immigrants to gain status in these countries (Lorenzi & Batalova, 2022). In this context, the lack of immigrant documentation carries with it a level of secrecy and shame that is not necessarily present for other populations of undocumented immigrants. This is clear from participants' insistence on maintaining this secret even from their closest family members. One participant stated of her status, "You wear it as if somehow, it's your fault; like it's a shame and it's your fault," while another admitted that she did not tell her husband-to-be about her lack of status until the night before the wedding, and others discussed how the assumption that they had permanent status helped them find work. Because of this, it was important that my use of snowball sampling did not require potential participants to disclose their status. I tried to keep the eligibility criteria broad on flyers as well as in communication with potential participants and those who might recruit them. While I cannot be sure that no one violated this request, I do believe that explaining why this measure was taken helped build trust among those sharing information about the study and increased the likelihood that they would follow protocol.

This method created challenges in verifying the eligibility of potential participants and maintaining participant confidentiality (Biernacki & Waldorf, 1981; Ellard-Gray et al., 2015). The family members and friends helping with recruitment were sometimes not clear on the inclusion criteria for the study, and I was determined to limit my contact with participants to protect their confidentiality. As a result, I had to confirm the eligibility of participants as part of the ongoing interview. It would have been counterproductive and intrusive to begin by asking directly about their immigration status, so I first discerned whether they were born in the Caribbean and had engaged in care work through a demographic questionnaire. Then, I started the interview with a question on their immigration journey. In discussing their journey, they usually provided information about their entry status and later changes in status through which I could glean if and when they were undocumented based on the study definition. The use of snowball sampling and kinship-friendship networks for recruitment also posed a problem in maintaining participant confidentiality. The method of providing my contact information to potential participants so they could decide whether to make initial contact helped maintain confidentiality between those referring and those being referred to the study. I did not personally know most participants, so conducting the interviews via WhatsApp voice call provided another layer of confidentiality for most participants.

Digital Methods in Interviewing
Face-to-face interviews are often understood as the ideal method for interviewing in general (Johnson et al., 2019; Khan & MacEachen, 2022) and more appropriate for working with hidden and vulnerable populations specifically (O'Connor & Madge, 2017). However, COVID-19 restrictions required that I explore digital methods for conducting my

research. These methods offered the opportunity for more inclusive research than may have been possible if I was limited to in-person interviews in specific physical locations (O'Connor & Madge, 2017). The major concern regarding digital methods is the quality of the data, specifically, the fear that interviews will lack richness and depth when mediated by technology (Khan & MacEachen, 2022; Thunberg & Arnell, 2022). Challenges include technological access, connection issues, participant absenteeism or withdrawal, difficulty in building rapport, lack of non-verbal cues, and ethical issues with the recording (Archibald et al., 2019; Johnson et al., 2019; O'Connor & Madge, 2017). In considering the method for conducting interviews, I thought of the possible effects of using certain modes of communication.

Digital methods for conducting the interviews allowed me to conduct synchronous in-depth interviews with participants without grappling with the restrictions and health risks of the pandemic. Research comparing in-person interviews with digitally mediated interviews (namely phone and videoconferencing) is limited and there are mixed views regarding the adequacy of these modes, though the common perception is that in-person interviews result in more depth and better quality (Archibald et al., 2019; Johnson et al., 2019; Thunberg & Arnell, 2022). To this end, videoconference software was the most appealing mode because of its ability to closely replicate in-person interviews in several ways. Phone or audio-only interviews are seen as less desirable because of an increased potential for misunderstandings, lack of visual cues, and difficulty building the rapport that results in the open in-depth conversations necessary for qualitative research (Johnson et al., 2019; Khan & MacEachen, 2022; Thunberg & Arnell, 2022). On the contrary, voice-only interviews are beneficial because participants do not have to worry about being seen with the researcher and associated with the study or having the researcher see them, which is especially helpful in studies with confidentiality concerns. As with the standardization of participants evident in REB protocols, academics often rely on traditional methods based on an ideal-type participant without considering the ramifications of these methods on vulnerable participants. I decided to give participants the option of conducting the interview via videoconferencing (Zoom), video-call (WhatsApp or Signal), or voice-only call (WhatsApp or Signal). I did lose the opportunity to interview some potential participants when they found out the interviews had to be conducted remotely, but those who did participate did not express many issues with the digitally mediated interviewing. Most of the care-worker participants chose WhatsApp voice-only calls. Those who provided a reason for this choice pointed to the ease of use, convenience due to time, and additional confidentiality of the WhatsApp voice-only call.

These interviews required a lot of reflexivity and flexibility on my part. The greatest challenge by far was building rapport. While I maintain that the richness of data should not be measured based on numeric factors such as the length of the interview and word counts, I was worried that the disembodied nature of the voice-only interviews would result in less depth due to the participants giving short answers. However, I found that most of the issues with building rapport had more to do with participants who were reluctant respondents than with the mode of the interview. I used various techniques to build rapport in a short time frame. First, I tried to engage in some small talk before gaining consent, discussing things like how their day was progressing and the weather. Second, I started the interview with a broad question about why they decided to leave the Caribbean. This elicited answers along the lines of getting a better life for their children and the lack of job opportunities. Starting this way removed the business-like nature of the interview, made it more of a conversation, and often allowed me to disclose my own similar experiences. Third, the interviews were semi-structured. I determined which question to ask next based on the direction that the participant had taken in answering previous questions and was often led to a probing question instead. I used probing questions to replace the non-verbal cues and fill in silences. I also did not have to be concerned about my own body language and visual cues. Code-switching from English to Patois[5] was also useful in building rapport and often led to a more conversational atmosphere throughout the interview.

During the pandemic, the burden of care largely fell to women at home and migrant women played a major role in filling the gaps in care in health-care (Bahn et al., 2020). Recognizing the limitations on time and capacity that this caused, the benefits of conducting the interviews via voice-only WhatsApp call outweighed the challenges because it made the research possible during the pandemic. As my research experience demonstrates, these modes of conducting interviews—especially with vulnerable undocumented immigrant groups—should be seen as not only viable options but sometimes the preferable mode based on the goals of the study.

After the Fieldwork

My main concern after conducting this research was that I would reveal the strategies these women used to secure employment and avoid detection in a system that sought to exploit them by limiting their choices in the labour market. This is a natural ethical concern for those researching undocumented immigrants (Olukotun & Mkandawire-Valhmu, 2020; Zapata-Barrero & Yalaz, 2020). I found two important factors that outweigh the concern I have with revealing these strategies. The first is that my interviews and investigation of immigration policies related to care work revealed these strategies as decreasingly viable options in this era of increased surveillance. Instead, because of the pre-employment screening for work authorization that is enabled by the ubiquity of surveillance, undocumented care workers are being driven further underground into the informal care-work market. In this context, my research highlights the vulnerabilities and marginalization that result from these strategies and will help advocate for policy changes. Second, the multi-level design of the study, which includes interviews with employers and policy analysis, shows these issues as structural rather than discussing the undocumented immigrants as criminal or deficient.

Conclusions and Recommendations

This chapter offers suggestions for conducting research with undocumented immigrants in the US and Canada. In it, I have discussed three areas of methodological consideration with specific attention to issues posed by conducting research remotely due to the COVID-19 pandemic: community-based and kinship-friendship network recruitment; privacy and confidentiality; and conducting interviews online or via phone. Here, I offer strategies used to overcome the challenges of pandemic research with community participants while acknowledging how these challenges were mostly two-fold in that they rectified certain issues but created others. Reflecting on my research experience, I find a gap exists in best practices for working with hidden populations, especially in regard to research that is made complex by participants' lack of legal status. As I have illuminated above, REBs and research methodologists need to approach undocumented immigrants as different from other populations that are considered hidden and vulnerable.

Based on my experience conducting research with undocumented immigrants during an era of heightened nativism and a global pandemic, I have a few recommendations for those hoping to conduct similar research. The first is for institutions, advisors, and mentors to advise doctoral students to view their dissertation as a starting project rather than the ultimate, career-defining research project we are often led to believe it to be. Academic institutions should reconsider expectations based on the scope of research that is possible given the constraints of time and funding, as well as the existing power imbalances in the research-approval process. Instead, graduate students should be encouraged to consider the scope of our project with our constraints in mind. The second is that REBs should educate researchers on their role and offer opportunities to openly discuss their projects before application (McCracken, 2020). This was especially helpful in my case but, as demonstrated, is not without its potential pitfalls. The notion that researchers are responsible for educating REBs about our subject area and what works with our population not only frames the process in adversarial terms but is also complicated by researcher positionality and our own marginalization in academia. Relatedly, all REBs should explicitly consider the positionality of the researcher vis-à-vis the potential participants when assessing research design, methods, risk, and mitigation (Lahman et al., 2011; McCracken, 2020; Peter & Friedland, 2017). This would be a reflexive process that questions the positivist insistence on impartiality that is largely unachievable. Some argue that researchers are responsible for educating REBs regarding the specifics of the population they are researching and their own positionality. Instead, I offer the suggestion that REBs query positionality through a direct question on the application. This recognizes the power dynamics at work in seeking institutional approval, especially for students and early-career researchers. It also has the added benefit of directing researchers to consider this as a factor in their design. Doing so would ward against some of the very dangers of privilege and power that led to the creation of REBs and aid in the legitimization of insiders who are also marginalized as researchers capable of conducting research within their own communities.

Notes

1. The operationalization of the term *undocumented* in this study is deliberately broad enough to capture the manner in which someone may come to be undocumented in both Canada and the United States. In this study, undocumented immigrants were defined as: "women and men who participate in the...labour force by legally entering the country and (a) not respecting the limits of their visa or (b) overstaying their visa permitted time, as well as by illegally entering the country, including those smuggled across the border" (Magalhaes et al., 2010, p. 2).
2. My research is particularly focused on the technologies of surveillance used to monitor the labour market participation of immigrants in care work; specifically, pre-employment screening technologies. In the study these are operationalized as any strategy or tool used to determine employment eligibility with regards to immigration status such as the use of E-verify, but also includes requiring proof of work authorization, bank account, fingerprints, social security number, SIN, or markers of immigrant status as well as the exchange of information and interoperable databases in use by both public and private institutions. The Electronic Eligibility Verification System (E-verify) is a federal internet-based system in the US that verifies identity and work authorization. It compares information the employee provides with data from the US Department of Homeland Security and the Social Security Administration to determine whether the person is authorized to work (Department of Homeland Security, 2018).
3. Institutional Review Board (IRB) as they are known in the US.
4. All but one of the undocumented care-worker participants in my study were Black women.
5. Caribbean dialect.

References

Adler, P.A., & Adler, P. (2011). The reluctant respondent. In J. Gubrium & J. Holstein (Eds.), *Handbook of interview research* (pp. 153–173). SAGE Publications.

Archibald, M.M., Ambagtsheer, R.C., Casey, M.G., & Lawless, M. (2019). Using Zoom videoconferencing for qualitative data collection: Perceptions and experiences of researchers and participants. *International Journal of Qualitative Methods, 18*. https://doi.org/10.1177/1609406919874596

Bahn, K., Cohen, J., & van der Meulen Rodgers, Y. (2020). A feminist perspective on COVID-19 and the value of care work globally. *Gender, Work & Organization, 27*(5), 695–699. https://doi.org/10.1111/gwao.12459

Bernhard, J.K., & Young, J.E.E. (2009). Gaining institutional permission: Researching precarious legal status in Canada. *Journal of Academic Ethics, 7*(3), 175–191. https://doi.org/10.1007/s10805-009-9097-9

Biernacki, P., & Waldorf, D. (1981). Snowball sampling: Problems and techniques of chain referral sampling. *Sociological Methods & Research, 10*(2), 141–163. https://doi.org/10.1177/004912418101000205

Bledsoe, C.H., Sherin, B., Galinsky, A.G., Headley, N.M., Heimer, C.A., Kjeldgaard, E., Lindgren, J., Miller, J.D., Roloff, M.E., & Uttal, D.H. (2007). Regulating creativity: Research and survival in the IRB iron cage. *Northwestern University Law Review*, *101*(2), 593–641.

Branker, R.R. (2017). How do English-speaking Caribbean immigrants in Toronto find jobs? Exploring the relevance of social networks. *Canadian Ethnic Studies*, *49*(3), 51–70. https://doi.org/10.1353/ces.2017.0021

Brigham, S. (2015). Mothering has no borders: The transnational kinship networks of undocumented Jamaican domestic workers in Canada. In G. Man & R. Cohen (Eds.), *Engendering transnational voices: Studies in family, work and identity* (pp. 135–153). Wilfred Laurier University Press.

Canadian Institutes of Health Research, Natural Sciences and Engineering Research Council of Canada, & Social Sciences and Humanities Research Council of Canada. (2018). *Tri-Council Policy Statement: Ethical Conduct for Research Involving Humans*. https://ethics.gc.ca/eng/documents/tcps2-2018-en-interactive-final.pdf

Clement, D. (2024). Background. *State Funding for Social Movements*. https://www.statefunding.ca/about/background/

Collins, P.H. (1986). Learning from the outsider within: The sociological significance of Black feminist thought. *Social Problems*, *33*(6), s14–s32. https://doi.org/10.2307/800672

Collins, P.H. (2015). Intersectionality's definitional dilemmas. *Annual Review of Sociology*, *41*(1), 1–20. https://doi.org/10.1146/annurev-soc-073014-112142

Department of Homeland Security. (2018). *Verify employment eligibility (E-verify)*. Homeland Security. https://www.dhs.gov/verify-employment-eligibility-e-verify

Dingwall, R. (2008). The ethical case against ethical regulation in humanities and social science research. *Twenty-First Century Society*, *3*(1), 1–12. https://doi.org/10.1080/17450140701749189

Dyer, S., & Demeritt, D. (2009). Un-ethical review? Why it is wrong to apply the medical model of research governance to human geography. *Progress in Human Geography*, *33*(1). https://doi.org/10.1177/0309132508090475

Ellard-Gray, A., Jeffery, N.K., Choubak, M., & Crann, S.E. (2015). Finding the hidden participant: Solutions for recruiting hidden, hard-to-reach, and vulnerable populations. *International Journal of Qualitative Methods*, *14*(5). https://doi.org/10.1177/1609406915621420

Ellis, B.D. (2015). The production of irregular migration in Canada. *Canadian Ethnic Studies*, *47*(2), 93–112. https://doi.org/10.1353/ces.2015.0011

Goddard-Durant, S.K., Doucet, A., & Sieunarine, J.-A. (2021). "If you're going to work with Black people, you have to think about these things!" A case study of fostering an ethical research process with a Black Canadian community. In C. Burkholder, F. Aladejebi, & J. Schwab-Cartas (Eds.), *Facilitating community research for social change* (pp. 17–32). Routledge.

Grayson, J.P., & Myles, R. (2005). How research ethics boards are undermining survey research on Canadian university students. *Journal of Academic Ethics*, *2*(4), 293–314. https://doi.org/10.1007/s10805-005-9005-x

Gutierrez y Muhs, G., Flores Niemann, Y., Gonzales, C.G., & Harris, A.P. (Eds.). (2012). *Presumed incompetent: The intersections of race and class for women in academia*. Utah State University Press.

Haggerty, K.D. (2004). Ethics creep: Governing social science research in the name of ethics. *Qualitative Sociology*, 27(4), 391–414. https://doi.org/10.1023/B:QUAS.0000049239.15922.a3

Haraway, D. (1988). Situated knowledges: The science question in feminism and the privilege of partial perspective. *Feminist Studies*, 14(3), 575–599. https://doi.org/10.2307/3178066

Harding, S. (1992). Rethinking standpoint epistemology: What is "strong objectivity?" *The Centennial Review*, 36(3), 437–470.

Henry, F., Dua, E., James, C.E., Kobayashi, A., Li, P., Ramos, H., & Smith, M.S. (2017). *The equity myth: Racialization and Indigeneity at Canadian universities*. UBC Press.

Hessler, R.M., Donnell-Watson, D.J., & Galliher, J.F. (2011). A case for limiting the reach of institutional review boards. *American Sociologist*, 42(1), 145–152. https://doi.org/10.1007/s12108-011-9122-5

Jach, E., Gloeckner, G., & Kohashi, C. (2020). Social and behavioral research with undocumented immigrants: Navigating an IRB committee. *Hispanic Journal of Behavioral Sciences*, 42(1), 3–17. https://doi.org/10.1177/0739986319899979

Johnson, D.R., Scheitle, C.P., & Ecklung, E.H. (2019). Beyond the in-person interview? How interview quality varies across in-person, telephone, and Skype interviews. *Social Science Computer Review*, 39(6), 1142–1158. https://doi.org/10.1177/0894439319893612

Khan, T.H., & MacEachen, E. (2022). An alternative method of interviewing: Critical reflections on videoconference interviews for qualitative data collection. *International Journal of Qualitative Methods*, 21. https://doi.org/10.1177/16094069221090063

Laforest, R. (2011). *Voluntary sector organizations and the state: Building new relations*. UBC Press.

Lahman, M.K., Mendoza, B.M., Rodriguez, K.L., & Schwartz, J.L. (2011). Undocumented research participants: Ethics and protection in a time of fear. *Hispanic Journal of Behavorial Sciences*, 33(3), 304–322. https://doi.org/10.1177/0739986311414162

Liamputtong, P. (2007). *Researching the vulnerable: A guide to sensitive research methods*. SAGE Publications.

Lorenzi, J., & Batalova, J. (2022, July 7). *Caribbean immigrants in the United States*. Migration Policy Institute. https://www.migrationpolicy.org/article/caribbean-immigrants-united-states

Magalhaes, L., Carrasco, C., & Gastaldo, D. (2010). Undocumented migrants in Canada: A scope literature review on health, access to services, and working conditions. *Journal of Immigrant and Minority Health*, 12(1), 132–151. https://doi.org/10.1007/s10903-009-9280-5

Maynard, R. (2019). Black life and death across the U.S.-Canada border: Border violence, Black fugitive belonging, and a Turtle Island view of Black liberation. *Critical Ethnic Studies*, 5(1–2), 124–151. https://doi.org/10.5749/jcritethnstud.5.1-2.0124

McCracken, J. (2020). Ethics as obligation: Reconciling diverging research practices with marginalized communities. *International Journal of Qualitative Methods, 19.* https://doi.org/10.1177/1609406920964336

O'Connor, H., & Madge, C. (2017). Online interviewing. In N.G. Fielding, R.M. Lee, G. Blank (Eds.), *The SAGE handbook of online research methods* (pp. 416–434). SAGE Publications.

Olukotun, O., & Mkandawire-Valhmu, L. (2020). Lessons learned from the recruitment of undocumented African immigrant women for a qualitative study. *International Journal of Qualitative Methods, 19.* https://doi.org/10.1177/1609406920904575

Palmer, B.J. (2017). The crossroads: Being Black, immigrant, and undocumented in the era of #BlackLivesMatter. *Georgetown Journal of Law and Modern Critical Race Perspectives, 9*(99).

Peter, E., & Friedland, J. (2017). Recognizing risk and vulnerability in research ethics: Imagining the "what ifs?" *Journal of Empirical Research on Human Research Ethics, 12*(2), 107–116. https://doi.org/10.1177/1556264617696920

Robb, J. (2021). Marginalised health communities: Understanding communities of "people without papers" as silent networks of survival. *Communication Research and Practice, 7*(4), 311–325. https://doi.org/10.1080/22041451.2021.1978627

Sabati, S. (2019). Upholding "colonial unknowing" through the IRB: Reframing institutional research ethics. *Qualitative Inquiry, 25*(9–10), 1056–1064. https://doi.org/10.1177/1077800418787214

Shedlin, M.G., Decena, C.U., Mangadu, T., & Martinez, A. (2011). Research participant recruitment in Hispanic communities: Lessons learned. *Journal of Immigrant and Minority Health, 13*(2), 352–360. https://doi.org/10.1007/s10903-009-9292-1

Thunberg, S., & Arnell, L. (2022). Pioneering the use of technologies in qualitative research—A research review of the use of digital interviews. *International Journal of Social Research Methodology, 25*(6), 757–768. https://doi.org/10.1080/13645579.2021.1935565

Whetung, M., & Wakefield, S. (2018). Colonial conventions: Institutionalized research relationships and decolonizing research ethics. In L. Tuhiwai Smith, E. Tuck, & K.W. Yang (Eds.), *Indigenous and decolonizing studies in education: Mapping the long view* (pp. 146–158). Routledge. https://doi.org/10.4324/9780429505010

World Health Organization. (2017). *Women on the move: Migration, care work and health.* https://apps.who.int/iris/bitstream/handle/10665/259463/9789241513142-eng.pdf

Zapata-Barrero, R., & Yalaz, E. (2020). Qualitative migration research ethics: A roadmap for migration scholars. *Qualitative Research Journal, 20*(3), 269–279. https://doi.org/10.1108/QRJ-02-2020-0013

/5
Community-Engaged Research with Refugee Communities During COVID-19

FAWZIAH RABIAH-MOHAMMED
and LEAH K. HAMILTON

Introduction

In March of 2020, COVID-19 led universities across Canada to physically close their doors. Academic life was disrupted for students, staff, and faculty alike. Courses shifted online, workplaces closed, and most students moved out of residence. In addition to its direct impact on teaching and learning, COVID-19 also impacted many scholars' programs of research. This chapter examines how COVID-19—and universities' inaction—impacted community-engaged research in general, and our research with refugee communities specifically. In our case, we were working with Syrian refugees on a five-year project to map the barriers faced by refugees and the support needed to find safe, adequate, and affordable housing. During COVID-19, many of our participants talked about feeling like they were "back to square one" with respect to language acquisition, employment, and housing (Hamilton et al., 2022). As the need for support increased amongst Syrian refugees during COVID-19, our research practices became more fraught. As we illustrate here, our role as researchers working in institutions that refused to take needed actions during COVID-19 clashed with the participants' growing need for better housing and financial stability in the midst of economic challenges caused by COVID-19.

This chapter is written using a reflective framework that is rooted in critical social science and centres on empowerment and notions of being rather than doing (Johns, 2017). It involves "being mindful of the self...in order to confront, understand and become empowered to act towards resolving contradictions between one's vision of desirable practice and one's actual practice" (Johns, 2017, p. 3). We employ this reflective framework to better understand "the contradiction between [our] vision of practice and [our] actual practice as recalled" (Johns, 2017, p. 3). Our focus on the inaction of post-secondary institutiones (PSIs) centres on our ongoing concerns about the lack of real-time guidelines adaptive to different stages of COVID-19 and the absence of clear instructions for supporting multi-barriered communities with growing needs during times of crisis. Our goal and vision for conducting community-engaged research was to improve people's lives through understanding their experiences and co-advocating for their needs; however, our actual practice was limited by our role as researchers in PSIs. We describe how our universities failed to acknowledge or provide guidelines for community-engaged researchers during the pandemic, and how this inaction negatively affected both our research and the communities with which we partner.

As we show in this chapter, while universities "closed their doors" during COVID-19 in 2020, the needs of Syrian refugees increased. With little guidance and an unwillingness of universities to provide pathways forward for our community-engaged research, we found ourselves navigating new terrain and, ultimately, letting down our community partners whose needs surpassed our capacities as researchers. We argue that, because of the university's inaction to support ongoing and community-grounded research, we felt a pressing need to amplify our participants' voices about their unmet needs and new struggles during COVID-19. During this process, we developed a close, empathetic relationship to support each other as we faced our own challenges during COVID-19. The close relationship we formed enabled us to pause our research, reimagine it, and centre the community's needs during a time when our institutions were silent on community-engaged research. We end with a series of recommendations for PSIS for supporting community-engaged scholarship during the next pandemic, or similar crisis.

About the Project

Our project, "Long-term housing outcomes of under-housed Syrian refugees" was supported by a Social Sciences and Humanities Research (SSHRC) Insight Grant that examines the housing experiences of government-assisted Syrian refugees in three cities in Canada: Fredericton (small city), London (medium city), and Calgary (large city). Using a grounded theory approach, this community-engaged project aims to understand the barriers and facilitators to achieve housing stability during the first five years post-migration. In each city, we aimed to interview fourteen to seventeen families once or twice yearly for five years.[1]

We began this project in 2018, two years prior to COVID-19. Although we, the researchers, have never met in person, the student-professor relationship grew steadily through regular and effective communication through emails, Zoom meetings, and phone calls. The challenges that COVID-19 brought to our research project softened the inherent power dynamics between a university professor and graduate student, which allowed us to foster a more empathetic connection. Despite our different locations (social and physical), we felt a shared connection as two women who both care deeply about the issues our participants are facing, and who strive to centre relationships as community-engaged researchers.

Leah describes the tension she experienced between her feelings of despair and recognizing her own privilege:

> I recognize the privilege I had in being a professor who was steadily paid throughout the COVID-19 pandemic and able to work safely at home. That said, I faced the challenge of trying to be the primary caregiver of a high-energy, needful five-year-old while my family was 3,500 kilometres away. I faced many of the challenges that have been well documented in the literature about how pandemic caregiving responsibilities impacted women in academia (e.g., Skinner, Betancourt, & Wolff-Eisenberg, 2021). Balancing work, caregiving, homeschooling, and household responsibilities with no support system (no extended family in the province) felt impossible. In the early days of the pandemic (March to June 2020), this ultimately

meant my child was largely ignored, online school was abandoned, and only the essential work responsibilities (teaching) were completed. My sleep deteriorated as my stress levels rose, and like many other mothers around the world, I felt simultaneously depressed and anxious. I felt like I was failing everyone in my life. At the same time, my family could collectively breathe after a challenging kindergarten year in which my child had to navigate an unwelcoming school environment.

When it comes to refugee communities specifically, I tried to support a family we had recently sponsored to come to Canada (they arrived in September 2019) as they transitioned three children to remote schooling. I also assisted some cultural brokers I had worked with on another community-engaged project. When two of these cultural brokers experienced job loss associated with the COVID-19 pandemic, I helped them access the local food bank, create and distribute a new resume, and provided emotional support. Throughout this time, I struggled with trying to reconcile my own feelings of despair with the knowledge that I had so much privilege and never had to worry about my job or food insecurity.

When COVID-19 began in Canada in March 2020, the project team had already conducted three waves of interviews with each family over two years and had formed relationships based on trust and deep listening. Deep listening entails hearing from a deep, receptive, and fully present place to better understand a person and their circumstances of living in inadequate housing, dealing with job losses, and experiencing social isolation and an uncertain future in the new country. For refugees across Canada, COVID-19 made securing safe and affordable housing an arduous experience (Rabiah-Mohammed et al., 2022). In our research, we found that several families began to depend on social assistance to meet basic needs, and this negatively impacted their mental health and well-being.

Over our two years of data collection with Syrian refugees prior to COVID-19, we learned that many Syrian refugees were struggling to meet their basic needs. However, opportunities for casual work were available to supplement low incomes, and some families frequently received food vouchers. These vouchers enabled families to buy food from Arabic and Middle Eastern grocery stores with Halal food, as opposed to accessing food banks, which often do not have Halal options. In the early stages of COVID-19, opportunities for casual employment were curtailed and community services were limited, including access to food vouchers. This intensified food and housing insecurity for many participants in our project.

Encountering Post-Secondary Inaction

During COVID-19, we were struck by our institutions' lack of acknowledgement of, and support for, community-engaged research, particularly during the first lockdown in March of 2020 when faculty were mandated to work remotely and move our courses online practically overnight. When COVID-19 reached Canada in March 2020, universities' immediate focus was on transitioning courses to online modalities as quickly as possible. This unprecedented, "frenzied chore" (Markov et al., 2021, p. 7) was challenging for administrators, staff, faculty, and students alike (Canadian Association of University Teachers, 2020). Importantly, we recognize the significant disruption this created for student learners (Doreleyers & Knighton, 2020), particularly as it pertains to exacerbating existing inequities. As Moore and colleagues (2021) state, "the social, cultural, and economic apparatuses that sustain online learning are inherently neoliberal, privatized, expensive, and discriminatory" (p. 14). These institutional responses to COVID-19 were a form of opportunistic disaster capitalism[2] that extended the neoliberalization of higher education in Canada (Moore et al., 2021). Indeed, for many scholar-teachers working in Canadian PSIs, universities' singular focus on teaching during the early days of COVID-19 was a vivid reminder of the capitalist "students as customers" model entrenched in PSIs (Newson, 2004). While teaching is a critical component of our jobs, so too is research.

Universities' silence about research—particularly community-engaged research—was palpable. As professors' teaching demands increased overnight, and universities simultaneously failed to take action to support ongoing research, projects stalled, experienced lengthy delays, and new research projects never left the ground. While emails were sent out about online teaching and managing student absences, there was no similar guidance about navigating our research practices, except for on-campus lab-based research. Universities' exclusive focus on teaching was followed shortly thereafter with directives about physical laboratory spaces on campus, but these directives completely omitted community-based research. Universities (e.g., the University of Calgary, where Leah is an adjunct faculty member) were quick to issue directives about animal-based research and physical laboratory spaces while ignoring community-based research with humans. Although the funding agency of our project (SSHRC) eventually extended our funding by one year to make up for COVID-19-related barriers, no guidance or consideration for community-engaged work was highlighted by the federal funding agency.

While most universities have been quick to incorporate community-engaged scholarship into their strategic plans to capitalize on funding opportunities for this type of work, when COVID-19 disrupted university life, administrators completely ignored the equity-deserving groups/communities at the centre of many community-engaged projects. This suggests that efforts by PSIs to incorporate community-engaged research into strategic plans are rooted solely in signalling without any actual desire to understand or positively impact these communities. As other scholars have highlighted (see Auerbach et al., 2022, for a powerful analysis), COVID-19 halted opportunities to build the trust and reciprocity that characterize participatory action research. Moreover, universities failed to consider that communities needed to refocus their energy on meeting basic needs (see Rabiah-Mohammed et al., 2022; Zhang & Gunderson, 2022), which had implications for project goals, timelines, and funding (Auerbach et al., 2022).

The lack of university guidance on how to continue community-engaged research under strict public-health measures that required physical distancing, and stay-at-home mandates, hindered our goal of pursuing a reciprocal relationship with the participants when they most needed our help. While many of the participants reported facing great difficulties meeting their basic needs, there were no clear instructions for community researchers to take on a more active role to lessen the consequences of COVID-19 on such communities. We were left with fewer resources to support the participants during an incredibly difficult time.

Pausing and Reimagining Our Project

During this time, we were concerned that continuing community-engaged research could be potentially perceived as extractive or exploitative, particularly because the timing of our planned data collection coincided with heightened food and housing insecurity for the participants. The full team was meeting periodically, and discussions about data collection were taking place. We decided to conduct a few interviews with actively engaged participants to gauge if participants were willing to be part of this round and ask how we could make the study more responsive to their needs. It was clear to us that community-engaged research should offer participants more than a symbolic honorarium to compensate for their time and willingness to share challenging stories about their housing and resettlement experiences. However, in the face of our inability to provide actual assistance to mitigate the impact of job losses caused by COVID-19 restrictions, our commitment and responsibility toward the participants intensified.

As we expected, the few interviews we conducted revealed that participants were struggling to meet their basic needs. In turn, this heightened our concern for the participants and made us question the essence of our project. The inability to provide immediate help during the reduced capacity of community services created a sense of dilemma in which continuing the study, as usual, was ethically questionable. We found ourselves grappling with a similar situation as Carieta Thomas (chapter 4 of this collection) describes, and it caused us to pause and rethink the purpose of our project.

For us, and many other community-engaged scholars, we received no directives or support from our universities' research offices during mandated lockdowns in which we could not physically be in the community. When these mandates were coupled with increased teaching and parenting demands, community-engaged research was unsustainable. Eventually, many months after the lockdowns, to avoid abandoning our project altogether, we made the difficult decision to transition our research online by conducting Zoom interviews, rather than interviewing people in their homes. In the past, all of our interviews happened in people's homes and these visits often involved tea, snacks, interacting with babies, and seeing participants' housing situations first-hand. These home visits are incredibly valuable for building trust and taking field notes about housing. However, there was a time in our research when we experienced so much uncertainty that we had no guidelines to support our plans. Ultimately, while we made the best decision given the constraints we were facing, transitioning community-engaged research to the virtual space impacted the nature of the collaborative relationships we established with our participants.

Moving the interviews online may have excluded those who have lower digital literacy or who do not have the right technology to connect with the research team (Salma & Giri, 2021). Fortunately, the relationship with the participants was established prior to COVID-19, which allowed us to form a sense of trust and close rapport in online interviews. Moving online precluded us from reaching out to the most marginalized and multi-barriered populations who did not have access to Wi-Fi, lacked technological literacy, or were burdened by excessive stress brought on by COVID-19. Not being able to reach out to multi-barriered participants precluded us from capturing their stories and experiences. Ultimately, this limits our understanding of the most marginalized population of Syrian refugees and limits our ability to provide tailored recommendations for the community we are interested in.

Research became an added load to Syrian refugees during a time when they could not even meet their basic needs due to income disruption caused by job loss. Participants indicated that sharing personal/vulnerable stories while losing face-to-face interactions felt less fulfilling to them compared to in-person home visits complete with tea and snacks. Ultimately, these challenges led to a one-year gap in data collection. We decided to suspend the data collection round in 2021 as the impact of COVID-19 on our participants' lives and work was heightened. Recognizing the growing feelings of anger and disappointment among participants stemming from the prolonged impact of COVID-19, we sought to pause and rethink the project.

The context of conducting community-engaged research during COVID-19 and meeting with participants virtually to discuss firsthand experiences that were still happening in their lives felt daunting. Participants started to question the benefits of participating in research as they needed immediate assistance with their housing and economic situations (Rabiah-Mohammed et al., 2022). For instance, as their economic situations deteriorated in the early days of COVID-19, participants asked how their responses to the interview questions would lead to fairly immediate policy changes that would benefit refugees. We were unable to promise participants immediate benefits, and this was understandably frustrating for some people. The compounded impacts of COVID-19 on the participants made the research team decide to not conduct the next wave of data collection. This decision was reached after a twenty-minute phone call between the two authors during which we acknowledged that expecting participants to share difficult experiences while actively living through them was not the right approach and would add another layer to the hardship they are facing. At the end of the call, we reached a conclusion that emphasized prioritizing community support over research outcomes.

While the purpose of community-engaged research is to co-create knowledge by collaborating with the people from the community of interest to benefit the larger community, we could not address the emerging and urgent needs of our participants created by COVID-19 (e.g., job loss). In this situation, the value of community-engaged research was questioned by both us and our participants, and the partnership felt strained. To address this issue and maintain trust, the principal investigator composed a video message tailored particularly to our participants to stay connected and confirm our commitment to continuing this project that we started together. A video message was chosen over a written message to enable the team to convey emotions. We took the opportunity to validate the challenging period everyone was experiencing, provide feedback, suggest a pause in the data collection, and outline a strategy for resuming the study. Ultimately, if not carefully managed, situations like these can result in public mistrust of research with multi-barriered communities and attrition in research studies (Khodyakov et al., 2017).

Fawziah expresses the emotions she was experiencing as she grappled with this:

> At this stage, I found myself grappling with overwhelming emotions that had long remained hidden. My interaction with the refugee populations and the isolation resulting from COVID-19 brought these emotions to the surface. Witnessing the intense hardship endured by the Syrian refugees triggered a complex mix of feelings. I felt a sense of anger at the persistent threat our region, the Middle East and North Africa, is subjected to, whether in the form of war, armed conflict, oppression, marginalization, poverty, or racism. This was compounded by the prolonged confinement that COVID-19 induced. This confinement felt similar to the feeling where women,

whom I know, would spend extended periods at home solely due to male-dominance ideologies. To the same extent, wearing a mask in public stimulates incidences of a lifelong wrestle with the niqab (face veil). As an Arabic-speaking woman who was born and raised in a male-dominant society, feelings of estrangement and insecurity, deprivation of basic human rights, and dealing with persistent gender-related concerns featured in my everyday life growing up crept in during the isolation of COVID-19.

The flood of thoughts and memories left me feeling unable to support the community I care for. With the intensity of the COVID-19 restrictions combined with the inability to provide tangible assistance to the Syrian refugees, I felt I was failing one of the most marginalized groups of people. Amid this profound challenge, the desire to give up was increasing. During this phase, contacting family through WhatsApp and other social media applications has helped me gradually gain a sense of normalcy, as Ethel Tungohan (chapter 7 of this collection) mentioned thriving through virtual life. Also, Leah and I maintained constant communication with encouraging words and a validating tone, recognizing the challenging period for everyone. These regular written communications and Zoom meetings were successful in dispersing my negative thoughts, allowing me to clear my mind and redirect my focus toward the potential of community-engaged research. We began discussing how the project could actually and immediately benefit our community partners.

Community Event and Public Scholarship

We shared a commitment to this community of refugees and were determined to continue in the spirit of community-engaged scholarship. We committed to amplifying the participants' voices during a time when they felt invisible to policymakers. When we sensed that our participants were no longer seeing the value in the project, we came together to re-centre their needs and adjust our data collection plan, ultimately abandoning one wave of data collection in favour of an in-person community event. This idea stemmed from several interviews with participants who indicated a pressing desire to engage with politicians. Participants wanted immediate solutions to their housing and resettlement challenges and felt this could be achieved via a community event that brought together participants, community members, politicians, and service providers.

Thus, political representatives and social service workers came to learn about the project and meet with the Syrian community to hear their housing concerns directly. The significance of carrying out this community event resides in responding to the participants' desire to meet face-to-face with politicians and community service providers to discuss their needs and challenges. The nature of community-engaged research permits implementing such an event to empower our participants and give them a voice, instead of us conveying their messages in a research paper. Our participants were passionate about telling their stories and got emotional in one-on-one conversations. Some participants had the chance to connect personally with local members of parliament and service providers.

In addition, we invested heavily in knowledge mobilization plans involving public scholarship (Hamilton et al., 2022) and different levels of government to steer policy change in regard to creating more safe, affordable housing for refugees (Rabiah-Mohammed et al., 2022). The effort of doing the community event and the knowledge translation felt rewarding especially when assistance related to job losses was not feasible. We felt like we were able to achieve a balance in community-engaged research where the participants became active agents in advocating for themselves within the framework of the community-engaged research.

Recommendations for Post-Secondary Institutions to Support Community-Based Research

COVID-19 revealed and exacerbated many inequities entrenched in the post-secondary system. University research offices and administrators must continue to build permanent support for community-engaged researchers and the multi-barriered communities with whom they work. Universities cannot feature community-engaged work in their marketing and communications when they want to look publicly engaged and relevant, and then turn their back on these communities in light of other pressing concerns, nor should they prioritize laboratory-based research in times of crisis simply because they are focused on physical spaces that are more tangible. While post-secondary institutions' inaction and lack of support for community-engaged research have always existed, the effects of this inaction were heightened during COVID-19. The COVID-19 context revealed that universities leverage this type of work for their own gain with little to no regard for the actual communities at the centre of this work.

Moving forward, truly supporting community-engaged scholars will mean major structural changes to research offices and procedures including: i) creating community-engaged research offices with dedicated resources; ii) offering (flexible) funding and support to make space for research projects that change course at the behest of the community being served; iii) recognizing and adjusting faculty and student workloads to allow for researchers to work in-depth with community partners; iv) redefining scholarly impact to include community-impacts that are not obvious "outcomes," e.g., adopting the Declaration on Research Assessment; v) revising hiring, tenure, and promotion criteria for community-engaged scholars; vi) training ethics boards on the emergent, co-design elements of this type of work; and vii) reconsidering graduate student thesis timelines and funding for those who are doing community-engaged work (see Milne & Hamilton, 2021). Moreover, it will mean committing to supporting community-engaged research—both researchers and communities—during times of disruption and crisis.

Corinne L. Mason and Irene Shankar (chapter 6 of this collection) speak about how they overcame their academic loneliness during COVID-19 through their connection and informal discussions, which resemble a phase in our academic relationship as well. Our empathic collaboration created a sense of trust that allowed for the opportunity to discuss uncommon practices in research, such as halting a data collection phase and replacing it with a community event for participants rather than continuing with the traditional research process. Our relationship with each other helped us to truly listen to participants and to reflect on how university structures and systems need to change to meaningfully support community-engaged research.

In addition, the university's involvement in advocacy for such communities is particularly needed during times of crisis. Advocacy campaigns organized by the university can galvanize funding and structural changes sorely needed by multi-barriered populations. Such structural changes and a more fulsome understanding of community-engaged research would have aided in continuing our research project during COVID-19 and would have resulted in better partnerships in times that are less tumultuous. This will help to build stronger, meaningful partnerships with multi-barriered communities that ultimately lead to positive community outcomes. A crucial lesson learned through conducting community-engaged research during COVID-19 is that, during times of crisis, researchers face a heightened need to prioritize community care and centre participants' needs. Responding to community needs means slowing down, pausing, and walking away from data collection and the pressure to publish. This may require researchers to resist the neoliberalization of the university, restructure workloads, and continue to push universities to improve their support for community-engaged research.

Notes

1. Fawziah Rabiah-Mohammed is the primary overall project research assistant in London and Leah Hamilton is a co-investigator on the project and the lead for the Calgary team.
2. Disaster capitalism can be defined as "the deviant behaviour of the unscrupulous individuals and organisations that extract private advantage in emergency situations" (Imperiale & Vanclay, 2021, p. 556).

References

Auerbach, J., Muñoz, S., Affiah, U., Barrera de la Torre, G., Börner, S., Cho, H., Cofield, R., DiEnno, C.M., Grady-Lovelace, G., Klassen, S., Limeberry, V., Morse, A., Nataajan, L., & Walsh, E.A. (2022). Displacement of the scholar? Participatory action research under COVID-19. *Frontiers in Sustainable Food Systems, 6*, 1–15. https://doi.org/10.3389/fsufs.2022.762065

Canadian Association of University Teachers (CAUT). (2020). *The impacts of COVID-19 on post-secondary education staff.* Canadian Association of University Teachers. https://www.caut.ca/sites/default/files/the_impacts_of_covid-19_on_post-secondary_education_staff.pdf

Doreleyers, A, & Knighton, T. (2020, May 14). COVID-19 Pandemic: Academic impacts on postsecondary students in Canada. *StatCan COVID-19: Data to insights for a better Canada* [Catalogue no. CS45-28/1-2020-16E-PDF]. Statistics Canada. publications.gc.ca/pub?id=9.887395&sl=0

Hamilton, L., Banerjee, P., & Rabiah-Mohammed, F. (2022, February 22). "I am back to square one": How COVID-19 has impacted recently resettled Yazidi and Syrian refugees. *The Conversation.* https://theconversation.com/i-am-back-to-square-one-how-covid-19-impacted-recently-resettled-yazidi-and-syrian-refugees-176121

Imperiale, A.J., & Vanclay, F. (2021). The mechanism of disaster capitalism and the failure to build community resilience: Learning from the 2009 earthquake in L'Aquila, Italy. *Disasters, 45*(3), 555–576.

Johns, C. (2017). *Becoming a reflective practitioner* (5th ed.). Wiley-Blackwell.

Khodyakov, D., Mikesell, L., & Bromley, E. (2017). Trust and the ethical conduct of community-engaged research. *European Journal for Person Centered Healthcare, 5*(4), 522–526. https://www.researchgate.net/publication/322133227

Markov, A., Yavnai, R., Lafrenière, G., Woodford, M., & Karki, K. (2021). *Surviving and thriving in a COVID-19 remote learning context: A survey of post-secondary students and instructors in Ontario*. ECampus Ontario. https://www.ecampusontario.ca/wp-content/uploads/2021/07/Surviving-and-Thriving-in-a-covid-19-Remote-Learning-Context-Report.pdf

Milne, E., & Hamilton, L.K. (2021). Navigating personal, professional, institutional, and relational dimensions of community-engaged research. *Journal of Community Engagement and Scholarship, 14*(1), 1–17. https://doi.org/10.54656/JGKP9815

Moore, S.D.M., Jayme, B.D.O., & Black, J. (2021). Disaster capitalism, rampant edtech opportunism, and the advancement of online learning in the era of COVID19. *Critical Education, 12*(2), 2–23. https://doi.org/10.14288/ce.v12i2.186587

Newson, J.A. (2004). Disrupting the "student as consumer" model: The new emancipatory project. *International Relations, 18*(2), 227–239. https://doi.org/10.1177/0047117804042674

Rabiah-Mohammed, F., Hamilton, L.K., Oudshoorn, A., Bakhash, M., Tarraf, R., Arnout, E., Brown, C., Benbow, S., Elnihum, S., El Hazzouri, M., Esses, V.M., & Theriault, L. (2022). Syrian refugees' experiences of the pandemic in Canada: Barriers to integration and just solutions. *Studies in Social Justice, 16*(1), 9–32. https://doi.org/10.26522/ssj.v16i1.2669

Salma, J., & Giri, D. (2021). Engaging immigrant and racialized communities in community-based participatory research during the COVID-19 pandemic: Challenges and opportunities. *International Journal of Qualitative Methods, 20*, 1–10. https://doi.org/10.1177/16094069211036293

Zhang, T., & Gunderson, M. (2022). The differential impact of COVID-19 on labour market outcomes of immigrants in Canada. *Canadian Public Policy, 48*(3), 473–490. https://doi.org/10.3138/cpp.2021-043

/6
Institutionalized Feminist Loneliness

An Exchange on Pandemic Disruptions to Research

CORINNE L. MASON
and IRENE SHANKAR

IT IS A LONG-RUNNING JOKE that academics are loners, so maladjusted and in fear of social interactions that they prefer to work in solidarity conditions.[1] An ableist and saneist discourse of the loner academic posits the scholar as a fundamentally flawed human who has actively chosen a lonely career due to their personal constraints (read as the lack of ability to engage with others). At the same time, the narrative of being a solidarity academic is often touted as a source of pride and a marker of true intellectualism. Beyond pride or rebuke, the structure of academia reproduces isolation for scholars. We are, often, expected to work alone and when together, we are habitually positioned in competition with each other. While collaborative research is rhetorically supported and encouraged by universities and external granting agencies, processes of tenure and promotion, which assess our work, are fundamentally solitary endeavours.

The solitary exercises of academia are taking their toll. When surveyed, faculty point to institutional barriers to connection as the source of mental-health challenges related to loneliness. According to a survey by Shaw (2014), two-thirds of more than 2,500 faculty respondents identified their mental unwellness as a direct result of their university job. Among the concerns cited were heavy workloads, bullying, lack of support, and isolation (Shaw, 2014). Some faculty members find themselves isolated due to the absence of meaningful connections and relationships with others in their workplace or larger discipline (Sibai et al., 2019). Faculty are not alone in their experiences of isolation. In 2019, 69.6 percent of Canadian post-secondary students surveyed reported feeling "very lonely" at least once in the past year; the number was even higher for female-designated participants at 73 percent (American College Health Association, 2019, p. 13).[2] These findings reflect the larger cultural context in which one in ten people in Canada identified themselves as "always" or "often" lonely ("Canadian Social Survey," 2021). While we recognize that isolation does not necessarily warrant loneliness or vice versa, in this chapter, we use both these terms to refer to our feelings of loneliness based on our experiences of isolation within a neoliberal institution of higher learning. Here, we reflect on how our preexisting isolation and loneliness were exacerbated through pandemic protocols and institutional responses (or lack thereof) to intensified inequities during this time. For us, the pandemic served to highlight and bring these experiences of isolation and feelings of loneliness to the forefront of our research collaboration.

In higher education advice writing, loneliness is regularly conceptualized as a personal responsibility, and behavioural changes are offered as a solution. For example, in Johnson's (2012) "The Lonely Life of the Academic," published by *Inside Higher Education*, readers are encouraged to stop procrastinating, start working, exercise, talk to someone, take comfort in the fact that you are not actually alone, manage your loneliness triggers, and be grateful for "me" time. Johnson describes being alone as part of "the nature of the beast!" and suggests learning to enjoy your own company. This individualization of loneliness, and the pathologization that often accompanies expressions of isolation, motivated Magnet and Orr (2022) to develop "feminist loneliness studies." Frustrated by the advice to seek out connections through exercise and hobbies when expressing her loneliness to mental-health professionals, Magnet began to identify time and energy for leisure under capitalism as a structural obstacle to connection. Orr, for their part, reflected on how they were able to identify their depression, anxiety, and loneliness, but only in jokes and banter. Perhaps because loneliness is so often filtered through the medical model of disability and mental-health distress it is understood as requiring a cure or to be altered in such a way as to allow someone to overcome it.

Moving beyond medical constructions of loneliness and writing against individualized pathways out of isolation, Magnet and Orr (2022) conceptualize feminist analyses of loneliness as taking up the complex relationships between isolation and systemic inequities. Feminist loneliness studies, then, offers a space to think critically and explicitly about "the ways that systems of oppression—white supremacy, settler colonialism, anti-queer bias, misogyny, neoliberal capitalism, and so on—create our lonely world" (p. 3). Focusing on systems that produce loneliness, rather than loneliness as an interior experience, Magnet and Orr demand that ways of writing and speaking about loneliness be troubled, and they reject ideas "that medical or psychiatric intervention, neoliberal achievement, an app or a traditional heteronormative nuclear family unit will 'cure' loneliness and make us feel 'happy'" (p. 9). Expanding Magnet and Orr's call to trouble loneliness, our exchange brings feminist loneliness studies into the academy. In other words, here we offer a conceptualization of "institutionalized feminist loneliness" as a way to articulate the academic isolation we experience as feminists in the university. This exchange is particularly inspired by Charania's (2022) article "Lonely Methods and Other Tough Places: Recuperating Anti-Racism from White Investments." In it, she wrestles with the expectations to research and write for white audiences, and the approval of the white academy. Charania challenges institutional commitments to expertise, objectivity, rigour, and productivity that create the conditions in which we become isolated from our research, from our participants, and often, from ourselves.

Writing about the formulation and enactment of her research about racialized violence in everyday life, Charania writes alongside M. Jacqui Alexander, Dian Million, Eve Tuck, and Audra Simpson who have long warned of the dangers of academic expectations to critique, disregard, and diminish the work of other scholars as a way of charting a new and original pathway as an "expert." As Charania reminds us, Million (2014, p. 35) maintains that the academy is a "place of unwritten rules, old implacable cultures, and high stakes" in which Indigenous and racialized women's lived experiences, expertise, and ways of knowing are discounted, ignored, erased, and silenced. In this context, isolation and loneliness are an ongoing experience for marginalized faculty where, as Ahmed (2012) outlines, the invitation to the university is not met with substantive inclusion in the academy. Following Charania's conceptualization of loneliness, here we flesh out our experiences of isolation and feelings of loneliness as an outcome of navigating white investments in academia. As we illustrate here, we have attempted (and sometimes succeeded) to meet the threshold of acceptable academic pursuits, which tend to be higher and often tenuous for historically and presently excluded faculty members. In working to meet these tenuous and ever-shifting expectations, we have become more isolated from ourselves and the communities with whom we desire to be connected and have found ourselves feeling lonely in the institution.

In what follows, we discuss our research collaboration on a Social Sciences and Humanities Research Council (SSHRC) funded project that focuses on how institutions take up (or do not) the in-house expertise of feminists as they respond to the systemic issue of sexualized violence on campuses across (what is colonially known as) Canada. Our exchange focuses on how our advocacy around sexualized violence at universities has ushered us into a complex relationship with institutional loneliness. We explore how our desire to connect with other lonely feminists brought us into a collaborative research partnership and solidaristic friendship with one another. In our exchange below, we focus on the structure of the institution and its white investments as the site but also the cause of our isolation. Reflecting on research collaboration and our experiences of "pressing on" during the COVID-19 pandemic, we express and expose the institutionalized loneliness in the academy where misogyny, white supremacy, and trans- and queerphobia are co-creators of our lonely worlds. Rather than create new forms of loneliness and isolation, the COVID-19 pandemic concretized and further exposed our ongoing experiences of institutionalized loneliness. As we describe below, the time away from the institution due to stay-at-home orders offered us a new perspective on our relationship with the university and to one another as research collaborators and friends.

Situating Ourselves

This chapter is based on informal discussions between us, Corinne and Irene, over the winter semester of 2023, culminating with an in-person recorded conversation on April 21, 2023. The final one-hour-long conversation was recorded and professionally transcribed. We have organized our conversation in this chapter for clarity and narrative coherence. We opted for an autoethnographic exchange to speak about our experiences of conducting research on faculty responses to sexualized violence during the COVID-19 pandemic. This chapter is specifically focused on our experiences of conducting research during the pandemic. At the start of the pandemic, we were working at different undergraduate teaching universities. Currently, we are employed in different departments within the same undergraduate institution. Both of us are dedicated to anti-racist, queer, and feminist epistemological frameworks and activism.

In February 2019, we were preparing to commence data collection for our SSHRC Insight Development Grant–funded research. Our project's objective was to examine how feminist researchers' expertise on sexualized violence informs their institution's policies and practices. As such, we set out to conduct focus groups and semi-structured interviews with feminist faculty about their roles in contributing to anti-sexualized violence policies and procedures at their institutions.

In this project, we sought to understand the complex ways in which scholarly expertise, particularly the expertise of racialized, queer, trans, disabled, and/or neurodivergent feminist faculty members, gets invoked or ignored within institutional sexualized-violence policies. We were hoping to mobilize the expertise of researchers by providing them with an opportunity to critically evaluate their institutions' sexualized-violence policies and practices and communicate concrete suggestions on how policies and practices can better meet the needs of universities. In addition, we hoped that this project would create opportunities for feminist scholars to share knowledge, forge research connections, and collaborate through focus groups and the resulting workshops. As we discuss below, pandemic lockdown measures were implemented as we were getting ready to fly out for our first interviews and focus groups. Thus, our data collection was moved online, and we conducted our interviews over Zoom.

What follows is an autoethnographic reflection on data collection and our experiences during the COVID-19 pandemic. Through personal reflexivity, we bridge the connection between personal and structural and how the pandemic heightened the exclusionary infrastructure of academia. Autoethnography requires looking inward to make sense of the larger cultural and societal structure (Adams et al., 2014). As such, our autoethnographic stories demonstrate how we have come to make sense of our experiences of loneliness and ourselves within academia.

Exchange

Loneliness as Impetus for Our Connection
Corinne: I am going to start…by asking you why we decided to do this project, to get us to start thinking about how feminist loneliness brought us into conversation with one another in this project.
Irene: I saw you on CBC [Canadian Broadcasting Corporation] and you were being interviewed for the non-disclosure agreement that Brandon University was making a student sign, and you did not hold back. As I was looking you up, I realized you were an assistant prof and not an associate, and then I got worried. So I emailed you…I don't know how it felt getting an email from a stranger at that particular point, but it was out of concern, but also knowing how risky talking about sexual violence is on campus, and that you were doing it in such a public venue, without the security of tenure.
Corinne: Yeah, I think I was so deeply lonely at that university and I was so alone in that advocacy. I understood the institutional risk of speaking out alongside the student, specifically about what they called a behavioural contract, in that she couldn't speak to anybody other than a designated counsellor on campus about her situation, and her speaking would be at the risk of expulsion. It felt lonely to both know her story and hold her risk, understanding that I could only say and do so much with the institutional pressures that she was facing. It was really scary thinking about her being removed from campus. So I wasn't thinking about myself in that context, I was thinking about trying to get her as many resources as possible, but I looked around and saw nobody with me. People had abandoned me at that moment. So, I was experiencing a deep loneliness. That incident exposed so much of what was wrong with the

university, including that there were not enough feminists on campus who were willing to stand up for her, and some were willing to let someone junior to them—and untenured faculty—go first.

I think that taught me a lot about feminist loneliness, specifically feminist loneliness in the institution; so looking around at an institution where people are both maybe appointed to women and gender studies, or who claim to be feminist, or articulate that they are going to be in solidarity with you, but when it comes time to step up and speak out...you kind of look around and you see yourself completely isolated and also alienated from them. That taught me a lot about institutional loneliness, specifically feminist loneliness, where I assumed people would work with me, and I assumed there would be a collective, or I assumed people would collectivize. When they didn't it felt like such an intense betrayal.

You showing up in my email was the opposite of that. I thought, "Okay, there are people who I can connect with, but maybe they are just not in my proximity, maybe they are not in the office beside me, maybe they exist at another campus." I think that is why I was so interested in continuing our relationship once we had built it—if I am lonely on my campus, who else is experiencing that same kind of feminist loneliness on their campus? How can folks like us connect with other people who are also experiencing that kind of loneliness?

Irene: I think part of the loneliness is the reason why I reached out...

I felt similar things. In graduate school, Dr. Malinda Smith educated us about disappearing white feminists, where white feminists show up around issues about sexism but will not be there for other issues of inequality—such as racism. So even though my expectations had been tempered before I got to my current institution, I was quite devastated by the reality of it. So for me, it was a bit different. For you, no one showed up, period. For me, it was the selective showing up.

For instance, in the first couple of years at my institution, Mount Royal University, I was fighting for pay increments during maternity leave and people who were not from working-class backgrounds didn't care about the issue. I am the main income earner. I don't come from money, and so the pay increment matters to me. The fact my feminist colleagues didn't or couldn't think about my concerns with those particular intersections of race, class, and gender is what made the loneliness so brutal. Some people showed up, but I always envisioned that once I got my tenure-track position, there would be a feminist community, but that community never happened. I have people, but it is like one person here, one person there. It was not the feminist community I imagined. I think that has been deeply lonely. I am still hopeful, but it just hasn't materialized in the way that I thought it would.

Corinne: That is so interesting because I, too, saw people selectively—or maybe I had an expectation of people showing up—but who didn't show up because it didn't serve them. One of the first things I heard from a colleague after I spoke out about this case of sexualized violence was that I had ruined the reputation of the university…I was ruining the reputation of the university, and I was taking her career down with me.

Irene: So you became constituted as a problem, as Sara Ahmed said?

Corinne: Yes, I exposed the problem, I became the problem. And of course, similarly around Sara Ahmed's notion of the "happy talk" of the institution, perhaps this colleague of mine was willing to hold up the reputation of the university in ways that I wasn't. Perhaps she was willing to do the happy talk of the institution, to put up all the window dressings. I was not as invested—or maybe not at all invested—in that kind of an institutional project.

Irene: Right, and when there was a collective—when people came together to work on issues, I found that there was an expectation to "be nice" and a refusal to criticize the institution. So I didn't fit in because I was too critical. People around the table were more willing to do the happy talk while I was not. That was one of the reasons I was so alienated and isolated. Another issue I worked on at my institution was sexualized-violence policies, which came about because one of my students was sexually assaulted, and he had nowhere to go because of the gender binaries that were constructed in the policy documents. None of the services available worked for him. So every time I would criticize the institutional policies on sexualized violence, it was seen as being ungrateful and for not understanding the institution.

As seen above, Irene's response to Corinne speaking to a news media outlet about sexualized violence was the impetus for our connection

(Mason & Shankar, personal communication, April 21, 2023). However, the connection was facilitated by the larger underlying loneliness both of us were experiencing due to our politics and advocacy on campus, and it is this shared politics and institutional loneliness that created the condition for an ongoing relationship. While we each had different relationships and connections within our institutions, we were trying to find "not simply coalition or solidarity across difference, but rather the enactment of a community of support based on shared politics" (Chowdhury & Philipose, 2016, p. 4).

It bears reiterating that our experiences are not unique or new as many other scholars have written about their experiences of isolation and loneliness due to their demands for social justice on or off campus. For instance, in 2016, Sara Ahmed left her position as a tenured faculty member after Goldsmith University refused to respond to students' experiences of sexualized violence. As explained by Ahmed (2016), feminists' identification or naming of a problem gets us constituted as a problem. Thus feminists, by bringing hidden inequities and problems to the forefront and refusing to do institutional happy talk are taken up as "killjoys," who bring others down by their insistence on addressing normalized problems. Speaking out about the institution violates "the implication…that feminist happiness within institutions depends on withholding complaints about the institution" (Ahmed, 2021, p. 67). By speaking out, Corinne was seen as compromising the reputation of the university, and as a result they were "dropped out of conversations and activities for not doing institutional work in the right way" (p. 67).

There is a long genealogy of activists being silenced and isolated. Audre Lorde (2007, pg. 137) in *Sister Outsider* speaks about her experience of "isolation and frustration" in the 1960s due to pressure to align with other folks' agenda and politics and from constantly having to deal with other people who were offended by her particular socio-political positionality and political stance. The consistent pressure to realign with institutional norms and politics along with the aggression of being deemed "too much" or "not enough" is a weight carried by historically or currently marginalized scholars within academia. Being cognizant of the genealogy of this loneliness is certainly helpful in framing and understanding the larger context of our struggles. Nonetheless, the experiences of isolation and loneliness remain painful.

Instead of finding ourselves wrapped in a community when we have spoken up about the injustices of the institution, both of us have experienced a selective showing up. Without shared politics among feminists on our campuses, each of us was positioned as difficult, as a traitor to the institution and our colleagues, and/or chastised for not understanding the institutional culture. As explained by Puwar (2004) in *Space Invaders: Race, Gender and Bodies Out of Space*, non-somatic bodies (read as anyone who is not an able-bodied heterosexual cisgender white man) are taken up as space invaders in privileged spaces, such as academia. As racialized or queer bodies, we are already bodies out of place, and any transgressions that violate the institutional norms of playing along or being quiet are further evidence of our not belonging in academia. In refuting the institutional mandate to keep quiet, those who speak out violate white investments in "professional collegiality" that requires silence and the prioritization of institutional reputation over all else.

As discussed above, being unhappy with aspects of our institutions, and an unwillingness to stay quiet or perform the happy talk of the institution, facilitated conditions of loneliness for both of us and also served as motivation to look beyond the institutional walls for connections.

Looking for Community Through Research
Stemming from our own experiences trying to advocate for feminist sexualized-violence responses on our campuses, we became interested in investigating how other faculty members experienced their institutions' responses to sexualized violence. Looking back, this project was also our way of looking for a community "within an exclusionary, alienating, and hierarchical academic culture" (Chowdury & Philipose, 2016, p. 4).

Corinne: It is interesting to think of loneliness as, of course, isolation, but our research project brought two lonely people together. Our research project...brought two isolated people together who were experiencing a similar kind of feminist loneliness in the institution into a conversation. We were both specifically looking for people who were—and definitely, we didn't articulate in this way at the time—similarly lonely to us! We were trying to figure out who was out there and if there were more of us with similar stories. We wanted to know what they were experiencing as faculty trying to respond to, provide expertise, or advise the institution as they were coming up with new policies or responding to legislation around sexualized violence, but also we wanted to find folks like us who were pushed aside—who were forced to divest in institutional transformation because we had been made to feel so alone in the process.

Irene: That was very much the impetus for us to start our project, because we wanted to see what happened to other feminists on campus. How was their expertise taken up or not taken up? When you constantly get shut down, not only are you lonely but also it takes a toll. That was part of our project. We were looking for other people's experiences of coping. What did they do? Where did they go? Did they find community and connection or were they further isolated by speaking up? When the institution refuses to hear you, how do you get heard? What did your experience feel like when you got turned down? Constantly being shut down means you get rendered invisible, you get erased from the institution, like you don't matter, and I wanted people to be seen. I think that is something that resonated with our participants. And when we did interviews, participants were like, "Oh, I want to tell you what happened." Interviews were a way of being seen and heard. As faculty, there are many institutional stories we can never tell because they are confidential and people sharing them knew they wouldn't be part of the data. But they wanted to come and tell us their experiences. That was one of the major motivations behind the project—to share our stories of both refusal and survival.

Looking for a community within academia is complex. Patel and Da Costa (2022) illustrate that universities are now instrumentalizing collaborations, especially across differences, in their commitments to equity, diversity, and inclusion (EDI). Rather than being a challenge to the neoliberal Western academy's conception of individual merit and knowledge production, they note that the emergence of "collaboratories" at universities is an example of the deradicalization of collaborative research, methodologies, and pedagogical practices. As Patel and Da Costa (2022) reveal in their reflections on the (im)possibilities of writing across caste lines, collaborations and friendships are complicit in structures of domination reproduced by the academy even when they resist structures of violence and harm. As they explain, the appearance of solidarity between faculty who are Indigenous and Black, Indigenous, and people of colour, for example, can be used as evidence of institutional decolonization and successful EDI measures to benefit the university's reputation. Here, our desire to find community—solidarities and accomplices—is bound up in "generational and ongoing complicities in the violence" of colonial white supremacy (Patel & Da Costa, 2022, p. 21). Friendship—including ours, which has merged across differences (queer and racialized, respectively)—is perhaps useful to this larger project of what Thobani (2021) calls "the equity/diversity/inclusion machinery" (p. 6). That is to say that we are aware that friendships and collaborations like ours are complicit in what Patel and Da Costa (2022) refer to as "instrumentalized collaborations" and what Ahmed (2019) conceptualizes as "structurally useful" within the university. However complicit (or potentially co-opted by the institution), academic friendships and collaborations bound by care are also resistant and subversive, as Tungohan explores in chapter 7 of this collection.

Silencing and Complaint
Reflecting on the potential complicity of our collaboration in the EDI machinery of the institution, and our romanticization of the feminist community within this context, led us to discuss other forms of feminist complicity in the violence of the university as a condition of loneliness. In our interviews, we spoke to some feminists who had, in some form, helped to shape policies and practices to respond to sexualized violence. Below, we discuss some of our hesitancies about working for the university, and within narrow frameworks, to respond to sexualized violence.

> Corinne: I think there is something specific about researching responses to sexualized violence that has allowed us to see our work as being about feminist loneliness in institutions. The way that the university largely deals with sexualized violence is such a lonely process for folks who come forward with a complaint. What we heard from folks we interviewed was that they were either part of complaint processes or had advocated alongside students, and once you entered into these arrangements with the institution you were

meant to go at it alone. What many of these policies do is create individual pathways where one person goes through a complaint process with the institution and sign[s] onto, often, privacy and confidentiality agreements. So, that survivor is told to tell their story, often multiple ways, in multiple locations, in front of multiple audiences, but they often do it all by themselves. Then the resources that they get in return are often limited to on-campus, short term, not sexualized violence–specific, maybe not queer-trans affirming, or they can't find support from someone who is embodied and understands the experiences and complexity of being racialized, having a disability, and/or being neurodivergent in those counselling offices. The experience can be so lonely, because you are told who to speak to, and told who you can't speak to, and no kind of collective organizing happens once you are in a complaint process.

And, once you are in a complaint process it is you, as an individual, alone with the institution. Whatever decision is handed down most often comes with a privacy and confidentiality agreement as well. So your experience of the complaint is also made private, made confidential, and so it is very difficult, I think, to be so alone in that process of making a complaint. For me, it is important to think about our roles as feminist faculty in trying to critically respond to and resist these institutional policies and procedures that create a new form of institutional loneliness.

Irene: Yes, there is that, the confidentiality of the complaint process, but there are all kinds of silencing built into the process. There are all kinds of loneliness built into how the university works, the various mechanisms put into place so you can't talk to anyone. Our experiences tend to be so specific to whatever we are going through at the institution, and it is hard to talk about it with other academics. For example, when you are on committees where horrible things have happened with dire consequences for faculty members, you can't talk about the experience. Also, operating from an anti-racist and feminist perspective, other people do not necessarily see what you see. Often, there is only one of you—a racialized woman, a non-binary faculty member—on a committee, so only you have noticed what has happened. It is so hard to describe and convince others of what you have observed, as well. So all kinds of loneliness are built into the structure of the university which makes us very isolated.

Often, campus complaints of sexualized violence are met with stringent requirements for confidentiality. Confidentiality of deliberations is justified to protect the privacy of the complainant and the accused. Such confidentiality requirements are also instituted by the university legal team to protect the institutional reputation and legal risk (Buss & Majury, 2020). For faculty and staff, not only can refuting the institutional mandates for confidentiality lead to job termination, it is also seen as a violation of professional collegiality or traitorous to publicly discuss institutional deficiencies. As explained by Corinne above, all of these mechanisms make the complaint process an intrinsically lonely experience. There is no way to collectively discuss and share our experiences with each other. This isolation and loneliness is by design.

As discussed by Irene above, many forms of violence happen in different contexts, including committee work. As racialized and queer faculty continue to be under-represented within academia (Smith, 2010), often we find ourselves alone in such contexts, which means that we are often alone in rooms when being subjected to acts of violence, harassment, or intimidation on committees (see, e.g., Thobani, 2021). Even if there are others in the room, they may not necessarily see or recognize acts of hostility as such. While some of us are marginalized and have a record of working on issues of inequity and are trained to identify discriminatory practices, when others around the table don't comprehend or acknowledge that something is "off," that is isolating. When speaking about the incidents, those targeted by violence are often met with "blank stares" (Ahmed, 2021) and silence, which further compounds our feelings of isolation and loneliness. As explained by Magnet and Orr (2022, p. 13), feminist loneliness comes up when we are told we are exaggerating or seeing things. This gaslighting creates the conditions for further loneliness and isolation within an already hostile environment.

Pandemic Disruptions
The COVID-19 pandemic was for us, like many scholars, a major disruption to our research. As we write elsewhere (Mason & Shankar, 2024), the COVID-19 pandemic has further entrenched existing inequities in academia (Davis, 2021; Górska et al., 2021; Oleschuk, 2020). For women, in particular, research and publication plans have been drastically affected, which will have a long-term impact on tenure

and promotion plans (Bohanon, 2020; Flaherty, 2021; Isselbacher, 2020). Beyond our career trajectories, institutionalized feminist loneliness has been compounded by the intensification of inequities during the pandemic. As we explore below, and as authors Ayesha Mian Akram (chapter 1), Fawziah Rabiah-Mohammed and Leah K. Hamilton (chapter 5), and Ethel Tungohan (chapter 7) take up within this collection, the institutional demands of productivity during the early days of the pandemic conflicted with our feminist ethics of care and political commitments to community to "press on" with our research.

Irene: The other thing with our study is we did have a lot of people who came and talked to us about their experiences of institutional isolation, and we are so grateful for that, especially because they took the time to connect with us during the pandemic. We had booked our flights, we had our data collection organized, like where we were going to go and who we were going to interview, and then suddenly the pandemic hit and everything closed down and we couldn't travel, so we had to do it all over Zoom. We moved really quickly. That brought its advantages and disadvantages. The advantage was we could do many more interviews than we originally thought possible, and so we connected with a lot more people.

But the other part was how we connected with people. Only certain people could find time to talk during the early days of the pandemic. People with very young kids [whose children were home because of school closures] and those who identified as currently and/or historically excluded groups couldn't connect with us. Due to my positionality, those were the folks I was eager to connect with. People weren't able to come and talk to us because they were so overextended. Black Lives Matter protests were happening at the same time, and so many people were working on local actions. Institutions also, more often than not, were at the same moment asking for all this labour on EDI issues from faculty. People were exhausted. I think that is a sadness I still hold about this project—all these people we wanted to talk to, all these people who wanted to talk to us, couldn't because of how overextended and exhausted they were.

Corinne: When we were inviting people to interview, we were very apprehensive about asking people for more labour in the midst of a pandemic. So much of the feminist response to the pandemic was about community care, slowing down, using COVID-19 as a portal…asking how we make new ways of relating. But the institution doesn't care about new ways of relating, slowing down, being community-focused, or being focused on our families. The expectation was that we would turn around our classes overnight, put them online, and then all of a sudden we would become online qualitative researchers, and we would just know how to move projects that were meant to be in-person onto Zoom. And for me and you, we were meant to be in person together—to spend time with participants but also to spend time with each other. The point was for us to be together, too, to work on our relationship in addition to building relationships with participants.

When we started, we specifically said we want to talk to people who are Black, Indigenous, or racially minoritized; we want to talk to queer and trans people, people with disabilities; we want to talk to people who are neurodivergent. We want to talk to the people who experience the most marginalization on their campuses, but also those whose communities are at the highest risk of sexualized violence, but who don't often get heard by the institution and whose experiences of sexualized violence don't match the kind of idealized or archetypal survivor that the universities most respond to. Of course, during COVID-19 those were communities who were most hit in terms of high transmissions and death rates—this is the demographic of people who were most likely to be working essential frontline jobs, people who were most underserved or ignored by public-health guidance and were offered such minimal resources.

A bunch of the feminist faculty we wanted to speak to were called into their community to do care work and community activism, which makes a lot of sense because we were also being called into our communities to do that work as well. At the same time, like all academics, we were not given any kind of relief to stop our projects, to slow them down, to say that we would collect data when lockdowns were over. Nobody knew when that would happen, of course, but there were no provisions, either with granting agencies or our institutions to spend the time we needed to spend taking care of ourselves, living through a pandemic, which was deeply frightening and isolating and lonely. We were also experiencing the loneliness and the isolation of being at home during the pandemic and trying to manage so much of what was left, largely, to women and femmes in households to just kind of deal with, which was the burden of care!

I think we also bypassed a lot of our intuition about ways of connecting with ourselves, with each other, with our families, friends, and our communities, to try and keep the project going, and I think that created its own kind of feminist loneliness.

Irene: There was a lot of institutional pressure to keep going. I wonder if I had more time to think it through, what questions or what other things could I have asked? What other things would I have seen that I didn't get to see? I think all kinds of barriers in place made the loneliness even more pronounced. Like, because of confidentiality requirements, I couldn't turn around and tell my partner about the traumatic things I had heard during the interviews. The only person we could talk to was each other, but we couldn't even show up to the interviews at the same time. One of the things you said was we were going to meet and do this together and spend time together, and about halfway through the interview I was like, Well, I can't come. I would spend a lot of time crying because I couldn't figure out how to make sure my parents were vaccinated. They are in a different town than I am in, and they are very vulnerable and immunocompromised. At the same time, I was trying to help my young child with her school work. It ended up being like, one of us would show up at each interview over Zoom, and so we missed out on that connection. Each of us connected with half of the participants—we didn't get to do it together. There wasn't enough time. I remember being so tired!

As Corinne notes above, we often bypassed our feminist commitments to care in our research, and limited our care work in the community, because of the rush toward completing our data collection. Against the ticking clock of a two-year research grant, we experienced an urgency to produce during a time that specifically called for us to slow down. In the article "White Supremacy Culture" (1999), Okun names urgency as a central organizing principle of white supremacist organizations. A "continued sense of urgency," she writes, "makes it difficult to take time to be inclusive, encourage democratic and/or thoughtful decision-making, think long-term, to consider consequences"; "frequently results in sacrificing potential allies for quick or highly visible results, for example sacrificing interests of communities of colour to win victories for white people (seen as the default or norm community)"; and "[is] reinforced by funding proposals which promise too much work for too little money and by funders who expect too much for too little antidotes" (p. 2).

During the COVID-19 pandemic, we found ourselves conforming to the conditions of white supremacy in our organizations that made it impossible to be inclusive in our interview recruitment. As Okun (1999) warns, we sacrificed potential allies under the pressure of institutional urgency that was reinforced by funding constraints. This sense of urgency from institutions was not limited to research during the pandemic. As Mian Akram explores in chapter 1 of this collection, universities added to the pressures facing marginalized faculty members by committing to new and laborious EDI initiatives at a time when faculty were experiencing high levels of burn-out—perhaps better articulated as labour exploitation (Dhamoon, 2020).

Faculty Burn-Out and Divestment

Unsurprisingly, the participants we interviewed so often spoke to us about their experiences of burn-out. Burn-out is a rampant issue across academia, but its fallout is particularly acute for marginalized faculty. For racialized women, in particular, sexist and racist microaggressions, tokenism, bullying, and service workloads are all cited in literature on this issue (Dhamoon, 2020; Duncan, 2014; Fossett, 2023; Fox Tree & Vaid, 2022; Hendrix, 2021; Lund et al., 2022). Williams (2021) highlights the labour of student interaction and mentorship as central to the disproportionate labour that racialized faculty experience. Alongside a disproportionate burden of service work, racialized women experience barriers to advancement into prestigious academic positions (Fox Tree & Vaid, 2022). Fox Tree and Vaid (2022) note that racialized women are cited less often, are less professionally recognized, and experience disparity in capturing recommendation letters, funding, and positive evaluations of training. For Pope-Ruark (2022), the white supremacist valuation of worthiness in academia sets up the conditions in which racialized women experience workplace bullying and gaslighting, all while being tasked with transforming the injustices of the university. As Dhamoon (2020) maintains, racialized faculty experiences of white hostilities sometimes develop into health and well-being issues that require faculty to take sick leave, move departments or faculties (as explored by Gabrielle Ellen Weasel Head in this collection), or leave academia entirely. However, most unions and faculty organizations have no framework for understanding this cost of racism.

Within this context, the COVID-19 pandemic not only entrenched long-standing inequities but made them more visible. As Weasel Head and Mian Akram reveal in their chapters within this collection, the toll of anti-racism labour became more extreme during the pandemic as calls for institutions to respond to anti-Black and anti-Indigenous racism were off-loaded to racialized faculty and students. Here, we offer our reflections on how expectations of labour, particularly for those the university would perceive as "equity-seeking," ramped up during COVID-19 as calls for EDI-based service increased. Additionally, we offer our thinking on what has changed for us as we "return to normal" at the university.

Corinne: Most of the participants talked about burn-out because...the work they were doing on sexualized violence was hard and brutal, and often an experience where they felt deep loneliness, and then that work kind of slid right into calls for those same people—sometimes, not always, but often—to pick up the slack, and keep going with the EDI work of the institution. And this was during the pandemic! The university was calling in folks who we wanted to talk to, who are most marginalized on campus, to do work on EDI around the same time. Because what the universities were seeing was a call from communities on and off-campus, to respond to Black Lives Matter protests, calls for deep, transformative anti-racist work, and in response, universities made new commitments to EDI. That created a new kind of institutional busywork.

Irene: One of the big realizations for me was how COVID-19 brought this question of EDI-based labour exploitation to the forefront. The pandemic allowed us to see how tired, exhausted, and burned-out people were, and how institutional practices have made people unwell. That was a huge realization; this veil had lifted, and we got to see people as they were struggling. Historically marginalized and/or currently excluded faculty members were tasked with EDI work without adequate supports or protection. As such, they were particularly burned out. The pandemic was the moment when we got to see that very clearly. It couldn't be hidden anymore.

Corinne: I have noticed that there are lots of people who have divested from the institution, and maybe not because of COVID-19 exactly, but maybe because the pandemic revealed how little the university cares for people. There was so little support, so few resources, and such high expectations during the pandemic. I think coming back to the university has meant a return to proximity to one another, but returning has been a lonely experience. I look around and see that people who were sometimes in solidarity with you, maybe weren't always collectivizing with you, but you could kind of rely on to show up in particular ways, are so divested from the institution because of their burn-out, because of how unwell they have become because of the institution. It means that loneliness, for me, has become more pronounced as we get "back to normal."

And, I think the expectations are higher. There is no time to ramp up; nobody got a break, and there wasn't like, "Oh, this part of the pandemic is over, and now we shall rest because we survived and we're collectively grieving." There was none of that. It was, "We better get back in person and we better catch up on everything that was missed over the past two and a half or three years." That, I think, has created a different kind of institutional loneliness where we're expected to squirrel away at our desks to make up for a global pandemic.

Irene: bell hooks talked about how feminism needs to tackle capitalism, and the pandemic revealed the relationship between academia and capitalism. And not that I didn't know this already, but to see it in practice during a global pandemic is to fully see how we have been commodified. I think the pandemic, in some ways, was a wake-up call for me.

Returning to the campus after being away during the lockdown has made me more cognizant of discriminatory institutional practices that I had previously shrugged off or ignored. I recently read an article by Hendrix (2021) where she talks about how "snipers" are everywhere. Returning after a bit of absence from campus has made me more attuned to all insitutional practices, particularly the racist and gendered aggressions, invisibility, and erasure of expertise that had somehow become normalized over the years. Now, there is no denying that there is violence in occupying a space that is not meant for you. The crude self-interest of the neoliberal post-secondary institutions has become quite clear.

The lack of due care and concern exercised by institutions during the pandemic (as described in this collection by Mian Akram, Borzoo et al., and Weasel Head) has laid bare the neoliberal self-interests of educational institutions, which have remained focused on business as usual—even during the most dire circumstances. Universities issued rhetoric of care that required individualized responsibility (such as rest and exercise) while refusing accommodations that would allow people to rest. For instance, tenure and promotion expectations were not changed to realign with the realities of the pandemic. Instead, at Irene's university, faculty were told to explain in their annual reports how their work had been impacted—requiring further labour of those already most acutely impacted by the pandemic. In addition, the additional labour that marginalized faculty members undertake in the care of students and working on social-justice issues—both within and outside of the campus—has remained invisible despite the pandemic heightening both of these important and necessary workloads for many faculty members.

Feminist Snap

In *Living a Feminist Life*, Ahmed (2016) describes her resignation from Goldsmiths University in the midst of conducting sexual-harassment advocacy as a "snap." A snap, for Ahmed, has a history, which means that a feminist snap is not rash and rushed, but rather exposes an accumulation of pressure. She writes:

> And when I think of snap, I think of a twig. When a twig snaps, we hear the sound of it breaking. We can hear the suddenness of a break. We might assume, based on what we hear, that the snap is a starting point. A snap sounds like the start of something, a transformation of something; it is how a twig might end up broken in two pieces. (pp. 188–189)

As we articulate below, the COVID-19 pandemic for some faculty is, perhaps, a moment of snapping, but only because the pressures that came before have established our precarious bonds with our institutions.

Corinne: We have both talked about the institution revealing itself during COVID-19; turning away, being divested from, or burning out from the institution; and seeing feminists and speaking to feminists in our interviews who are doing the same thing. We have seen lots of people turning away from the institution. What do we, as feminists, do to connect with others to counter, or make sense of, our own institutionalized loneliness?

Irene: One of the emerging findings of this research, and maybe fuel for our next project, is the question of divestment from the institution as a result of feminist loneliness. I think that because of this experience of loneliness, we have found a new pathway for connecting.

Corinne: Yes, I think articulating our own experiences of loneliness, as a way of building relations in response to this deep desire to connect, is a way forward. I think this is because of how the institution of the university has created the conditions for isolation and the conditions in which we are asked to go it alone.

There are interesting things to learn from feminists who are navigating their own pockets of the university in ways that are very specific to this moment, specifically this "post-COVID" moment. This is a moment where the university has committed us to their project of EDI without actually resourcing any of us who have expertise in the things that they say they want to do! And in this moment, when so many folks who are so burdened with all kinds of care labour outside of the institution because of the pandemic are so very tired. I think there is something in this moment that would allow us to see even more how deeply isolating the institution makes us feel, and how the institution often makes us feel responsible for our own isolation.

Irene: I want to be clear that it is not everyone experiencing isolation; it is the people who refuse to do the happy talk of this institution. This reminds me a lot of Sara Ahmed and Charmaine Nelson—two amazing scholars whom I look up to—who left their institutions because they refused to do the happy talk. Dr. Nelson left during the pandemic and Dr. Ahmed left before the pandemic, but I still think about that, what it took for them to leave. Financially, I don't have the ability to leave, and I don't think you do either. So for me, it means thinking through what to focus on and how to navigate academia with this reorientation that we have experienced.

Corinne: This is so interesting to me. Ahmed calls this a "feminist snap." And it is not that the snap just happens, it is in the works—there is pressure building up that causes the snap. It isn't rash, but the reasons are often made invisible. But snapping is also world-making. Ahmed (2017) calls being a feminist killjoy a world-making project. I think only by articulating our experiences of being lonely in our feminism at our institutions—and where, how, and why we "snapped"—can we actually connect with people in the ways that we want to. We need to ask each other, "How did you experience feminist loneliness at your institution? What made you snap? What feminist worlds are you building now?" I think these questions have the potential to bring us into a relationship with one another in really exciting ways.

Importantly, for Ahmed (2016), a feminist snap is not only the breaking of a bond but should also be understood as "an opening, a new way of proceeding" (p. 187). The feminist snap requires acknowledgement that we are not "personally responsible for the shortcomings of an institution that is only willing to recognize a single model of knowledge and knowledge sharing" (Monture, 2010, p. 28). Accordingly, in reflecting on snapping her familial bonds to live a feminist queer life, Ahmed (2016) offers the feminist snap as not a sad moment, but as the "relief from pressure" (p. 193). Bonds to the institution of the family for Ahmed, and for us bonds to academic institutions, are binds that can get in the way of living a feminist life. For us, this feminist snap under the immense pressure of COVID-19—and all of the other pressures that mounted before the pandemic—is worth exploring because snaps can be "a lifeline" (Ahmed, 2016, p. 194). As Ahmed maintains, "A snap is not a starting point, but a snap can be the start of something" (2016, p. 194). Thus, as we end our exchange, we carry with us the lessons imparted by feminist experts we have interviewed and feminist scholars we read. For instance, we carry hooks's (2000) lessons that our personal experiences are due to larger political infrastructure and relations, and that we should continue to push for a transformation of the entire system instead of performative transformations. Thus, we recognize that our loneliness is created by the broader structure of the neoliberal post-secondary education system, and we need to continue to rally against this institutional loneliness by adhering to

Simpson's lesson to "resist colonial and capitalistic forces and exercise our autonomy" (Simpson, 2017, as cited in Magnet & Orr, 2022, p. 13).

Conclusion

Throughout this exchange, we have identified the broader conditions for our personal experiences of loneliness within our institutions and demonstrated the structural constraints and barriers to connection that create the conditions for our feminist loneliness. Since our research together during the COVID-19 pandemic, specifically during the first two years that were marked by proximal loneliness at the behest of "lockdown" and social distancing public-health policies, we have addressed how our experiences of institutional alienation and isolation were intensified as we sought to "pivot" our research online. As scholars attempting to use our research to build feminist networks and connections, we discussed how our attempts to cope with loneliness were hindered by the pandemic context, and we explored how we continue to be motivated by our experiences of institutionalized feminist loneliness to connect to other feminist killjoys in the academy.

Notes

1. This chapter is a feminist collaboration in which each author contributed 50 percent. Author names are presented in alphabetical order.
2. We recognize that there are major limitations to how sex and gender data were collected in this survey. Only those respondents who selected "female" for both "sex" and "gender identity" and selected "no" to the option of "transgender" were designated as "female." This way of collecting information about sex and gender excludes trans women from the category "female." Moreover, regardless of their answers for sex or gender identity, those who responded "yes" to transgender were designated "non-binary," which is an incorrect use of the term; and those whose reported sex and gender identity were "inconsistent" with each other were also designated "non-binary." If a respondent skipped any of the sex or gender questions, researchers designated their gender as "unknown" (American College Health Association, 2019, 2).

References

Adams, T.E., Holman Jones, S., & Ellis, C. (2014). *Autoethnography: Understanding qualitative research*. Oxford University Press.

Ahmed, S. (2012). *On being included: Racism and diversity in institutional life*. Duke University Press.

Ahmed, S. (2016). *Living a feminist life*. Duke University Press.

Ahmed, S. (2017, May 21). *Snap!* Feminist Killjoys blog. https://feministkilljoys.com/2017/05/21/snap/

Ahmed, S. (2019). *What's the use? On the uses of use.* Duke University Press.

Ahmed, S. (2021). *Complaint!* Duke University Press.

American College Health Association. (2019). *National College Health Assessment II: Canadian Consortium Executive Summary Spring 2019.* https://www.acha.org/wp-content/uploads/2024/07/NCHA-II_SPRING_2019_CANADIAN_REFERENCE_GROUP_EXECUTIVE_SUMMARY.pdf

Bohanon, M. (2020, September 15). Pandemic expected to cause additional barriers to tenure for marginalized academics. *Insight into Diversity.* https://www.insightintodiversity.com/pandemic-expected-to-cause-additional-barriers-to-tenure-for-marginalized-academics/

Buss, D., & Majury, D. (2020). Shadow matters: Campus sexual violence and legal forms. In D. Crocker, J. Minaker, & A. Nelund (Eds.), *Violence interrupted: Confronting sexual violence on university campuses* (pp. 243–262). McGill-Queen's University Press.

Canadian Social Survey: Loneliness in Canada. (2021, November 24). *The Daily.* Statistics Canada. https://www150.statcan.gc.ca/n1/daily-quotidien/211124/dq211124e-eng.htm

Charania, G.R. (2022). Lonely methods and other tough places: Recuperating anti-racism from white investments. *Feminist Theory, 23*(1), 61–75. https://doi.org/10.1177/14647001211062725

Chowdhury, E.H., & Philipose, L. (2016). Introduction. In E.H. Chowdhury & L. Philipose (Eds.), *Dissident friendships: Feminism, imperialism, and transnational solidarity* (pp. 1–8). University of Illinois Press. https://doi.org/10.5406/illinois/9780252040412.003.0001

Davis, J. (2021, March 2). University survey shows how COVID-19 pandemic is hampering career progress for women and racialized faculty. *The Conversation.* https://theconversation.com/university-survey-shows-how-covid-19-pandemic-is-hampering-career-progress-for-women-and-racialized-faculty-153169

Dhamoon, R.K. (2020). Racism as a workload and bargaining issue. *Socialist Studies, 14*(1). https://doi.org/10.18740/ss27273

Duncan, P. (2014). Hot commodities, cheap labor. *Frontiers: A Journal of Women Studies, 35*(3), 39–63.

Flaherty, C. (2021, March 10). Covid-19: A moment for women in STEM? *Inside Higher Education.* https://www.insidehighered.com/news/2021/03/10/covid-19-moment-women-stem

Fossett, K. (2023, February 9). Burnout, racism and extra diversity-related work: Black women in academia share their experiences. *Politico.* https://www.politico.com/newsletters/women-rule/2021/07/09/nikole-hannah-jones-black-women-academia-493523

Fox Tree, J.E., & Vaid, J. (2022). Why so few, still? Challenges to attracting, advancing, and keeping women faculty of color in academia. *Frontiers in Sociology, 6,* article 792198

Górska, A.M., Kulicka, K., Staniszewska, Z., & Dobija, D. (2021). Deepening inequalities: What did COVID-19 reveal about the gendered nature of academic work? *Gender, Work & Organization, 28*(4), 1546–1561. https://doi.org/10.1111/gwao.12696

Hendrix, K.G. (2021). There are no awards for surviving racism, sexism, and ageism in the academy: Contemplations of a senior faculty member. *Communication and Critical/Cultural Studies, 18*(3), 246–262.

hooks, b. (2000). *Feminist theory: From margins to centre*. South End Press Classics.

Isselbacher, J. (2020, July 9). *Women researchers are publishing less since the pandemic hit. What can their employers do to help?* STAT. https://www.statnews.com/2020/07/09/women-research-covid19-pandemic/

Johnson, M. (2012, August 14). The lonely life of the academic. *Inside Higher Education*. https://www.insidehighered.com/blogs/gradhacker/lonely-life-academic

Lorde, A. (2007). *Sister outsider*. Crossing Press.

Lund, S., D'Angelo, J.D., Jogerst, K., Warner, S.G., Busch, R., & D'Angelo, A.-L.D. (2022). Revealing hidden experiences: Gendered microaggressions and surgical faculty burnout. *Surgery, 172*(3), 885–889.

Magnet, S., & Orr, C. (2022). Feminist loneliness studies: An introduction. *Feminist Theory, 23*(1), 3–22. https://doi.org/10.1177/14647001211062734

Mason, C.L., and Shankar, I. (2024). "Sorry, my child is kicking me under the desk": Intersectional challenges to research during the COVID-19 pandemic. In C. Carter, C.T. Jones, & C. Janzen (Eds.), *Contemporary vulnerabilities: Reflections on social justice methodologies* (pp. 215–240). University of Alberta Press.

Million, D. (2014). There is a river in me: Theory from life. In A. Simpson & A. Smith (Eds.), *Theorizing Native studies* (pp. 31–42). Duke University Press.

Monture, P. (2010). Race, gender, and the university: Strategies for survival. In S. Razack, M. Smith, & S. Thobani (Eds.), *States of race: Critical race feminism for the 21st century* (pp. 23–36). Between the Lines.

Okun, T. (1999). *White supremacy culture*. Dismantling Racism. https://www.dismantlingracism.org/uploads/4/3/5/7/43579015/okun_-_white_sup_culture.pdf

Oleschuk, M. (2020). Gender equity considerations for tenure and promotion during COVID-19. *Canadian Review of Sociology, 57*(3), 502–515.

Patel, S.A., & Da Costa, D. (2022). "We cannot write about complicity together": Limits of cross-caste collaborations in Western academy. *Engaged Scholar Journal, 8*(2), 1–27.

Puwar, N. (2004). *Space invaders: Race, gender and bodies out of place*. Bloomsbury Academic.

Pope-Ruark, R. (2022). *Unraveling faculty burnout: Pathways to reckoning and renewal*. Johns Hopkins University Press.

Sibai, O., Figueiredo, B., & Ferreira, M.C. (2019, January 29). *Overworked and isolated: The rising epidemic of loneliness in academia*. Phys.org. https://phys.org/news/2019-01-overworked-isolated-epidemic-loneliness-academia.html

Shaw, C. (2014, May 8). Overworked and isolated—work pressure fuels mental illness in academia. *The Guardian*. https://www.theguardian.com/higher-education-network/blog/2014/may/08/work-pressure-fuels-academic-mental-illness-guardian-study-health

Simpson, L. (2017). *As we have always done: Indigenous freedom through radical resistance*. University of Minnesota Press.

Smith, M. (2010). Gender, whiteness, and "other Others" in the academy. In S. Razack, M. Smith, & S. Thobani (Eds.), *States of race: Critical race feminism for the 21st century* (pp. 37–58). Between the Lines.

Thobani, S. (2021). *Coloniality and racial (in)justice in the university: Counting for nothing?* University of Toronto Press.

Williams, W. (2021, June 18). Lightening the burden. *Inside Higher Ed*. https://www.insidehighered.com/advice/2021/06/18/advice-how-colleges-can-lift-some-emotional-burden-bipoc-faculty-opinion

/7
"Dissident Friendships" During COVID Times

ETHEL TUNGOHAN

Introduction

The neoliberal academy has long been a site of rampant gender and race inequities. Academic norms assume that all professors are childless, male faculty without caring obligations, forcing scholars from underrepresented communities—namely women, Black, Indigenous and people of colour (BIPOC), disabled, and first-generation scholars—to conform to these norms. Despite research documenting the diversity gap in academia that penalizes women and BIPOC in evaluations of teaching, research, and service (Chávez & Mitchell, 2020; Henry et al., 2017; Winslow & Davis, 2016) and that places more labour on them (Dhamoon, 2020), universities appear resistant to change. This is notwithstanding the numerous equity, diversity, and inclusion (EDI) initiatives that they promote. In fact, neoliberal academic structures remain intact. Government austerity programs that reduce university funding forces universities to impose "measures" of academic value when evaluating programs and, by extension, faculty, to the detriment of minority academics who already face extra scrutiny in evaluations of "merit" (Kınıkoğlu & Can, 2021).

The COVID-19 pandemic amplified these existing inequities. Numerous research studies extensively document the gender gaps in publishing during the pandemic and the reduction in academic productivity (Malisch et al., 2020; Shalaby et al., 2021). Women of colour with caring responsibilities—especially Black women with children—experienced the biggest reduction in productivity (Staniscuaski et al., 2021). In my field, political science, female professors were less productive during the pandemic due to magnified caregiving responsibilities. Female educators in primary, secondary, and post-secondary institutions also faced increased expectations to provide support to students and colleagues through an increase in service roles (Dogra & Kaushal, 2022). Working conditions during the pandemic were so untenable that many decided to leave. The trend of academics fleeing academia became so widespread that some dubbed this mass exodus "the great resignation" (Gewin, 2022).

To say that I was impacted by the pandemic is to make an understatement. When I read the aforementioned research highlighting the gendered and racialized impacts of the pandemic, I felt validated, knowing that my experiences were reflected in others. Discussions of toxicity in academic spaces resonated deeply with me, particularly Plotnikof and Utoff's (2022) description of how "greedy universities moving into our homes during the pandemic" required "all-consuming" productivity (p. 1260). These expectations then magnify the imposter syndrome of women—and, I would add, racialized academics—who find it impossible to meet research productivity expectations because of enhanced caring responsibilities. What I found especially taxing was the unstated expectation that women, especially women of colour, assume emotional labour to provide support for their students and their colleagues as institutions crumble around them, thereby necessitating the provision of care work at home *and* work. Yet, in some ways, these studies only reflected a fraction of the pressures I faced.

Being a professor with young children is only one part of my identity. I am also a daughter and a niece, with familial ties around the world. My extended family is dispersed across several national borders, living across Canada, the United States, and the Philippines. I saw the uneven impacts of COVID-19. Global South countries like the Philippines were more affected by the pandemic because of inadequate and insufficient health-care systems. The coronavirus spread in these countries was exacerbated by "vaccine apartheid," which refers to the uneven distribution of vaccines globally as a result of wealthy Global North countries' vaccine monopoly (*A Dose of Reality*, 2021).

Consequently, much of my time during the pandemic was spent connecting virtually with family members abroad. I was especially concerned because many loved ones worked in essential health-care fields, placing them in direct contact with the public. Given that many health-care workers are in the Filipino community, it is unsurprising to see that some of the first COVID-19 deaths across the world were from the Filipino community (Almendral, 2020). I acknowledge this intersection between race and COVID-19 spread in a blog post that I wrote about COVID-19's impacts (Tungohan 2020; see also Ajadi & Thompson, 2021). During the first year of the pandemic, two of my family members died. One of my relatives was living in the United States and working as an undocumented health-care worker in a long-term care home. Because of fears regarding the pandemic spread, his wife and children were unable to be with him in his last moments. Another uncle in the United States also died during this period, not from COVID-19, but from being unable to go to the hospital due to health-related complications because hospitals were at capacity. Also, during this first year, vaccines were not widely available, and many family members got COVID-19, including another uncle in the Philippines, a doctor, who thankfully recovered after days in the intensive-care unit. Many family members got sick before COVID-19 spread became more rampant. Getting COVID-19 in those early days was seen almost as a sign of irresponsible individual behaviour rather than a sign of institutional failure. Rather than considering structural factors that led to increased COVID-19 spread—such as how racialized, working-class communities tend to be concentrated in areas of high density (thus making it hard to abide by social distancing regulations), and how many members of these communities work in so-called essential public-facing, low-paid jobs that made COVID-19 more likely—the belief in "individual responsibility" led to much stigma.

As a community advocate and an immigration researcher, I also saw just how vulnerable migrant workers were during the pandemic. COVID-19 spread was rampant among workplaces such as manufacturing plants, warehouses, farms, and long-term care homes, i.e., workplaces that were considered essential. Some migrant workers in these spaces would later contract COVID-19 in the first and second waves of the pandemic because of inadequate workplace protections such as the provision of personal protective equipment and insufficient enforcement of occupational and workplace safety regulations like social-distancing requirements (see Tungohan et al., 2021). Based on conversations with migrant workers in these spaces, it was clear that many of them were abandoned by their employers and their government. The ongoing stigma that they faced then and still face now, when we are supposedly transitioning into a post-COVID society, was exacerbated by dire conditions such as low pay, an absence of benefits, and a lack of health and safety protections. Despite statements by government leaders calling migrant workers heroes, it remains clear that policies needed to protect migrant workers' labour rights and their occupational health and safety were not implemented. The disjuncture between discourses of heroism and the absence of much-needed occupational health and safety policies made migrant workers "expendable essential workers" (Pandey et al., 2021, p. 1287). In some cases, migrant workers were instead blamed for getting COVID-19. Alberta's chief medical officer of health, Dr. Deena Hinshaw, for example, said that Filipino cultural norms of hard work and their propensity to live in households with their extended family members were the reason COVID-19 spread in the Cargill meatpacking plants (Kinney, 2020). Such victim-blaming narratives conveniently ignore larger socioeconomic factors, such as work policies that penalize migrant workers for absences, or the lack of affordable housing and housing discrimination that necessitates cohabitation, and serves to increase the risk of COVID-19 transmission (Kinney, 2020).

Professional, family, and community pressures, combined, made the COVID-19 pandemic an extremely stressful time. I was pulled in many different directions: I had to continue teaching, doing research, and providing service while simultaneously facing a multitude of caring responsibilities toward my children, my extended family, and my community. Bearing witness to so many instances of institutional indifference to the experiences of migrant and essential workers, and experiencing so much grief, led me to the epiphany that I needed to reprioritize what mattered the most to me, namely my family and my community's needs.

Being embedded in various virtual "communities of care" (Francisco-Menchavez, 2018) allowed me to survive these challenges. Through WhatsApp and Facebook group chats, Zoom hangouts, and Twitter, friends and family members asynchronously checked in with each other. I succeeded in carving out a space of care amid a constant onslaught of challenges. In this chapter, I delve into the various virtual communities of care that enabled my survival. These virtual communities of care embodied the "dissident friendships" grounded in an ethic of care (Chowdhury & Philipose, 2016) that see one's communities as being essential to healing (hooks, 2000). These communities of subversive friends "counter fear and speak truth to power in a unique way by embodying and experiencing mutual and heart-centred connections with unlikely interlocutors" (Chowdhury & Philipose, 2016, p. 3). Forming and strengthening these friendships is fundamentally a political act for they are formed within the context of institutional indifference to our lives, as in the case of state institutions that only pay lip service to care workers' "heroism" without corresponding labour protections or in the case of neoliberal academic institutions that continuously disregard faculty, student, and staff well-being. That these friendships can even flourish amid a "necrocapitalist" (Tyner, 2019, Preface) pandemic context that demands that women—namely, working-class, racially minoritized women—continuously provide care even at the expense of their health shows why they are also sites of resistance; dissident friends recognize and affirm their intrinsic worth rather than accepting institutional imperatives that see people as being instrumental and not as being good-in-themselves. Hence, these friendships are not merely solidaristic but constitute an essential network from which different norms can flourish (Nguyen et al., 2016). Ultimately, I argue that dissident friendships in these "virtual" communities are crucial in creating an *alternative* value system where care and strategic subversion are prioritized over competition and compliance with institutional norms and rules. Centring care runs counter to academic norms that assume that academics are "autonomous" individuals without caring obligations and that assumes that the default academic is a cisgender, heterosexual man whose sole priority is research.

This chapter is divided into three sections. In the first section, I discuss how virtual communities of care through my podcast, *Academic Aunties*, which I produce with Wayne Chu and Nisha Nath (Tungohan,

Chu, & Nath, 2021), Facebook group chats, and Zoom hangouts were crucial in helping me navigate academia while facing family obligations and community responsibilities. These virtual communities of care, more significantly, helped me and my dissident friends establish a subversive set of practices that are counter to how the neoliberal academy operates. In the second and third sections, I expand on these points, discussing how *Academic Aunties* and other virtual spaces, including friendship networks and research projects that centred care, provided a crucial site for connection. They became places of subversive joy and affirmation away from the corrosive realities of academia. Collectively, these spaces helped me pursue alternate values and practices that prioritized my and my communities' needs, which at times ran counter to academic priorities.

The Academy Won't Love You Back
At the height of the pandemic in May 2020, when universities instituted virtual schooling, and university instructors had to adapt their courses to online teaching, I was pre-tenured, had children who were four years old and eleven months old, and was worried about meeting my professional obligations. At that point in my career, I had internalized the academic "hustle culture" that venerated overwork (Kern, 2019). While I understood that multiple structural barriers prevent female and BIPOC professors from succeeding in the academy (see Gutierrez y Muhs et al., 2012; Rockquemore & Laszloffy, 2008), I felt that the solution to this was simply to just hustle harder.

This meant that, during the early months of the pandemic, I worked triple shifts, barely sleeping. During the day, I took care of my two daughters, devising different activities to keep them entertained, and keeping up with needed household work. At night, after my children were asleep, I graded papers, wrote lectures, applied for grants, and tried to complete my research. I was also part of two major service committees, including an EDI task force that was mandated to instill research equity across the university. I showed up to all of the meetings and participated extensively, learning which Cocomelon videos were exactly an hour long so I could park my kids in front of the television while I sat in meetings. I also tried to show up for my students, oftentimes staying after class was over to talk people through the challenges that they were facing during the COVID-19 pandemic. Because a large percentage of students at my university were first-generation, working-class, and/or immigrants, many of them had to continue working in essential jobs to support themselves. Some of my students also had to take care of their younger siblings while their parents worked essential jobs. In short, I tried to be a good professor; I did everything I was supposed to do, and more. That these expectations were racialized and gendered was not lost on me, given widespread assumptions about women and women of colour's availability to provide emotional labour. Nevertheless, despite knowing the expectations I faced that my white, male, cis, heterosexual colleagues did not, I felt an obligation to support students who were experiencing the full brutalities of the pandemic.

Although my university provided *some* relief to faculty members who were facing challenges during the pandemic, including tenure-clock extensions and extra funding for faculty members to pay guest lecturers to "free" them from course preparation, for the most part, the message that faculty members received was to keep going, as usual. Every week, my university sent emails on "Wellness Wednesdays" to the faculty listserv, all of which included peppy messages reminding faculty members to "take care" of themselves. An email sent on May 20, 2020, was especially annoying, what with its advice to "make time for yourself." "How can I do that?" I remember thinking. The email included these "tips on balance and work-life harmony, to help create and sustain a sense of well-being":

Balance
Working from home or on campus under these unprecedented circumstances, along with a potentially disrupted family life, can pose challenges in establishing and/or maintaining a sense of balance and harmony in our lives. Here are some tips on balance and work-life harmony, to help create and sustain a sense of well-being:

- *Separate your work and home life when working at home.* As much as possible, maintain a separation between your work and home life. Human Resources has developed some materials to provide some tips and suggestions for doing this on our Working Remotely resource page.

- *Schedule time for yourself.* Make time in your day for the things you enjoy and contribute to your well-being. This could be for exercise, rest, a hobby, time with your family, a phone call to a friend, or even a nap!
- *Enjoy some vacation time.* Just because you may be working from home doesn't mean you don't need a break. The need for rest and time away from work may even be more present during these unprecedented times, with increased stress levels, family and work demands. Be sure to take time off and enjoy a "staycation" to rejuvenate and recharge. (University communication, 2020, May 20)

Such messages felt deluded in that they completely ignored how taking better care of ourselves was not a matter of will; rather, our inability to care for ourselves was the direct result of structural failures that made the pandemic worse for some communities more than others.

As the months went by, with no end in sight to lockdown provisions and with family and community members dying of COVID-19, I felt numb. "It would all be worth it," I thought, "once I get tenure." In the spring and summer of 2020, as I prepared my file for tenure, I felt a tremendous feeling of accomplishment. Seeing my dossier showed how much I accomplished since starting as an assistant professor in 2016. "Once I get my tenure letter, I can finally rest," I thought.

Yet I never got my letter. A colleague—a fellow BIPOC assistant professor who was also going up for tenure—and I later found out that despite completing our tenure files, and getting accolades from our colleagues, the department chair's office "forgot" to send up our tenure files. The union intervened on our behalf, allowing my file to be considered by the University Senate despite the delays. The University Senate ruled three in favour and two against me and my colleague getting tenure, with two senate committee members voting against us, not because of the contents of our files, but because they found the delays caused by the department as being so irregular that they believed my file had to be evaluated again. Thankfully, the other three members of the senate committee assessed our files as being excellent and argued that we should not be punished for procedural irregularities. While both my colleague and I ended up receiving tenure, this experience scarred me. Though internal investigations found that our files were not forgotten on "purpose," the fact that all my years of work, which culminated in an

FIGURE 7.1 Trying to work while nursing a two-week old baby. (Photo courtesy of the author.)

excellent CV and countless hours of service, did not ultimately matter in the end because the department chair's office simply *did not care enough about my file to make sure it got sent to the proper channels* was gut-wrenching. Hustling harder did not matter, not when working within a neoliberal institution that rendered our work inconsequential. Put differently, I have seen the files of white, male professors handled with care; I was heartbroken that our files were simply forgotten.

At this specific juncture, I had the trite epiphany that institutions can never love us—*love me*—back. All the "yeses" I said to invitations to sit on service committees, to review files, to join student committees, to produce report after report documenting EDI problems within the institution, alongside my receipt of grants and publication opportunities, were inconsequential. I also felt immense regret, because all the time I spent making sure that I was a badass who would not let pregnancy or childbirth—or even a pandemic!—affect my output meant that I did not prioritize my family, my children, or myself. Rather than being content to spend time with my two-week-old baby, I decided to *work*—as you see in figure 7.1. I posted this photograph on social media to much acclaim from friends who cheered me on for working. I look at this photograph now, and I think, "Wow, you let the academy steal your first few moments with your daughter."

It was during this period in 2021 that I started my podcast, *Academic Aunties*. The toxic work environment, the feelings of desperation that I felt but could not express, and the increasing dissatisfaction with my work life culminated in a desire to reach out to my friends—mostly other racially minoritized women in the trenches of the academy—to talk about our experiences. The conceit of the show, paying credence to the long lineage of "auntiehood" in many BIPOC communities, is that all the guests in the podcast would gather as aunties to dispense "auntie-wisdom" to our listeners. My partner, Wayne, and I spontaneously decided to create this podcast after another endless day of sheltering-in-place, during which Wayne observed me toggle from one group chat to the next, giving advice and getting advice from my virtual community of care. I remember my friend Jessica asking me what she should wear on her first day as an assistant professor in one group chat, my friend Shaista bemoaning the endless days of online teaching in another group chat, and my friends Nisha, Mariam, and I griping about pandemic parenting in another group chat. Bemused, Wayne told me that my friends and I should all be on a podcast to give advice. Playing along, I asked Wayne, well, would a podcast of "academic aunties" work? We tossed around a few ideas and then Wayne asked what the tagline of the podcast would be. Immediately, and without much thought, I said, "Take care, be kind to yourself, and don't be an asshole." Wayne, and then, later, Nisha Nath, became producers for the podcast.

In the years since launching the podcast, it has generated multiple conversations across different online platforms with different women and women of colour academics. Similar to how Corinne L. Mason and Irene Shankar in chapter 6 of this collection discuss gravitating toward each other in the face of their loneliness and betrayal after seeing so-called feminists remain indifferent to institutional cruelty, the podcast became a way to seek out those who shared a similar subversive mindset. Many have reached out to me sharing their heart-wrenching experiences in academia and their stories of subverting academic norms. Each episode reaches more than a thousand listeners, and, as of February 2024, it has been downloaded 65,000 times. Episodes deconstruct the "hidden curriculum" of academia, providing space for me and my guests to address topics including—but not limited to—why academics are assholes (Tungohan, 2021a), with my friends Nisha Nath and Mariam Georgis; trying to find joy in academia, with my best friends Shaista Patel and Krittika Ghosh (Tungohan, 2021b); why academic parents need to show their children that they do not see their worth as being equated with their work in order to break intergenerational cycles of chronic overwork, with one of my favourite parent-friends and allies Yolande Bouka (Tungohan 2022a); what *really* happens when job search committees deliberate, with respected colleagues Sailaja Krishnamurti and Sharry Aiken (Tungohan, 2022b); why it is important to carve out spaces of rest and find activities that are not work-related, with Nisha Nath and Rita Dhamoon (Tungohan, 2021c); reflections on decades of fighting for space and overturning toxic academic norms, with Joyce Green (Tungohan, 2022c); and talking through the harms wrought by toxic productivity, with Ayendy Bonifacio (Tungohan, 2022d), based on an article he wrote that went viral (Bonifacio, 2022). The podcast also frequently features new books by feminist heroes, including Sara Ahmed, who spoke about different ways to be a feminist killjoy (Tungohan, 2023).

Through *Academic Aunties*, I realized when conversing with our guests how important it is to carve out a space that challenges existing academic norms, prioritizes self-care alongside community care, and plants the seeds for critical change within the flawed structures of the neoliberal academy. Black feminist theory was decisive in instilling my awareness regarding the subversive nature of care. Bearing in mind Lorde's (1988) oft-cited invocation of how self-care is "self-preservation and an act of political warfare" (p. 130) alongside hooks's (2000) reminder that "healing is an act of communion" (p. 215) and Riley's (2023) observations that "self-care alone won't save you, community is a necessary risk," I saw the ethic of care that animates the podcast as being distinct from endemic neoliberal calls for self-care. Rather, care becomes a subversive practice done in a community with fellow academic "fugitives" (Moten & Harney, 2004) who resist neoliberal academic norms and structures.

Podcast conversations have helped me attempt to unlearn hustle culture, specifically toxic productivity, to "divest" from corrosive institutions that do not give me "returns" on all the time and energy I have invested—a concept that Kristine Alexander talks about in an episode of *Academic Aunties* (Tungohan, 2022e) and also via our Facebook messages, and, more importantly, to dream about and move toward the vision of "another university" that sees education as emancipation and that is untethered from neoliberal demands (Emejulu, 2017; Moten & Harney, 2004). Even today, I occasionally listen to previous episodes of the podcast whenever I am feeling unmoored and stressed out. When I listen to these episodes, I remember my purpose: to unlearn toxic academic norms and "do the work that feeds me and my community," to quote Rita Dhamoon (Tungohan, 2021c).

"Are We Praying Tonight?": On the Power of WhatsApp and Zoom Hangouts

For transnational families with different members living across different time zones, the ease of communication via Voice Over Internet Protocol (VOIP) through Skype, FaceTime, Zoom, etc., enables instantaneous connections. Researchers such as Francisco-Menchavez (2018) and De Leon (2018) even highlight how such technologies allow different family members to show their love for each other, with migrant parents working abroad using these technologies to supervise their children and with children using these technologies to show their parents that they love them back through, for example, liking their parents' posts on Facebook. When the pandemic first started in 2020, many Filipino migrants joked that finally, the rest of the world was catching up to the use of these technologies.

For my family, the use of VOIP was vital in helping us support each other, particularly while grieving over the deaths of our family members. Although our family communicated via Facebook Messenger even before the COVID-19 pandemic, our use of Facebook Messenger escalated during the pandemic. When news about family members getting sick and then, later, dying from COVID-19 circulated, my mom organized virtual novenas, where family members could gather and pray. When Facebook Messenger could not accommodate the large numbers of family members who wanted to be part of our virtual novena, I stepped in and organized these gatherings via Zoom. I am not religious but being part of these vigils grounded me and helped me process my grief. Lockdown provisions meant that travel and large gatherings were

FIGURE 7.2 Sending silly FaceTime photos via our family group chat. (Photo courtesy of the author.)

prohibited, so having the opportunity to collectively grieve through VOIP provided solace to me and my family during a very sad time.

In year two of the pandemic, when lockdown restrictions were eased to allow immediate family members to gather for my uncle's funeral, family members who could not attend in person watched the live stream of the funeral through the funeral home's YouTube channel. Afterwards, family members virtually gathered via Zoom, singing, sharing recollections of my uncle, and reliving memories from my uncle's and my father's childhood. We shared a photograph of everyone gathered via Zoom with my cousin so he could see how much love family members around the world had for his father.

Aside from presenting us with the opportunity to develop new mourning rituals, these virtual gatherings also gave my transnational family members new ways of connecting. Every day, either my mom or one of her siblings would message the group chat, asking, "Are we praying today?" followed by one of them calling the entire group. While the virtual praying sessions provided an excuse to "pray together," what I find the most meaningful about these family hangouts are the conversations that we have after praying. Our conversations engendered empathy and solidarity. For example, learning about how a cousin was struggling with working while supervising his daughter's online schooling helped both of us laugh about our shared challenges. These spaces also enabled sharing photographs of our daily lives, such as those of my kids making a volcano using baking soda and vinegar, the baked goods my cousin made, and even silly photos of my niece and my kids using different FaceTime filters (see figure 7.2). These seemingly mundane moments provided me with small moments of joy, particularly in the face of toxic work politics.

During the pandemic, these virtual connections with my family anchored me. Our online prayer sessions, our hangouts, and our group chats reminded me that I was part of a larger community of aunties, uncles, and cousins who supported and loved each other unconditionally. At this juncture in our lives, in the face of so much loss, it became clear to me that I needed to reprioritize my family, which includes my biological family and my chosen family. These spaces were nurturing and supportive, providing the perfect antidote to the corrosiveness of academia.

"We're Not Alone After All": *Kuwentuhan* ("Talk-Story") Sessions Through Zoom

In May 2020, I was disheartened with how the bulk of newspaper coverage on the pandemic's health care "heroes" only featured doctors and nurses, leaving behind the experiences of other health-care workers. Family members and friends shared posts on Facebook and Twitter of their experiences as personal support workers during the pandemic, so I knew that there were other health-care workers whose experiences were being omitted by media narratives. I contacted my friend, Mithi Esguerra, a fellow organizer with the Filipinx feminist organization Gabriela-Ontario and a staff member at Migrant Resource Centre Canada (MRCC), about organizing a project that focused on the experiences of frontline Filipina health-care workers. Mauriene Tolentino, Conely De Leon, and Jessica Ticar—all of whom are members of Gabriela-Ontario—as well as friend and fellow community advocate Marissa Largo, also got involved. Together, we put together a project proposal that involved using photovoice to understand Filipina health-care workers' experiences during the COVID-19 pandemic. Although we initially faced challenges conceptualizing what a community-based research project could be like during COVID-19 because our universities (as Fawziah Rabiah-Mohammed and Leah K. Hamilton point out in chapter 5 of this collection) did not issue research guidelines, we used to our advantage the lack of protocol to create a "just-in-time" research project that tried to capture, in real time, care workers' challenges (Roberts et al., 2021). Following our receipt of ethics approval from York University's research ethics board, an onerous process that was similar to Carieta Thomas's descriptions of the challenges she faced in her research with undocumented Caribbean care workers (see chapter 4), we recruited Filipina support workers, in-home care workers, and licensed practical nurses to participate in our project.

We then placed different women into "pods" consisting of two to four people, placing women in the same field together. Each pod met three times over Zoom. They each shared photographs that they took of their lives in answer to the question, "What is your life like during COVID?" and shared stories of their lives. Each session had two members of the research team present, with one person hosting and asking questions, and another taking notes. At the beginning of each session, after we realized that people needed to disconnect from their daily lives and focus on our conversation, we spent one minute on a guided meditation and a few minutes asking people how they were doing. Only after everyone felt comfortable enough to participate did we officially start our sessions. Using kuwentuhan (loosely translated as "talk-story"), which is a "Philippine cultural practice of storytelling that can be used to exchange essential information" (Francisco-Menchavez et al., 2021, p. 56), the women in each pod started each session describing the photographs that they took following the suggested list of questions that we provided.

Often, the discussions generated during our kuwentuhan sessions deviated from the photographs, with women sharing their various experiences at work and home, shifts in their family lives during the pandemic, challenges with immigration policies, and many more. Frequently, they gave advice to each other, sharing tips on dealing with restrictive employers, discussing ways to do better on the English language tests that caregivers under the Caregiver Program had to pass to get Canadian permanent residency, and how to deal with family separation.

What was interesting to observe was how conversing with one another led to shifts in their understanding of their place in Canadian society. For example, one participant who worked as a live-in caregiver summoned the courage to approach her employer to ask her to buy Filipino ingredients after other participants said that she needed to be more assertive when claiming her entitlements. Given that her employer deducted part of her salary for room and board, all the women reasoned that she had the right to request grocery items. Another example of someone whose behaviour shifted during the pod was a woman who, prior to the sessions, admitted that she was reluctant to make waves. Being part of a pod with care workers who were also community organizers with the Filipinx migrant justice organization, Migrante, however, emboldened her to also become an organizer. These pods, then, became a catalyst for change.

Each session was only supposed to last for an hour, but there were sessions that lasted longer, with many of the women reluctant to say goodbye. Some shared that our conversations were the only time that they could talk to people outside of home and work. They appreciated the opportunity to speak to fellow care workers who could relate to their stories. In these spaces, they did not have to put on a brave face, as they would when talking to, say, their employers, whose goodwill they wanted to maintain, or their family members, whom they did not want to vicariously stress out.

Although the research team and I were initially reluctant to use Zoom because we were afraid that it would be hard to establish rapport, we soon discovered that many of the women were part of transnational families and were used to communicating through VOIP. In fact, in some ways, I believe that most of the women would have preferred meeting through Zoom rather than meeting in person even if lockdown regulations were not in place. Having the option not to keep the camera on, to use a different name, and even to communicate primarily through the

FIGURE 7.3 *Matatag* Launch, November 2021. (Photo by the author.)

chatbox function gave them the ability to choose how they wanted to interact with the group. As such, Zoom facilitated the creation of virtual communities of care with each pod. To my knowledge, some of the women who met each other through the pods are still in contact.

Being part of this research project at the beginning of COVID-19 was one of my few sources of fulfillment. Amid workplace and family challenges, being in community with migrant women through our kuwentuhan sessions gave me a brief respite from everyday stresses. Not only did our participants become dissident friends who collectively brainstormed on ways to subvert the system, we also used our findings to write policy briefs and to advocate for better labour conditions for care workers. In addition, our findings led our research partners, Gabriela-Ontario and MRCC, to develop programming that aligned with care workers' needs. The photographs taken by our participants also helped shift public conversations on the value of care when they were shown as part of our art exhibit *Matatag* (loosely translated as "strong" in Tagalog), at Toronto's A-Space gallery (November 2021–May 2022; see figure 7.3 for a photo of the poster from our closing community event); at Barrie City Hall (August 2022); at the International Women's Alliance meetings in Montreal (October 2022); and at the Carework Network conference in Costa Rica (June 2023).[1]

As a scholar-activist, seeing the project lead to positive social change is gratifying. I have written before about how my commitments to research are tied irrevocably to my commitment to progressive social change (see Francisco-Menchavez & Tungohan, 2020; Tungohan, 2019). I was happy to have played a role in making sure that migrant care workers' lived experiences were centred, in direct opposition to the widespread perception that their lives were "expendable" (Pandey et al., 2021). Working on this project during the pandemic ensured that I did the work that "fed me and my community," to once again quote Dhamoon (2020). In choosing to work on this project, I prioritized work that mattered to me, abandoning conventional assumptions in my field of political science about "good" research. Rather than accepting the discipline's dictates on what "counts" as legitimate research, being part of this project allowed my personal commitments to community advocacy *and* research that leads to social good and community justice to be aligned. In addition, heeding the imperatives of the "slow" scholarship movement (Berg & Seeber, 2016), which asks that researchers be more intentional about the work that they produce and stop falling prey to publish-or-perish mindsets, my fellow researchers and I have prioritized community outputs (e.g., gallery showings, petitions, policy briefs) over academic publications. Only now are we considering what academic publications to pursue. Seeking to follow timelines that work for me, rather than the academy, and centring ethical, collaborative research practices was a way for me to rebel. I am mindful, of course, of how my status in the academy as a tenured professor gives me more room to resist publish-or-perish pressures; as such, I constantly strategize with early-career scholars who do community-engaged work on ways they can publish without compromising community goals.

Conclusion

As dreadful as the pandemic was, one thing it helped me learn, once and for all, is the importance of community. Prior to the pandemic, and all the losses it brought, I prioritized my career over everything else, including my family. The pandemic helped me realize that the academy will never love me back and that equating my self-worth with how productive I am is a damaging mindset. The pandemic helped me pivot and prioritize family; it helped me reorient my approach to research to one that prioritized community. The various communities of care I formed—whether through *Academic Aunties*, transnational family group chats via Facebook Messenger, or Zoom kuwentuhan pods—helped me and those participating in these spaces shift the way we navigated the world. Having a space that helped us recognize that our needs were important, too, despite institutions telling us otherwise, was cathartic and healing. In this way, then, I see communities of care as being essential to our collective survival.

Note

1. Our project website, www.filipinacareworkers.com, showcases some of these photos.

References

A dose of reality: How rich countries and pharmaceutical corporations are breaking their vaccine promises. (2021, October 21). UNAIDS. https://www.unaids.org/en/resources/presscentre/featurestories/2021/october/20211021_dose-of-reality

Ajadi, T., & Thompson, D. (2021, May 22). Opinion: The two pandemics of anti-Black racism and COVID-19 are tied together. *The Globe and Mail*. https://www.theglobeandmail.com/opinion/article-the-two-pandemics-of-anti-black-racism-and-covid-19-are-tied-together/

Almendral, A. (2020, July 15). Crucial yet forgotten: The Filipino workers stranded by coronavirus. *Nikkei Asia*. https://asia.nikkei.com/Spotlight/The-Big-Story/Crucial-yet-forgotten-the-Filipino-workers-stranded-by-coronavirus

Berg, M., & Seeber, B.K. (2016). *The slow professor: Challenging the culture of speed in the academy*. University of Toronto Press.

Bonifacio, A. (2022, October 25). My career as a professor is soaring: I've never been so depressed and anxious. *Slate*. https://slate.com/technology/2022/10/academia-latinx-communities-depression-success-therapy.html

Chávez, K., & Mitchell, K.M.W. (2020). Exploring bias in student evaluations: Gender, race, and ethnicity. *PS: Political Science & Politics*, 53(2), 270–274. https://doi.org/10.1017/S1049096519001744

Chowdhury, E.H., & Philipose, L. (2016). Introduction. In E.H. Chowdhury & L. Philipose (Eds.), *Dissident friendships: Feminism, imperialism, and transnational solidarity* (pp. 1–8). University of Illinois Press. https://doi.org/10.5406/illinois/9780252040412.003.0001

De Leon, C. (2018). *"Pagod, dugot, pawis (Exhaustion, blood, and sweat)": Transnational practices of care and emotional labour among Filipino kin networks* [Doctoral dissertation, York University]. https://yorkspace.library.yorku.ca/xmlui/handle/10315/35480

Dhamoon, R.K. (2020). Racism as a workload and bargaining issue. *Socialist Studies, 14*(1), article 2. https://doi.org/10.18740/ss27273

Dogra, P., & Kaushal, A. (2022). Underlying the triple burden effects on women educationists due to COVID-19. *Education and Information Technologies, 27*(1), 209–228. https://doi.org/10.1007/s10639-021-10645-6

Emejulu, A. (2017, January 12). *Another university is possible.* Verso. https://www.versobooks.com/en-ca/blogs/news/3044-another-university-is-possible

Francisco-Menchavez, V. (2018). *The labor of care: Filipina migrants and transnational families in the digital age.* University of Illinois Press.

Francisco-Menchavez, V., Celemen, E., & Osorio, K. (2021). Filipino formal caregivers to the elderly and normalized exploitation in the workplace. *Alon: Journal for Filipinx American and Diasporic Studies, 1*(1). https://doi.org/10.5070/LN41149607

Francisco-Menchavez, V., & Tungohan, E. (2020). Mula sa masa, tungo sa masa, from the people, to the people: Building migrant worker power through participatory action research. *Migration Letters, 17*(2), 1–8.

Gewin, V. Has the "great resignation" hit academia? *Nature, 606*(7912), 211–213. https://doi.org/10.1038/d41586-022-01512-6

Gutierrez y Muhs, G., Flores Niemann, Y., Gonzales, C.G., & Harris, A.P. (Eds.). (2012). *Presumed incompetent: The intersections of race and class for women in academia.* Utah State University Press. https://doi.org/10.2307/j.ctt4cgr3k

Henry, F., Dua, E., James, C.E., Kobayashi, A., Li, P., Ramos, H., & Smith, M.S. (2017). *The equity myth: Racialization and Indigeneity at Canadian universities.* UBC Press. https://doi.org/10.1017/S0008423920000116

hooks, b. (2000). *All about love: New visions.* HarperCollins.

Kern, L. (2019, January 1). *Academic hustle culture: Why are we glorifying burnout and overwork?* Leslie Kern Coaching. https://lesliekerncoaching.com/2019/01/30/academic-hustle-culture-glorifying-burnout/

Kim, E., & Patterson, S. (2022). The pandemic and gender inequality in academia. *PS: Political Science & Politics, 55*(1), 109–116. https://doi.org/10.1017/S1049096521001049

Kınıkoğlu, C.N., & Can, A. (2021). Negotiating the different degrees of precarity in the UK academia during the Covid-19 pandemic. *European Societies, 23*(sup1), S817–S830. https://doi.org/10.1080/14616696.2020.1839670

Kinney, D. (Host). (2020, May 4). *Alberta's most expendable workers* (No. 36) [Audio podcast episode]. In *The Progress Report.* Progress Alberta. https://www.theprogressreport.ca/filipino_community_and_covid_19

Lorde, A. (1988). *A burst of light and other essays.* AK Press.

Malisch, J.L., Harris, B.N., Sherrer, S.M., & Deitloff, J. (2020). In the wake of COVID-19, academia needs new solutions to ensure gender equity. *PNAS, 117*(27), 15378–15381. https://doi.org/10.1073/pnas.2010636117

Moten, F., & Harney, S. (2004). The university and the undercommons: Seven theses. *Social Text, 22*(79), 101–115. https://doi.org/10.1215/01642472-22-2_79-101

Nguyen, N., Nastasi, A.W., Mejia, A., Stanger, A., Madden, M., & Mohanty, C.T. (2016). Epistemic friendships: Collective knowledge-making through transnational feminist praxis. In E.H. Chowdhury & L. Philipose (Eds.), *Dissident friendships: Feminism, imperialism, and transnational solidarity* (pp. 11–42). University of Illinois Press. https://doi.org/10.5406/illinois/9780252040412.003.0002

Pandey, K., Parreñas, R.S., & Sabio, G.S. (2021). Essential and expendable: Migrant domestic workers and the COVID-19 pandemic. *American Behavioral Scientist, 65*(10), 1287–1301. https://doi.org/10.1177/00027642211000396

Plotnikof, M., & Utoft, E.H. (2022). The "new normal" of academia in pandemic times: Resisting toxicity through care. *Gender, Work & Organization, 29*(4), 1259–1271. https://doi.org/10.1111/gwao.12778

Riley, Cole Arthur [@blackliturgies]. (2023, May 9). *"Self-care alone won't save you. Community is a necessary risk"* [Photograph]. Instagram. https://www.instagram.com/blackliturgies/p/CsBtRG4ucvB/

Roberts, J.K., Pavlakis, A., & Richards M. (2021). It's more complicated than it seems: Virtual qualitative research in the COVID-19 era. *International Journal of Qualitative Methods 20*(1), 1–13. https://doi.org/10.1177/16094069211002959

Rockquemore, K.A., & Laszloffy, T. (2008). *The Black academic's guide to winning tenure without losing your soul.* Lynne Rienner Publishers.

Shalaby, M., Allam, N., & Buttorff, G.J. (2021). Leveling the field: Gender inequity in academia during COVID-19. *PS: Political Science & Politics, 54*(4), 661–667. https://doi.org/10.1017/S1049096521000615

Staniscuaski, F., Kmetzsch, L., Soletti, R.C., Reichert, F., Zandonà, E., Ludwig, Z.M.C., Lima, E.F., Neumann, A., Schwartz, I.V.D., Mello-Carpes, P.B., Tamajusuku, A.S.K., Werneck, F.P., Ricachenevsky, F.K., Infanger, C., Seixas, A., Staats, C.C., & de Oliveira, L. (2021). Gender, race and parenthood impact academic productivity during the COVID-19 pandemic: From survey to action. *Frontiers in Psychology, 12.* https://www.frontiersin.org/articles/10.3389/fpsyg.2021.663252

Tungohan, E. (2019). Equality and recognition or transformation and dissent?: Intersectionality and the Filipino migrants' movement in Canada. In J. Irvine, S. Lang, & C. Montoya (Eds.), *Gendered mobilization and intersectional challenges: Contemporary social movement in Europe and North America* (pp. 208–225). ECPR Press/Rowman & Littlefield.

Tungohan, E. (2020, May 1). *Filipino healthcare workers during COVID-19 and the importance of race-based analysis.* Broadbent Institute. https://www.broadbentinstitute.ca/filipino_healthcare_workers_during_covid19_and_the_importance_of_race_based_analysis

Tungohan, E. (Host). (2021a, March 31). A-holes in the academy (No. 1) [Audio podcast episode]. In *Academic Aunties.* https://www.academicaunties.com/episodes/a-holes-in-the-academy/

Tungohan, E. (Host). (2021b, June 30). Searching for joy (No. 4) [Audio podcast episode]. In *Academic Aunties*. https://www.academicaunties.com/episodes/searching-for-joy/

Tungohan, E. (Host). (2021c, December 22). After hours (No. 9) [Audio podcast episode]. In *Academic Aunties*. https://www.academicaunties.com/episodes/after-hours/

Tungohan, E. (Host). (2022a, January 26). Pandemic parenting, part II (No. 10) [Audio podcast episode]. In *Academic Aunties*. https://www.academicaunties.com/episodes/pandemic-parenting-part-ii/

Tungohan, E. (Host). (2022b, April 13). The ultimate Academic Auntie (No. 16) [Audio podcast episode]. In *Academic Aunties*. https://www.academicaunties.com/episodes/the-ultimate-academic-auntie/

Tungohan, E. (Host). (2022c, August 24). The real deal with job search committees (No. 18) [Audio podcast episode]. In *Academic Aunties*. https://www.academicaunties.com/episodes/the-real-deal-with-job-search-committees/

Tungohan, E. (Host). (2022d, September 7). Back to school (No. 19) [Audio podcast episode]. In *Academic Aunties*. https://www.academicaunties.com/episodes/back-to-school/

Tungohan, E. (Host). (2022e, November 2). Battling toxic productivity (No. 23) [Audio podcast episode]. In *Academic Aunties*. https://www.academicaunties.com/episodes/battling-toxic-productivity/

Tungohan, E. (Host). (2023, October 4). The feminist killjoy handbook with Sara Ahmed (No. 40) [Audio podcast episode]. In *Academic Aunties*. https://www.academicaunties.com/episodes/the-feminist-killjoy-handbook-with-sara-ahmed/

Tungohan, E., Chu, W., & Nath, N. (Executive Producers). (2021–present). *Academic Aunties* [Audio podcast]. https://www.academicaunties.com/episodes/a-holes-in-the-academy/

Tungohan, E., Ticar, J., Esguerra, M., De Leon, C., Largo, M., Tolentino, M., Panjaitan, M., Seardon, B., Jaymalin, M., & Natial, A. (2021, June 8). *Araw araw, tinataya aming ang buhay aming (Everyday, we gamble with our lives): Filipina migrants in Canada and care work—Carework network responds*. Carework Network. http://careworknetworkresponds.com/2021/06/08/araw-araw-tinataya-namin-ang-buhay-namin-everyday-we-gamble-with-our-lives-filipina-migrants-in-canada-and-care-work/

Tyner, J. (2019). *Dead labour: Towards a political economy of premature death*. Kindle edition. University of Minnesota Press.

Winslow, S., & Davis, S.N. (2016). Gender inequality across the academic life course. *Sociology Compass, 10*(5), 404–416. https://doi.org/10.1111/soc4.12372

III
A Future Otherwise

/8
Resisting Racism Through a Pedagogy of Blackfoot Resilience

GABRIELLE ELLEN WEASEL HEAD

Introduction

The stories of Indigenous peoples' experiences in Canada are largely told through a Western lens with the aim of protecting Eurocentric nation-building, knowledge systems, and advancing a narrative of Indigenous deficit that is reflected in government statistics, perpetuated in media, and reinforced in the education systems. This narrative of Indigenous deficit is rooted in the notion that the current marginalization of Indigenous peoples is a result of their own cultural failings (Ponting & Voyageur, 2001) and is one that has been constructed on a foundation of Euro-settler racism. Utilizing a critical race theory and postcolonial lens to analyze the educational failure of marginalized students in Western countries, Valencia (2020) asserts that the deficit-thinking model is a collective mindset of international scope that is based in Eurocentric and racist ideology, yet purported to hold scientific, evidence-based validity. The deficit-thinking paradigm frames Western/Eurocentric understandings and approaches to trauma attached to Indigenous people's experiences with settler colonial violence (Pihama et al., 2017), as well as shapes a limited view of resilience that is then applied to Indigenous peoples (Lindstrom et al., 2021). Strength-based discourses in higher education and social serving fields might attempt to analyze Indigenous lifeways using resilience as the site for analysis (see Kirmayer et al., 2011; Ungar, 2013), but these discourses emerge from a Eurocentric paradigm (de Finney, 2017). This too is problematic since common understandings of resilience are insufficient in helping system educators, administrators, and policymakers reframe deficit thinking surrounding Indigenous peoples' histories and realities—resiliency measures often reduce human experiences of suffering and strength to person-centred, individually conceptualized protective and/or risk factors (Ungar, et al., 2007).

This limiting narrative of Indigenous deficit is ubiquitous in Canada and has been passed along settler generations and reinforced in homes, education, religion, and government. Indigenous deficit shapes intergenerational and intercultural transmission of anti-Indigenous racism, which is the heartbeat of settler colonialism in Canada and a requirement for resource extraction via the continuous and relentless destruction of Indigenous identities, bodies, spirits, and lands. While global economies, travel, and individual "freedoms" were brought to a standstill due to the COVID-19 global pandemic, the image of a polite and benevolent Canada was shattered in the face of the ongoing recoveries of Indigenous children from mass graves—children who never made it home from the Indian Residential Schools.

These events foreground the reflections and provide the backdrop to my discussion of the findings that have emerged from a research project that advances a definition of resilience from a Blackfoot lived-experience perspective, which is currently under way at the time of this writing. This chapter is a reflective journey on the tumultuous racial tensions that seemed to intensify during the pandemic all while I was writing up my research findings. The research allowed me to carve out a conceptual space wherein I could push back against the narrative of deficit and tell another story, a story that offers much-needed clarity around what motivates and inspires Indigenous people to persevere despite overwhelming barriers. The research project also opens another avenue for making meaning from events that occurred during the global pandemic in ways that have strengthened me to persevere both in academia and beyond.

As some critical scholars point out (Greidanus & Johnson, 2016; Ponting & Voyageur, 2001), defining Indigenous lifeways within a series of negations normalizes the perception that Indigenous peoples are not anything more than problems to be solved. Too often Indigenous experiences are conceptualized and defined in the context of settler colonial forces. Concepts such as resilience and trauma are used to describe the experiences of Indigenous peoples, yet they are filtered through a Euro-Western frame of reference and thus insufficient in capturing the embodiment of cultural continuity that is at the heart of Indigenous people's ontological responsibilities (Bastien, 2004). Instead, Indigenous scholar de Finney (2017) encourages us "to reject limited, overly Eurocentric psycho-social notions of resilience" and locate it within "complex kinship networks, across generations, and in relationship with ancestors, lands, and all relations" (p. 10).

Here, I provide an overview of the findings from my Indigenous research project titled "Mokakit Iyikakimaat: Towards a pedagogy of resilience from a Blackfoot perspective," conducted through a small undergraduate university in western Canada. Repeat conversation-style interviews were held with Blackfoot Elders to develop a distinct embodied definition of resilience as experienced and understood from a Blackfoot perspective. I also held two focus groups with both Indigenous and non-Indigenous students to determine their understanding of resilience and how this understanding might manifest in a post-secondary classroom. While the focus groups were not interrupted by the pandemic, the interviews with Elders were, which delayed the data-gathering process. This delay was serendipitous since the analysis of the findings became such a significant source of strength as I navigated systematic oppression within the institution and beyond. My research was concerned with dismantling the deficit constructions of Indigenous people by advancing the embodiment of resilience as experienced from a Blackfoot perspective. The Blackfoot words *Mokakit Iyikakimaat* are roughly translated in English as "a process wherein one becomes wise through continual perseverance in life despite ongoing challenges." Stories of strength, humility, and suffering came to life through the voices of Blackfoot Elders and the post-secondary experiences of both Indigenous and non-Indigenous students as they engaged in Indigenous Studies courses. While many non-Indigenous members of mainstream society have constructed an inaccurate image of Indigenous people based on assumptions and cultural biases, this research demonstrates a way to push back against deficit thinking within the post-secondary classroom through a process of unlearning colonial ideologies and centring Indigenous embodied laws of truth, humility, kindness, and compassion.

This chapter centres Blackfoot conceptualizations and embodiments of resilience that are grounded in a cultural paradigm that is inherently anti-racist. It is organized into two main sections. In the first section, I offer a narrative overview, focusing on my own resilience, of how the COVID-19 pandemic impacted me on both a personal and professional level, including the institutional challenges I experienced as an Indigenous scholar. In the second section, in offering the context and overview of the research findings, I demonstrate how the process of conducting this research enabled me to persevere and strengthen my identity as a Blackfoot woman despite the ongoing legacy of settler colonial racism. In keeping with the methodological approach of the research project, this chapter is written in accordance with an autoethnography that is oriented from a personal perspective. I employ autoethnography in an Indigenous research context in an effort toward self-determination. The use of this method originates from research in "which the dominance of traditional science and research is questioned and many ways of knowing and inquiring are legitimated" (Wall, 2008, p. 39). Here, I begin by positioning my identity in the context of the issues I explore in this chapter.

Researcher Self-Location

Nistoo nitanikoo Tsa'piikani. Nii'moohk'to'to Akainaiwa. My Blackfoot name is Tsa'piinaki, which translates to Slanted-Eyed Woman. I am from the Kainai Nation, also known as the Blood Tribe, located on what is now the Blood Indian Reserve #148, the largest Indian reserve in Canada. The Kainai Nation is part of the Blackfoot Confederacy, which is an ancient, or "long-time" alliance of the Blackfoot-speaking First Nations, consisting of the Siksika, Kainai, Piikani, and Ampskapi'pikunni. The traditional territories of the Blackfoot Confederacy are expansive and extend south to the Yellowstone River in what is now the United States, west to the eastern slopes of the Rocky Mountains, north up to the North Saskatchewan River, and east into what is now known as the province of Saskatchewan, located on the northern plains in what we now call Canada. The peoples of the Blackfoot Confederacy are currently situated on three separate reserves in Alberta, Canada, and one reservation in Montana, USA. I was born and raised on the Blood Reserve and spent most of my adult life there. I now identify as a Kainai'aki, a Kainai Woman and a citizen of the Kainai Nation. This was not always so. For many years, I was estranged from my cultural identity, and like numerous other Indigenous people in the settler colonial state of Canada, I was unaware of both the contexts of my oppression and the fact that my people have inherited a legacy of perseverance, strength, and fortitude, for the only messages that I heard from mainstream society was that my people's existence was never on par with Western culture. Our languages and knowledge systems did not matter. Although I was ignorant to the reality that resilience was part of my genetics, I instinctively knew that being put on reserves ran counter to what I was taught by my parents and Elders and required that I develop a strength of character that would ensure I continue on despite a reality of ongoing social exclusion. What I observed and experienced in my community in terms of respecting people's right to personal autonomy and the preservation of basic human dignity were entirely different from what I experienced while off the reserve. These experiences combined with the embodiment of cultural preservation shape the research project that is central to this chapter.

The act of self-location in one's research is part of an Indigenous research paradigm and has multi-layered purposes ranging from researcher transparency to relational accountability. Anishnaabe scholar Kathy Absolon (2011) refers to self-location as a deeply personal act of "storying and re-storing" (p. 13). As Indigenous researchers, it is an act that comes first when preparing to research, and is enacted again during the research process, and again when sharing the results of research (Wilson, 2008). Self-location also presents the opportunity to connect with the past (Peltier et al., 2019) in deeply reflexive (Kovach, 2009) and transformative ways. This connection serves as a conduit for bridging ancestral knowledge and situating it as a relevant and necessary element of academic research. Self-locating one's identity is part of a reflexive research design that lends an additional layer of rigour and accountability to research relationships.

Being an Indigenous Scholar During a Pandemic
Looking back to the first week of March 2020, I can vividly remember how my life was unfolding. I was halfway to tenure and had successfully

earned federal funding to conduct original research. I was mentoring two Indigenous undergraduate students as research assistants and had been nominated for a prestigious early-career research recognition award at the small university where I held an appointment at the assistant-professor rank. My greatest joy, career-wise, came from teaching and building relationships with students. The classroom provided a space for authentic connection and offered me an opportunity to create ethical space (Ermine, 2007) with others through meaningful and honest dialogue about the history and experiences of Indigenous peoples within settler colonial Canada. I always envisioned my time in the classroom as a chance to impart to my students the kind of knowledge that I did not receive while in my post-secondary education programs. It was my classroom experiences that provided the impetus for exploring the connection between transformative learning experiences (Mezirow & Taylor, 2009), Indigenous conceptualizations of resilience, and how these two concepts might intersect in teaching the settler colonial history of Canada.

I deliberately utilized Indigenous pedagogies that I feel create the optimal conditions for transforming our relationships and illuminating the violence of settler colonialism in ways that do not detract from individual responsibility to move toward self-development. Indeed, I saw my teaching as a source of healing and was inspired by students' struggles with difficult knowledge (Simon, 2005). I realized that my non-Indigenous students needed healing just as much, if not more, than myself. I wanted to elevate student voices and support their experiences as they explored the truth of settler colonialism.

The threat of a pandemic did not seem immediate, but in looking back to that time, I realize how inevitable it was that the virus should reach my corner of the world. Indeed, Alberta was thrust into lockdown in mid-March of 2020. During the lockdown, I heard many people complaining about the social exclusion associated with it, but exclusion was not a new experience for me. My childhood and most of my adult years were spent on my reserve where I was largely segregated from local settler society. My parents' house was in a rural area, and the only time we would leave was to get food and household supplies. Residents of the small, neighbouring city and nearby towns made it very clear that "Indians" were not welcomed. Despite the worry I had for the elderly and others who were most at risk of dying from COVID-19, I felt safe in my home during the lockdown because it was such a familiar situation for me. Career-wise, like thousands of other university professionals, my classroom teaching as well as my research projects were essentially brought to a full stop. This standstill continued throughout the spring of 2020. Little did I know that a major controversy was just around the corner.

The racism-fuelled murder of George Floyd in the spring of 2020, and the ensuing social outrage, allowed me to hope that perhaps our society would mobilize and begin to push back against racism. Local universities released statements condemning racial violence and some installed equity, diversity, and inclusion leadership positions as a commitment to anti-racist action. Other institutions—such as mine—were criticized for only providing lip service. As we were not able to meet in person, the systemic racism deeply entrenched within academia's social climate appeared on social media. This platform seemed to function both as a vehicle for racist rhetoric and a means to push back against racism. The divisiveness I saw on social media amongst academics was further intensified when the momentum of the Black Lives Matter movement was going full force during the summer of 2020—all of this amid a global pandemic. At this time, I was also facing cyber-bullying from another faculty member within my institution, and the lack of support from the university leadership only confirmed that the academy was built on White supremacy despite the university's public statements claiming otherwise. The racial tensions surrounding that summer, coupled with the ongoing losses of family members and friends due to COVID-19, cancer, and opioid overdoses, proved a breaking point for me, and I requested medical leave from my university appointment.

While people continue to describe COVID-19 as unprecedented, the global pandemic did not bring new suffering and loss within my Blackfoot Nation. We have always dealt with loss. Since the coming of settlers to the Americas, Indigenous peoples have been experiencing a hidden genocide (Hinton et al., 2014; Whitt & Clarke, 2019). Indeed, racism and bullying were also not new to me, and near-daily encounters with racism shaped both how I interpreted my experiences with settler society and how I perceived myself as a Blackfoot woman. I have been in a constant internal struggle to unlearn colonial thinking and relearn Blackfoot knowledge. The pandemic only added a layer of anguish to the Indigenous lifeway, which was already over-capacitated with grief and loss.

As the fall of 2020 turned into winter, racial tensions escalated at my university, and I felt the need to move on. Despite being over the halfway point to achieving tenure and waiting for an imminent appointment to a prestigious faculty research position, I left my university and took another academic position at a larger research-intensive institution. My new position was a far cry from my classroom teaching experiences and the first year of my academic appointment was spent nearly entirely in front of a computer screen. The role involved incorporating Indigenous ways of knowing across the university in both pedagogy and curricula. It was a massive undertaking for one Indigenous person, and I was often left feeling overwhelmed and tokenized despite the good intentions and attempts to support me. I worked with primarily non-Indigenous faculty and engaged with university leadership. Not only was it daunting trying to impart meaningful knowledge about Indigenous ways of knowing through a virtual lens, but attempting to support settler and non-Indigenous faculty was frustrating because some either wanted me to do the work for them or remained resistant to the inclusion of Indigenous perspectives in teaching and learning. My time working with faculty helped me realize that my greatest joy came from being with students in a university classroom and dedicating myself to Indigenous research.

Despite being at another institution, the pandemic raged on as did systemic racism. I learned that regardless of the institutional packaging, academia was never built for Indigenous minds, bodies, and spirits. As losses due to premature deaths piled up in my community, so did my workload and expectations for unpaid labour. Once again, I found myself needing to make another change. When my old position came up for competition, I reapplied and was the successful candidate. Many of my former colleagues found it odd that I was trying to get back into the institution while others were trying to get out for reasons similar to my own. Recreating relationships with students and regaining the academic autonomy of a traditional faculty role were motivators that would not allow for me to pass up the opportunity. Some of my colleagues advised that moving between institutions was not good for my academic career and indeed, transitioning set my tenure eligibility back by three years and delayed the completion of my grant-funded research project due to the grant needing to be transferred between institutions. This delay proved to be a blessing in disguise since it coincided with the data analysis on the research project. The findings that emerged from the research serve as a source for my continued perseverance because they remind me that struggle is part of growth and healing, that despite the ongoing violence of systemic racism, Blackfoot cultural continuity is located within personal challenges and collective meaning-making, which I expand on below.

Becoming Wise and Persevering

My exploration into Blackfoot resilience was initially inspired by my doctoral dissertation (Lindstrom, 2018), within which I looked at the interplay between trauma and resilience in the post-secondary learning experiences of Indigenous students. While the findings from my doctoral study are nuanced and much too dense to unpack here, I discovered how the embodiment of resilience from an Indigenous worldview could be used as a framework to shape adult learning pedagogy. I was moved to action by Brazilian critical educator Paulo Freire's (2000) vision of a liberatory pedagogy. When I entered my doctoral program, the outcomes-driven Western education model had been deeply normalized in my life, and I realized the extent to which I had internalized the deficit perspectives and stereotypes of Indigenous peoples (Lindstrom, 2020; Lindstrom et al., 2021). In addition to learning about Freire's theory of education, I also discovered Blackfoot scholar Betty Bastien's (2004) book wherein she intentionally articulates a Blackfoot model of learning based on Blackfoot ontological responsibilities and Blackfoot epistemology. These two visionaries moved me to build on my doctoral research through a sustained exploration of Blackfoot Elder knowledge and students' learning experiences so that I might begin an articulation of a pedagogy of resilience from a Blackfoot perspective.

Findings

The findings that emerged from the voices of the Elders and students offer robust, relevant, and provocative insight into the ontology of Blackfoot perseverance and cultural lifeways, and the experiences of both Indigenous and non-Indigenous students in taking Indigenous studies courses. The findings from the Elders' voices are conceptualized within a teleological framework encompassing how life was prior to colonization, what happened during colonization, and how life is today for the Blackfoot people. This framework was shared by one of the Elders in the study and is a useful way of understanding the processes of change and the ultimate purpose of life within Blackfoot culture.

How Life Was

This theme is understood in the context of precolonial Blackfoot realities. What is clear is that the Blackfoot Elders continue to hold our long-time knowledge in their minds and spirits, and they shared it in the interviews through stories, practical examples, humour, and easy-goingness that made us, as researchers, feel welcomed. Prior to colonization, Blackfoot systems were derived in accordance with Natural Laws. Resilience is not simply a response to hard times from which we bounce back. The ability to persevere is a gift from the Creator and is one cultivated at the moment of conception. Blackfoot people held a collective consciousness, and perseverance was more about a collective commitment to carrying on our way of life. Everyone worked together to improve the safety of our communities, and we supported each other to maintain Natural Laws. The notion of individual self-governance came up in the talks with Elders. Each person was responsible for their own individual self-governance because it was important to respect yourself and maintain personal autonomy—to walk in a good way. Helping oneself was done so you can help others. Protocols and social norms contribute to our resilience because they ensure balance and collective harmony. Another prominent finding was the revelation around the role of children. Children are at the centre of the Blackfoot communities, and ensuring we had healthy, vibrant, secure, and joyful children meant that they would grow to be adults who walked with integrity; adults who were living their lives with Blackfoot values of generosity, sharing, strength, respect, and kindness.

Based on this reflection upon the precolonial lifeways of my Blackfoot culture, I cultivated my individual self-governance by pushing back against racism while also refraining from allowing conditions that were out of my control to force me into reflecting that same kind of negative energy outward. On a collective level, I watched the Blackfoot Confederacy's response to the pandemic, which included offering a vaccination clinic that was open to the general public, which demonstrated attempts at restoring collective balance and maintaining good relations with the local settler community. These were being made despite the long-standing racism that characterizes the southern Alberta region.

What Happened?

All Elders in the study recognized how colonization has been a rupture in the pattern of Blackfoot resilience. Rather than our resilience being a response to colonization, the collective traumas we encountered have taken a toll on our communities. We cannot hope to understand Blackfoot resilience without also exploring and understanding the deliberate acts on the part of the government to destroy our culture. These ruptures related to the process of settler colonization continue to reverberate throughout our communities and include diseases such as smallpox and tuberculosis; colonial policies aimed at eradicating Indigenous identity; segregation through an apartheid reserve system; imposition of man-made laws to replace Natural Law; Indian Residential Schools orchestrated to solve the "Indian problem"; and the ravages of alcohol and drug abuse on the part of Indigenous people to quell the ongoing losses and cultural upheavals.

These happenings shaped the Indigenous experience of Canada, one that is underpinned by systemic racism, both historically and contemporarily. The COVID-19 pandemic revealed deeply entrenched inequities in terms of access to culturally safe and racism-free pandemic-related health services (Persaud et al., 2021), and while not surprising, they were sources of toxic stress and anxiety. I feared for the well-being of my elderly parents and other vulnerable groups who might need to access the health-care system. The findings from this research demonstrate that colonization is an ongoing process. Illness and disease continue to ravage Indigenous populations at a higher rate than the mainstream, and alcohol, still a coping mechanism for some, has been replaced by deadly opioids, the use of which is now reaching epidemic proportions on my reserve. The reserves are still apartheid structures and a source of mixed emotions—my reserve is simultaneously a place of segregation and poverty but also the last vestiges of our traditional territories wherein we are free from settler racism.

How Things Are Now

Elders shared how Blackfoot resilience is in our cultural continuity and epitomized through the smudge and our long-time governance systems. These governance systems include those protocols that have held our collective and individual self-determination. One thing is clear, the Blackfoot are always pushing forward. Today, culture- and language-revitalization programs strengthen our Blackfoot identity and function to empower us to realize that our resilience and strength rest in the power of being Blackfoot. Power is never seen as an individual tool to be wielded over others, but rather, power is understood as collective strength and is used to fortify Blackfoot identity against ongoing traumas. Our resilience is in our mentorship models, our ability to live in a bicultural context, and our willingness to be open-minded and accepting of the Creator's gift. The return to Blackfoot ways transforms lives and corrects patterns of dysfunction. The Elders further expressed that we need to try hard, "Iyikakimat," in life and that we must always move forward. One Elder stated, "No matter what they put on us, what they do to us, we still got that power," (G. Lindstrom, personal communication, n.d.) and we can still push forward today. There is a need to focus on resisting the internalization and adoption of colonial ideologies to survive through negative influences. If we resist, we will survive. If we survive then we have a choice to heal.

As I reflected on and made meaning from how things are now for my people, I realized that my individual experiences with systemic racism are part of the contrasting nature of life. While COVID-19 might have presented modern challenges, the illness continues to devastate Indigenous communities, for we have dealt with these since the time of first contact with Euro-settler peoples. As a Blackfoot person, it is part of my nature to move through these experiences while remaining connected to my ancestral teachings, so that I might create meaning and a sense of agency and self-empowerment from the otherwise violent and disconnecting experience that is racism.

Student Voices

A goal of this research project was to better understand how we might mobilize an Indigenous-derived embodiment of resilience into post-secondary classroom pedagogy. Through facilitating two talking circles and being supported with the space to smudge on campus, students were able to answer guided questions regarding resilience within their own learning and personal lives. The student findings have been categorized into the following points: transformative learning, balance, and experience.

Transformative Learning: The more granular findings related to transformative learning clearly highlighted that through their learning experiences in Indigenous Studies courses, students reframed their understanding of resilience. Several spoke of how we don't simply bounce back from difficulties and return to a previous state of wellness. Struggle changes us, and we are never the same afterwards. Resilience is about being reshaped by struggle, so one becomes a better person. While suffering is inevitable, it should help us develop our spirit, not change us for the worse. One student talked of self-control through reflexive growth and how we must all resist allowing negative experiences to change the essence of who we are. Many Indigenous students used the Indian Residential Schools as an example of resilience. One of the questions asked students about their self-concept and if they saw themselves as being resilient. Many student participants recognized their growth and changes and highlighted how learning is about growth, "learning and seeing who I want to be…I want to change to the new form."

The notion that higher education can change you for the better if one is provided with transformative learning opportunities was a consistent theme. Indigenous Studies courses offer human connection. Students explained that education has been their source of resilience due to its impact on their personal growth because it required them to acknowledge their connection to their lived experiences, embodied knowledge, and each other.

Balance: With regard to resilience within the classroom, the findings illustrate that balance is required in identifying the new information that one needs to sit and reflect on, and what one needs to let go of—what one must unlearn in order to learn new knowledge. These opportunities provide students with the ability to control how traumatic experiences shape them. Balance is required in resiliency to overcome obstacles. One student stated, "Education can feed into one's ego causing them to struggle with the privilege that education systematically provides. Resulting in a 'god' complex of power and economic gain." In response to this statement, another student emphasized that, "Regardless of race we each feel the same emotions that alone should unite us as one. [This] creates empathy towards all."

Experience: Students shared how resilience is a state of being that can't necessarily be taught by others. One must experience pushing through life on a consistent basis. The notion of pushing back, resisting, and overcoming were common descriptors used by the students. Resilience was described as being connected to healing and always taking something positive from negative experiences. One student shared, "Part of healing was realizing that the things that I have been through were really, really hard, but that they could be used in a good way. They changed me in a way that could be made good." This involved more than simply looking at the "bright side of things," but experiencing suffering and hardship and interpreting those experiences as opportunities to learn. One student also shared that resilience isn't just about going through extreme hardship and talked about how they never really had to be resilient because they felt they grew up in a very privileged way—as a White cisgender person from a well-to-do family. They now see resilience as also about trying hard in life and that resisting colonial thinking and challenging oneself in all aspects of life is part of being resilient. This finding is consistent with the Elders' perspective—that resilience is about challenging yourself. Resisting racism, pushing back against colonial oppression, and deconstructing one's privilege allowed settler students to experience a struggle in ways that enabled them to move beyond the shame that's often associated with discussions around racism.

Teaching for Resilience
The Elders shared how teaching for resilience means educating the whole self—learning as Niitsitapi; as "a real person." To be real means to know yourself, your knowledge, and your identity and to see yourself in relation to everything and everyone around you. Experience in relationships forms the basis for knowledge. We learn from the hard times and good times. Some of the Elders shared Napi (trickster) stories to demonstrate how we learn through trial and error, and it is this process through which we continue to foster our resilience. Our resilience lies

in having the humility to accept our mistakes and learn from them. When humility is fostered and mistakes normalized, then learning is seen as a gift. We learn to enhance ourselves and not simply affirm what we already know. The interviews with Elders highlighted how, as Blackfoot, we have always had our education systems, and that a teacher's role is to believe in all students' abilities. Curriculum needs to reflect the Indigenous identity, and non-Indigenous people need to learn about the experiences of Indigenous people in Canada, and who we are (a true representation of who we are as we understand ourselves), from us. In general, today's teacher education programs are also ineffective in preparing Indigenous teachers to teach from an Indigenous perspective. One Elder said, "We're trying to teach like White people." The focus must be more on our stories and less on learning about Western culture. Schools need to be a site of cultural continuity. One Elder shared, "There's a lot of these young people now lost, they don't know where to turn, what to do, who they are or even have a basic understanding or even a basic understanding of Blackfoot."

The findings from the conversations with Elders and the student talking circles point to a complexity of experiences that mainstream conceptualizations of resilience simply do not capture. Although there is an acknowledgement that "[t]here is no unified Indigenous view of resilience" (Andersson, 2008, p. 1), in the literature there is a tendency to fit Indigenous lifeways, experiences, cultural continuity, and individual and collective responsibilities within Western discourses of resilience, especially with regard to risk/protective factors (see Fleming & Ledogar, 2008; Pratt et al., 2013). I argue that the embodiment of Blackfoot cultural continuity, individual perseverance, and collective strength must be understood within a Blackfoot context using Blackfoot concepts, language, and models as opposed to using a Western frame of reference, Western definitions, and Western measurements as the entry points for engaging with Blackfoot lifeways. Based on the pattern of poor relationships between Canadian settler society and Indigenous peoples, the Western/settler colonial frame of reference is insufficient in engaging with Indigenous concepts. Indeed, the spirit of cultural embodiment becomes lost in translation. This argument is consistent with other critical Indigenous perspectives that push back against attempts to fit Indigenous lifeways into Western/settler colonial frameworks (Battiste, 2013; Nakata, 2002).

Resisting and Pushing Forward

With the insights from the Blackfoot resilience project, I have been better able to not only see but accept that the nature of human existence is framed within a series of contrasting experiences—resilience is about balance. Looking back to those times when COVID-19 and racism were front and centre in the world, I struggle to narrate those challenges adequately and appropriately because disease and the relational disconnects brought on by racial violence are not new. As Blackfoot people, these have been our experiences since the coming of settlers. Changes were always a part of my life, yet these past two years have challenged me in many unexpected ways. The loss of close family members and the ever-present reality of racially constructed marginalization and oppression were intensified through media coverage and social-awareness initiatives that illuminated the struggles of Black people, Indigenous people, and people of colour in North America. Many things, in terms of my research, were on hold but, there were also many projects that I was able to either start or complete.

When I did return to the Blackfoot resilience research project and finally got around to coding the interview and talking-circle data, I found that the process of making meaning from the voices of Elders and students was in itself a source of my own perseverance. The findings from the Elders' conversations reminded me that I must always look back to "how things were" and explore "what happened" in order to make sense of "how things are now." Too often, deficit discourse has framed how settler society perceives Indigenous culture. Resilience is a way to push back against focusing on negative aspects of life (Andersson, 2008) as well as enabling a re-storying of trauma experiences into narratives of resilience (Denham, 2008), but understanding resilience must be undertaken in the context of Indigenous lifeways and values (de Finney, 2017; Kirmayer et al., 2011). There has been limited exploration of Indigenous resilience in the context of higher education (see Hansen & Antsanen, 2016), but there has been nothing written that outlines how institutes of higher education might mobilize the embodiments of resilience from a distinct Indigenous cultural location in ways that avoid pan-Indigeneity or essentialist approaches. Moreover, autoethnography is a powerful methodology for this project because it allows me to also use my own story and experiences as points of reference (MacDonald & MacDonald, 2007; Whitinui, 2014).

Being philosophically oriented from a Blackfoot perspective, autoethnography illuminates Blackfoot science and technologies embedded in our oral system that provides a blueprint for cultural continuity and inner development—these include ceremony, language, humour, love, generosity, and kindness. These are all components of the Blackfoot ways of knowing.

Conclusion

The Western paradigm drives settler colonialism and encourages a lack of accountability to our relationships, to our learning, and even to ourselves. Student voices highlighted how the Western Eurocentric education system prevents them from creating a deeper relationship with their knowledge. Bastien (Bastien, 2003; Bastien, 2016) has suggested that Eurocentric knowledge privileges individualism and operates from a set of ontological assumptions that distort our responsibilities to our relational alliances by creating an objective reality wherein rationality, theorizing, and empirical methods become the primary ways of understanding the human experience. This research offers a glimpse into a Blackfoot world of experience, relationship, and knowledge. What I think is central to Blackfoot resilience is that it is a state of being that one must experience. One of the Elders in the research stated that our Blackfoot methods are our gifts and that we suffer for our gifts. These gifts connect us to our spirituality. To be resilient means I am connected to my spirituality. Blackfoot resilience, then, is about embracing discomforts so we can be transformed through our suffering and to be transformed is to be changed through our own as well as others' suffering. Within a Blackfoot resilience based on the embodiment of caring and ethical relationships as being central to cultural continuity, there is no space for racism.

References

Absolon, K.E. (2011). *Kaandossiwin: How we come to know* (1st ed.). Fernwood Publishing.
Andersson, N. (2008). Affirmative challenges in Indigenous resilience research. *Pimatisiwin*, 6(2), 3–6.
Bastien, B. (2003). The cultural practice of participatory transpersonal visions: An Indigenous perspective. *ReVision*, 26(2), 41–49.

Bastien, B. (2004). *Blackfoot ways of knowing: The worldview of the Siksikaitsitapi*. University of Calgary Press.

Bastien, B. (2016). Indigenous pedagogy: A way out of dependence. In K. Burnett & G. Read (Eds.), *Aboriginal history: A reader* (pp. 15–25). Oxford University Press.

Battiste, M. (2013). *Decolonizing education: Nourishing the learning spirit*. UBC Press, Purich Publishing.

de Finney, S. (2017). Indigenous girls' resilience in settler states: Honouring body and land sovereignty. *Agenda, 31*(2), 10–21. https://doi.org/10.1080/10130950.2017.1366179

Denham, A.R. (2008). Rethinking historical trauma: Narratives of resilience. *Transcultural Psychiatry, 45*(3), 391–414. https://doi.org/10.1177/1363461508094673

Ermine, W. (2007). The ethical space of engagement. *Indigenous Law Journal, 6*(1), 194–203. https://jps.library.utoronto.ca/index.php/ilj/article/view/27669

Fleming, J., & Ledogar, R.J. (2008). Resilience and Indigenous spirituality: A literature review. *Pimatisiwin, 6*(2), 47–64.

Freire, P. (2000). *Pedagogy of the oppressed: 30th anniversary edition*. Continuum.

Greidanus, E., & Johnson, J.L. (2016). Knowledge as medicine: The use and efficacy of a youth treatment program integrating aboriginal cultural education. In F. Deer & T. Falkenberg (Eds.), *Indigenous perspectives on education for well-being in Canada* (pp. 107–122). ESWB Press.

Hansen, J.G., & Antsanen, R. (2016). Elders' teachings about resilience and its implications for education in Dene and Cree communities. *International Indigenous Policy Journal, 7*(1), 1–17. https://doi.org/10.18584/iipj.2016.7.1.2

Hinton, A.L., La Pointe, T., & Irvin-Erickson, D. (2014). Introduction. In A.L. Hinton, T. La Pointe, & D. Irvin-Erickson (Eds.), *Hidden genocides: Power, knowledge, memory* (pp. 1–18). Rutgers University Press. https://www.jstor.org/stable/j.ctt5hjdfm

Kirmayer, L.J., Dandeneau, S., Marshall, E., Phillips, M.K., & Williamson, K.J. (2011). Rethinking resilience from Indigenous perspectives. *Canadian Journal of Psychiatry, 56*(2), 84–91. https://doi.org/10.1177/070674371105600203

Kovach, M. (2009). *Indigenous methodologies: Characteristics, conversations and contexts*. University of Toronto Press.

Lindstrom, G. (2020). Looking back while moving forward: A narrative journey toward self. In S. Eaton & A. Burns (Eds.), *Women negotiating life in the academy* (pp. 119–130). Springer. https://doi.org/10.1007/978-981-15-3114-9_10

Lindstrom, G., Baptiste, S., & Shade, S. (2021). "Mokakit Iyikakimaat": Autoethnographic reflections as a movement toward a pedagogy of resilience. In J. Macdonald & J. Markides (Eds.), *Brave work in Indigenous education* (pp. 29–40). Dio Press.

Lindstrom, G.E. (2018). *Trauma and resilience in Aboriginal adult learners' post-secondary experience* [Doctoral dissertation, University of Calgary]. https://prism.ucalgary.ca/items/5e309ca9-31f8-4351-861c-296f2b5e9e29

MacDonald, N., & MacDonald, J. (2007). Reflections of a Mi'kmaq social worker on a quarter of a century work in First Nations child welfare. *First Peoples Child & Family Review, 3*(1), 34–45. https://doi.org/10.7202/1069525ar

Mezirow, J., & Taylor, E.W. (Eds.). (2009). *Transformative learning in practice: Insights from community, workplace, and higher education*. Jossey-Bass.

Nakata, M. (2002). Indigenous knowledge and the cultural interface: Underlying issues at the intersection of knowledge and information systems. *IFLA Journal*, 28(5–6), 281–290. https://doi.org/10.1177/034003520202800513

Peltier, C., Manankil-Rankin, L., McCullough, K.D., Paulin, M., Anderson, P., & Hanzlik, K. (2019). Self-location and ethical space in wellness research. *International Journal of Indigenous Health*, 14(2), 39–53. https://doi.org/10.32799/ijih.v14i2.31914

Persaud, N., Woods, H., Workentin, A., Adekoya, I., Dunn, J.R., Hwang, S.W., Maguire, J., Pinto, A.D., O'Campo, P., Rourke, S.B., & Werb, D. (2021). Recommendations for equitable COVID-19 pandemic recovery in Canada. *Canadian Medical Association Journal (CMAJ)*, 193(49), E1878–E1888. https://doi.org/10.1503/cmaj.210904

Pihama, L., Smith, L.T., Evans-Campbell, T., Kohu-Morgan, H., Cameron, N., Mataki, T., Te Nana, R., Skipper, H., & Southey, K. (2017). Investigating Māori approaches to trauma informed care. *Journal of Indigenous Wellbeing*, 2(3), 18–31.

Ponting, R., & Voyageur, C.J. (2001). Challenging the deficit paradigm: Grounds for optimism among First Nations in Canada. *Canadian Journal of Native Studies*, 21(2), 275–307.

Pratt, K., Stevenson, J., & Everson, P. (2013). Demographic adversities and Indigenous resilience in Western Alaska. *Inuit Studies*, 37(1), 35–56. https://doi.org/10.7202/1025253ar

Simon, R.I. (2005). The touch of the past: The pedagogical significance of a transactional sphere of public memory. In R.I. Simon (Ed.), *The touch of the past: Remembrance, learning, and ethics* (pp. 87–103). Palgrave Macmillan US. https://doi.org/10.1007/978-1-137-11524-9_6

Ungar, M. (2013). Resilience, trauma, context, and culture. *Trauma, Violence, & Abuse*, 14(3), 255–266. https://doi.org/10.1177/1524838013487805

Ungar, M., Brown, M., Liebenberg, L., Othman, R., Kwong, W.M., Armstrong, M., & Gilgun, J. (2007). Unique pathways to resilience across cultures. *Adolescence*, 42(166), 287–310.

Valencia, R.R. (2020). *International deficit thinking: Educational thought and practice*. Routledge.

Wall, S. (2008). Easier said than done: Writing an autoethnography. *International Journal of Qualitative Methods*, 7(1), 38–53. https://doi.org/10.1177/160940690800700103

Whitinui, P. (2014). Indigenous autoethnography: Exploring, engaging, and experiencing "self" as a Native method of inquiry. *Journal of Contemporary Ethnography*, 43(4), 456–487. https://doi.org/10.1177/0891241613508148

Whitt, L., & Clarke, A.W. (2019). *North American genocides: Indigenous nations, settler colonialism, and international law*. Cambridge University Press. https://doi.org/10.1017/9781108348461

Wilson, S. (2008). *Research is ceremony: Indigenous research methods*. Fernwood Publishing.

/9
Abolishing Grades

"Ungrading" to Foster Freedom, Creativity, and Autonomy in the Pandemic Classroom

HEE-JUNG S. JOO, ERIN KEATING, and NARDOS OMER

Introduction

In the summer of 2021, I started working as an undergraduate research assistant for my professors Dr. Joo and Dr. Keating, gathering data and information on the topic of ungrading/abolishing grades. "No grading?"; "What does that even mean?"; "How does that even work?" were my initial thoughts on joining the project. Abolishing grades entirely sounded too radical; it was hard to imagine how it could be done to produce the same or better results than traditional grading. However, as I started my research, my perspective began to shift. I read what felt like hundreds of articles about ungrading in schools, what it looked like in the classroom, and what it meant for students. Some common themes I noticed were the idea that students take fewer risks in their work when graded, and that ungrading reduces students' anxieties and stress in the classroom overall. As a student myself, I found these claims to be compelling. As unconventional as the idea of ungrading seemed to me, I couldn't help but feel an immediate sense of relief knowing that I would not have to stress over my grades in at least one of my classes.

The account above, from undergraduate research assistant and coauthor of this chapter Nardos Omer, captures a common student reaction to ungrading—feeling skepticism about whether they would actually learn anything and if ungrading "works," combined with a curiosity that perhaps there are other ways to learn and for their work to be assessed. In April 2020, early into the COVID-19 pandemic, Roy noted that the pandemic was "a portal, a gateway between one world and the next" (section 4). Writing on the (mis)management of the pandemic in India, and thinking globally about the consequences of the pandemic for all of us, she concludes:

> We can choose to walk through it dragging the carcasses of our prejudice and hatred, our avarice, our data banks and dead ideas, our dead rivers and smoky skies behind us. Or we can walk through lightly, with little luggage, ready to imagine another world. (section 4, final para.)

While learning institutions pivoted educators and students alike to a remote teaching environment that many of us were unfamiliar with, if not skeptical of, the authors of this piece became deeply curious about the pedagogy of ungrading, sometimes referred to as the movement to abolish grades and grading. Knowing that there was no way to deliver an in-person course seamlessly online, we abandoned the pretense altogether and chose to step through the portal.

For those of us invested in pedagogies of resistance committed to anti-racism, abolition, and decolonization, we knew there was no "going back to normal," as we have always known that "normal" was not ever the solution or a safe place. A handful of days after Roy's article was published, Winnipeg police killed Eishia Hudson, a sixteen-year-old Ojibwe member of Berens River First Nation, in our city, followed by the police killing of George Floyd in nearby Minneapolis in May of 2020. COVID-19 may have thrust the world into a new kind of upheaval, but there were also too-familiar injustices that continued, and resistance continued to bloom. Locally in Winnipeg, a grassroots collective, Justice

4 Black Lives, organized a massive rally in June of 2020, joining similar protests across Turtle Island against police brutality and racism.

We, as professors, were pushed to explore other ways of teaching in the face of the uneven and unequal conditions that the COVID-19 pandemic exposed. Early on, our department did what it could to help ease the transition to remote learning, including asking all instructors to adhere to compassionate grading (grades would not fall below what the student already held), suspend late penalties on assignments, and have flexible attendance policies. We realized that many of these policies worked surprisingly well. For example, eliminating late penalties on assignments did not cause the massive chaos that we anticipated, as students generally want to meet due dates to keep their lives in order. At the same time, we also noticed an increase in students who disappeared from our classes, usually because of reasons completely unrelated to the course—they were ill, tending to family, dealing with personal issues, or working "front line" jobs that took priority. The pandemic laid bare the deep structural inequalities in society, including in our classrooms. As we entered into another term and another year of remote teaching, we wanted to rethink many of our assumptions about what we thought was best for our students and their learning.

With this social context in mind, this chapter traces the recent experiences with ungrading from the viewpoint of two literature professors teaching three different courses and an undergraduate student research assistant who read and compiled materials on ungrading before taking classes from both professors. We reside on Treaty One territory in what is now called Winnipeg, Manitoba (Canada). Our positions as settlers (two women of colour, one white woman) inform our teaching and learning values. Situating ourselves as such, deliberately within the history of settler colonialism and settler education on this land, reminds us of the residential school system's aim to "assimilate" Indigenous children into settler society by attempting to strip Indigenous children of their languages, cultures, and relations. We sought to understand how ungrading systems might help unsettle the structures and underlying colonial assumptions of our traditional university classes leading to a more equitable space for learning. To that end, we incorporated versions of ungrading into the various English literature classes we were teaching: a second-year class on superheroes, a second-year class on abolition literature, and a third-year class on British Restoration literature. Our findings are that many aspects of ungrading can be implemented successfully and creatively at multiple levels, topics, and historical periods.

Our chapter provides a mix of theoretical, practical, and self-reflective approaches to ungrading, allowing for a holistic and rooted analysis that itself practices scholarship in ways that exceed colonial standards of knowledge production. In the first section, "Grading and Ungrading," we provide a brief overview of scholarship on ungrading and the history of graded systems of evaluation, situating ungrading practices within anti-racist and anti-colonial approaches to education. Our approach can be seen as similar to what Gabrielle Ellen Weasel Head (see chapter 8) suggests is a "pedagogy of resilience," in that an anti-colonial approach needs to address methods and structures, not merely the content delivered in the classroom. In the second section, "Practical Details of Ungraded Classes," Joo and Keating provide specific details on how we implemented ungrading pedagogy into our classes, and Omer recalls how she navigated these classes. We found that scholarship on ungrading often lacked such nuts-and-bolts specifics, and we wanted to share concrete examples. In the third section, we conclude with reflections from all of us on what we think went well and what didn't, and what institutional support is necessary for this kind of innovative pedagogy. Overall, we argue that in the context of COVID-19 lockdowns and online education, ungrading operated as a harm-reduction strategy, offering flexibility and decreasing stress for our students. Ultimately, ungrading liberates both students and teachers, providing concrete ways to challenge some of the harmful norms of the colonial institution of the university.

Grading and Ungrading

In settler countries like Canada, universities are settler educational institutions, physically built upon occupied or stolen Indigenous land. As paperson (2017) states clearly, "Universities are land-grabbing, land-transmogrifying, land-capitalizing machines" (para. 12). Moreover, they are constructed to discipline students into docile citizens by teaching—and thus continuously asserting the superiority of—colonial, Eurocentric canons and ways of knowing. Education is a core method of how colonial powers attempt to ensure their continued cultural dominance

(Freire, 2000; Spivak, 1988; Tuck & Yang, 2012). The current scramble to "indigenize" higher education and the frenzy of equity, diversity, and inclusion administrative initiatives are proof of the fact that universities were created as settler colonial institutions of exclusion.

Yet, universities laud themselves as beacons of democracy and equality, of inclusion and diversity, and, above all, of meritocracy. One of the keys to this meritocracy is the supposed objectivity of grades. Echoing capitalism's myth of the Protestant work ethic, universities encourage students to work hard to get the grades they deserve. Both professors and students have taken for granted that grades reflect the quality of the work that has been submitted. This is perhaps why so many professors agonize over grades; we want to ensure they accurately reflect students' achievement.

However, significant research has proven that grades do not achieve what many of us, both inside and outside of education, think they do: they do not motivate students, they do not measure merit or effort, and they do not promote academic rigour (Blum, 2020; Kohn, 2018; Singh, 2021). As Kohn (2018) has summarized, the three main criticisms of traditional grading systems are that they diminish student interest, create "preference[s] for the easiest possible task," and diminish the quality of the students' thinking and learning (p. 29). Perhaps most devastatingly for humanities classes, grades do not inspire innovative, risk-taking student work. Rather, they often work to police and punish students in ways that induce anxiety and stifle their critical thinking—the opposite of the goals of a university humanities and liberal arts classroom as a site of the "practice of freedom" (Freire, 2000, p. 81). Even students who consistently receive high letter grades on assignments often suffer from grade anxiety. Being motivated by rewards, such as A+ grades, or even words of praise, what Kohn (2018) describes as "bribes," can be as damaging as being punished, as students are trained to pursue external validations instead of exploring and cultivating their actual interests and curiosities. By measuring students' "ability to conform to racialized, gendered, classed and neurotypical standards of behaviour" (Singh, 2021, para. 1), grades reinscribe colonial, white supremacist ideologies and reward the internalization of those ideologies (McGowan, 2021). Thus, in many ways, grades uphold the university as a settler institution.

Letter grades as we know them are a fairly recent implementation, only coming into wide use in the 1940s. Equally surprising as the short history of letter grades, perhaps, is the fact that the letter-grade system has been challenged by educators since at least the 1930s, nearly coinciding with when they began to be widely implemented (Crooks, 1933; de Zouche, 1945).[1] The earliest recorded reference to a grading system in North America was in 1785 at Yale University (Schinske & Tanner, 2014, p. 189) and the first letter grades were used at Mount Holyoke in 1897 (Singh, 2021). Unlike our current letter/number system, the categories were initially used solely by administrators to evaluate and rank students for bureaucratic purposes. Grades were not shared with students, as they were not tied to assignments. Rather, they were used as an efficient way to rank students according to one uniform, homogenized scale that could be translated across departments and with other universities. Singh (2021) analogizes this to how the United States Department of Agriculture grades meat.

In fact, this practice of assigning letter grades to evaluate students parallels the rise of factory work under industrial capitalism. Like Ford's assembly line, ranking or "quality control" assured its own standards by rejecting aberrations. As Stommel (2020) puts it, "Grades are currency for a capitalist system that reduces teaching and learning to a mere transaction" (p. 28). Freire (2000) refers to this transactional understanding of education as the "banking model," wherein teachers "deposit" information into supposedly empty students, a model that easily "dehumanize[s]" them as "automatons" by ignoring the knowledge and backgrounds they bring with them into the classroom (pp. 74–75). This standardization of higher education via letter-grade systems often disadvantages students of colour and other marginalized students (McGowan, 2021; Singh, 2021). In fact, standardization is often the very source of their marginalization. In this sense, ungrading can be regarded as not only an innovative pedagogy but a potentially anti-capitalist and anti-racist one as well. Our interest in experimenting with this pedagogy was to see whether it would create a better environment for student learning than the traditional classroom and whether it might facilitate the creation of a more equitable classroom. The new terrain of remote learning prompted by the pandemic, one that most students and professors found unsatisfying, was the perfect opportunity to imagine something radically different.[2]

Ungrading methods vary widely—they can include pass/fail assignment structures, assignment contracts, student self-grading, assignment bundling, learning portfolios, and more. What they all have in common, however, is that the students are assigned a high degree of agency in their learning process. Their work is assessed based on their own learning goals and desires rather than on an evaluation process led by external standards that pits them against one another. As well, instructors engage directly with student work in a more detailed fashion, providing extensive feedback that is not focused on justifying a particular grade.[3] In this way, ungrading liberates instructors from traditional grading systems as well.

In sum, ungrading fundamentally rethinks the power dynamics of pedagogy, focusing on a curriculum that provides students with agency and autonomy in their own learning so that they have a bigger claim to their own education (Pulfrey et al., 2011). One of its core aims is to encourage an intrinsic motivation to learn in students. It eschews an environment of student competition that can be fostered by grades in favour of student collaboration and peer learning. Ungrading rejects the logic of scarcity (higher letter grades as rare and in finite supply), a fundamental logic of capitalist dispossession, in favour of fostering an environment focused on the process of learning and community collaboration.

Practical Details of Ungraded Classes

English 2190: Literature and Abolition (Professor: Hee-Jung S. Joo)
I was curious about ungrading for a long time, and the COVID-19 pandemic—both how it changed the world and how it did not—enabled me to take the jump and rethink my entire pedagogy. When universities rolled out surveillance software such as Panopto (which tracks subtle body movements through cameras) and Respondus (including its LockDown Browser that prohibits internet use while taking remote exams) to curb student cheating, I knew that this was not the learning community I wanted to foster online. These surveillance software systems, named after carceral vocabulary ("panopticon," "lockdown"), are part of a massive industry of mining student data that further contributes to their dehumanization and exploitation.[4] Though I had no

idea how to teach a remote class, I knew that I did not want to be a cop, particularly in a class on the topic of abolition and literature.

My second-year course (enrolment: 45) started with the first two weeks devoted to critical readings on ungrading, the history of letter grades, their ineffectiveness in inspiring internal motivation, and critiques of the settler educational system. What better class to ungrade than a class on abolition and literature? We then moved into literature that discussed the impacts and legacies of the residential school system, and students were able to quickly make the links between schools and prisons from this settler colonialist context, even before we read Michel Foucault.

In terms of assignments, I was committed to: i) providing a wider range of assignments to encourage multiple modes of critical expression, ii) assessing assignments on a full credit/no credit model with the opportunity to resubmit if warranted, and iii) de-emphasizing due dates. Course assignments consisted of nine weekly and casual discussion posts, three online group annotation projects that showcased close reading and critical questioning in action, three shorter critical-response papers that were more formal (with creative options), and a final self-reflective exam. My goal was to provide a variety of ways in which students could express what they were learning and critically questioning, instead of asking them to echo back what I was lecturing. Particularly for a class on the topic of abolition and its relationship to settler colonialism, racial capitalism, and histories of slavery and displacement, what was important was that they were able to understand how these ideas were circulating within the context of their own lives. I would have rather read papers on students' critical doubts surrounding abolition than cookie-cutter responses that hit all the "right" points. Ungrading helped both students and me focus on working through and tackling difficult ideas—in other words, the actual process of learning. Considering the enrolment cap, it was imperative that I have teaching assistant (TA) support to assist with the extensive feedback; more on this follows in the next section.

Discussion posts were maintained inside groups of five so that students could form connections and foster trust. The group annotations enabled students to tackle denser material together in a safer environment. The critical responses were formal papers with frequent options for creative responses (with specific guidelines on how to incorporate theory into them). For example, one option was for students to write a hypothetical letter to someone they had hurt or harmed in the past, including reflecting on what they thought they did well or could have done better, drawing from our literary and theoretical readings on transformative justice. Another option was for students to continue to write beyond the end of a poem or short story we had read, accompanied by a critical explanation. The final exam gave students the space to reflect upon what they had (or had not) learned that term. For example, one of the final exam questions (students chose four questions out of eleven) asked them to trace their own assumptions around abolition at the start of the term and the end, and what accounted for this change (if there was any). Another question asked them to identify a concept covered in the course they found challenging or difficult to agree with: what questions lingered with them, and what would they need to learn more about to consider revisiting that idea.

Alongside these broader ways of asking students to express their ideas and opinions, students were given a clear outline of how many assignments they had to submit and receive "full credit" on to obtain a certain grade at the end of the term (see appendix 1). Final course grades at the University of Manitoba require a letter grade, so ungrading could only extend to assignments.

English 2190, Superheroes and the Critique of Individualism, and English 3620, Aphra Behn and the London Literary World (Professor: Erin Keating)
In *Teaching Community*, hooks (2003) calls for pedagogy that "serve[s] to educate students for the practice of freedom rather than the maintenance of existing structures of domination" (p. 46). Inspired by this, my goal when designing my ungraded classes was to create an environment for my students that encouraged agency, rewarded creativity, and enabled them to pursue the learning outcomes that best aligned with their interests and current abilities. The aim was to meet students where they were and to create lessons and assignments with the built-in flexibility to meet a variety of learning needs, interests, and schedules that had been made more crowded and unpredictable by the COVID-19 pandemic and the challenges created by online learning.

I designed a soft-contract model of ungrading, adapting models and insights from the experiences shared by Potts (2010), Stommel

(2020), Blum (2020), and Gibbs (2020) among others, that was based on both meaningful class contribution and completing assignments that fulfilled transparent criteria and learning objectives. I used this method of assessment in two English literature classes during the 2021–22 school year: a third-year class (enrolment: 19) and a second-year class (enrolment: 39). In what follows, I focus on three aspects of the assessment model that are portable across many types of classroom situations and easily adaptable to individual instructor needs: community-set learning objectives, flexible assignments, and assignment revision.

To set the tone of the classroom as a community that required each student "to be an active participant, not a passive consumer" (hooks, 2003, p. 14), the course learning objectives were listed as "To Be Determined" on the syllabi. In the first two weeks of classes, as a group, we discussed what students wanted out of the course both in terms of content interests and skills, using both synchronous Zoom conversations and an online discussion board to encourage full participation in the exercise. I used these conversations to generate a menu of possible learning objectives for the class and its assignments. For each assignment, students picked two or three learning objectives that they were working on, and these would be used in the assessment of their work. This was a simple way for students to signal to me their interests and needs while giving them agency in getting the most out of each assignment and, ultimately, the class.

Building on the flexibility of the learning objectives menu, there were choices between assignments and within assignments; for example, one required assignment could be completed as a traditional literary critical essay or a creative non-fiction essay. Both these choices required research elements, equivalent word counts, and were assessed according to the standards of the form and engagement with the subject matter, assuring fairness between students, while also giving them the agency to choose the format that best fit with their learning goals.

The method of assessment for the written assignments emphasized learning as an ongoing process rather than an end grade. As Gibbs (2020) writes, "Learning...is not about being perfect and never making mistakes; instead learning is about being able to understand your mistakes and act on them" (p. 97). I would add that learning in a humanities classroom is also about interrogating what defines a mistake, and what is hidden within the systems and structures that define correctness in a university setting. To encourage this reflective approach to criteria and "mistakes," I needed to be extremely transparent about the goals and criteria for each assignment, as well as meaningfully taking into account the learning objectives that the students had chosen for themselves. To that end, each written and oral assignment had a sheet that described the assignment and included a list of basic criteria that needed to be met. Each student received extensive written feedback on the assignments based on the criteria and the learning objectives that they had chosen to pursue. The feedback was tailored to identify strong points as well as areas for improvement and engaged both the ideas of the assignment and its structure/mechanics. Students received one of three possible assessments: Satisfactory, Revise, or Edit (Potts, 2010). Both the A and the B ranges of the grade contract required all Satisfactory assignments to be achieved, so students aiming for these categories were required to revise or edit assignments that didn't meet the Satisfactory designation the first time around (see appendix 2). Though time-consuming from both an instructor and student perspective, this approach emphasized the process of learning within the class rather than the testing of knowledge and abilities against a purportedly objective standard or set of expectations.

Navigating Ungraded Courses (Student: Nardos Omer)
Before taking Dr. Joo's and Dr. Keating's courses, I had already done one year of remote learning. I struggled during my first year online due to the limitations caused by COVID-19: not being able to meet in person, little to no class engagement, lagging internet connections, and the overall stress from being in a pandemic. One of my professors added two more assignments to the syllabus due to the belief that we would "slack off" with classes being online. They seemed to believe that remote learning meant classes were easier, completely ignoring the fact that life also got much harder for students who were stressing about school on top of their health, families, job security, and safety.

Working with Dr. Joo and Dr. Keating during the summer allowed me to mentally prepare myself for being in their ungraded classes that upcoming year. Still, after all the research I had done, I found myself feeling quite anxious. Part of it came from the fact that after being in school for many years, they were switching from the only teaching style I knew; another reason came from the uncertainty of whether this method was going to work. For both my fall and winter semesters, I was enrolled in three English classes: two graded and one ungraded.

I took Dr. Joo's ungraded course on abolition and literature in the fall. In her class, there was less emphasis on deadlines for assignments. She made it clear early on that, for our benefit, we should complete these assignments on the scheduled days, but the choice was ours if we needed to extend it. Because of this option, I was able to schedule my study time for Dr. Joo's class around my other two courses. This is not to say that her class was getting less of my attention, but there was breathing room to complete roughly eight readings and three discussion posts every week. My main thought during this semester was that if I was going to stray from her schedule, then it was all on me to properly manage my time. With my other two courses having strict deadlines, I did not have to worry about assignments overlapping or life getting in the way. My ungraded course eased my stress not only in that class but in my graded ones as well.

The second semester with Dr. Keating consisted of a different approach to navigating my ungraded courses with graded ones. My graded courses had a majority of our grade based on assignments with participation comprising only a small percentage of our final grade in the class (usually no more than 10 percent); in contrast, my ungraded one had almost an equal amount of participation and completion of assignments required (a minimum of 90 percent participation for an A). As a result, I was more focused on understanding the material so that I could engage in meaningful discussions in my ungraded course than my graded ones. In my graded Shakespeare course, for example, I often thought about what the professor wanted to hear so that I could use it for my essays as opposed to forming my own opinions. With Dr. Keating's course, I noticed critical discussions were more frequent as everyone had various opinions, and there was no fear or incentive of grades directing the conversations. Where discussions in my graded courses felt almost robotic and calculated, discussions in my ungraded courses felt liberating and genuine.

Reflections

Nardos Omer

I would first like to get into the specifics of my courses with Dr. Keating and Dr. Joo to convey both what being in an ungraded course was like, and why this method made the most sense for pandemic learning. My ungraded course with Dr. Keating was anxiety-reducing from the very beginning. There were clear deadlines set for her class (though she emphasized giving extensions if needed); however, due to her grading system of getting a Satisfactory, Edit, or Revise, I noticed this automatic sense of relief before I even started any assignments. With the pandemic causing significant disruptions in my life, it was comforting to know that I would essentially be given a second chance with my assignments. This sense of relief is what allowed me to take more risks in my writing. I noticed I was no longer motivated by a letter grade to do well, but rather that I desperately wanted to challenge myself with my writing.

There was one assignment, mentioned above by Dr. Keating, that allowed me to do just that. We had two options to choose from: We could write a traditional research essay on a chosen topic, or we could write a creative non-fiction piece, what was called an "un-essay." In past courses, anytime the word "creative" was mentioned for any assignment or project, I always ended up choosing the alternative option by default. Creativity has never been my strong suit, so I have always taken the "safe" route in my assignments for fear that I would get a bad grade. In the ungraded class, I felt motivated to step outside my comfort zone and I asked myself when I would ever be given another chance to experiment with my writing without being discouraged or "punished" for it. Because I was in an ungraded course, I decided to go with the creative option for once and see if this was something I could do. In short, and to my surprise, the un-essay assignment ended up being my best-written work for that class. I chose a topic I understood the least throughout the semester (neoliberalism) and the option I was least comfortable with (creative essay); both these factors are what made this assignment my most challenging one, and in turn, the most rewarding.

Early on in the pandemic, there were few opportunities to get extra help with assignments in-person from professors, classmates, or peer-review centres at the university; therefore, I could not afford to take any risks in my writing out of fear of failing. In contrast, Dr. Keating's course allowed me to take risks in my writing that I otherwise never would have taken had it not been an ungraded course. I knew that I could push myself and try something different for once, and the worst that could happen was I would be asked to revise it. There was no fear that I was setting myself up to fail by not being creative enough. I tried my absolute hardest for that assignment in hopes that I would exceed my own expectations at best, or get thoughtful feedback to work on at worst.

One problem with Dr. Keating's ungraded course was how time-consuming the revisions were. Because I did not have to write any revisions in that class myself, I do not know what that process was like; however, I spoke with classmates who did do revisions, and they all had similar comments about them, many positive but also some negative. One student said they wished there was an option to settle for a lower grade and move on rather than having to revise to reach a Satisfactory grade. Although they appreciated the extensive feedback that was given, they felt like the revision process made them do twice as many assignments than there actually were, and that the extensions would often overlap with other responsibilities and course assignments. Traditional grading in this sense would have allowed this student to accept whatever letter grade they were given, knowing they earned marks for what they did complete, and work harder for the next assignment. Instead, they were essentially required to resubmit the same assignment in hopes of meeting a Satisfactory level.

Dr. Joo's course was set up similarly to Dr. Keating's in that students determined what grade they were aiming for and then needed to meet the requirements for that letter grade. Taking Dr. Joo's abolition course during the pandemic resulted in some of my most reflective pieces of work. Her class felt like a safe space to not only push the limits of my writing, but my way of thinking too. It was easy to relate to ideas of abolition and reform when there were drastic changes happening all around the world at the time as well, due to COVID-19. Ungrading allowed for a more critical lens when discussing topics on prison abolition, decolonization, and critical race theory. In our second week of classes, we had intense conversations surrounding the abolition of prisons, mostly if we were for the idea, against it, or for reform. Initially, I was for the reforming of prisons; however, as classes went by, I noticed the connections between the pandemic, prison abolition, and ungrading. I realized that both traditional grading and prisons were concepts that people, including me, were conditioned to think we could not live without. Similarly, with the world going into complete shutdown within weeks, life during the pandemic—masks, social distancing, capacity limits, and remote learning—seemed too extreme to keep living this way for some. In a span of a few days, I already saw my thinking changing because of the classroom setup. If classrooms could abolish letter grades, and the world could adapt so quickly to a change in learning and working environments, then why couldn't the same be possible for prisons? In addition to gaining this new insight, I experienced only minimal stress when completing assignments for this course. A big part of that was due to there being extensions on due dates, as well as the agency surrounding topics and lengthy feedback. Because extensive feedback was given in this course, the feedback was acknowledged and felt meaningful compared to other classes. Though this acknowledgment is the goal for most courses, when a letter grade is attached to an assignment that cannot be resubmitted, feedback can have the opposite effect and can feel discouraging.

One challenge in Dr. Joo's ungraded course was the need for good time-management skills. I was lucky enough to organize myself pretty well throughout the semester; however, some learners need fixed deadlines and clear instructions with assignments to succeed. I even found myself getting lost at times because of the over-quantifying of assignments. It is easy to get overwhelmed in a course such as this where you must keep track of how many discussion posts you did, how many annotations, how many critical responses, etc., to meet the requirement for your desired grade. It felt like we were trying so hard to move past numbers and grades, but we somehow added more numbering than there was with traditional grading.

Overall, where my other courses seemed to crave a sense of normalcy in very abnormal times, my ungraded courses accepted the reality that the world was in a pandemic. This did not mean that our learning was placed on hold; by implementing ungrading, Dr. Joo and Dr. Keating created a classroom environment that students like myself could easily adapt to given the state of the world at that time. Their ungrading method supported the overall well-being of students during a pandemic and promoted a more meaningful learning experience.

Erin Keating

Though there was initially a lot of confusion and anxiety early on in the term, students seemed to come on board with the idea of ungrading quite quickly (certainly more quickly than I initially did) once the reasons, goals, and procedures were laid out for them. To that end, it is vitally important to be clear about how grades are harmful and the inequities that ungrading seeks to address early in the class. I also learned from my experience with my first ungraded class to make sure that there is an early assignment so that students get an example of the procedure in the first few weeks of the course. Students were much less anxious about the process in my second ungraded class, which I attribute to Nardos's enrolment in that class, as well as the presence of other students who had taken my or Dr. Joo's ungraded class the previous term. There is nothing like peer knowledge and experience for alleviating student anxiety, which is why I now include an "Advice from Former Students" section as part of my syllabus. I expect that as more students take multiple courses from me and Dr. Joo, it will become easier to teach in this manner.

In exit surveys collected from both classes, students were overwhelmingly in favour of this type of assessment, with the majority of respondents answering that they would either definitely (65% for English 3620; 76% for English 2190) or probably (30% for English 3620; 24% for English 2190) take another ungraded class if given the opportunity.[5] What emerged from these surveys was a sense of relief from the students—relief from anxiety over their grades, relief from making mistakes that they couldn't fix; relief from trying to read their professors' minds in terms of the unwritten conventions and expectations that accompany so many academic assignments. There was also a very rewarding recognition on the part of the students that they were learning and improving their work throughout the semester. Though, as Nardos mentions in her reflection, many pointed out the additional work created by the revisions, most felt the value in being able to revise their work rather than being stuck with a grade that they weren't happy about. One student noted the affective shift enabled by the ungrading system; they reported being "miffed" when first getting a "Revise" grade but then traced the way that they were mollified when they considered that an initial low grade in another course might make them drop the course entirely. This student's experience, and eventual pleasure in being able to learn from their mistakes and achieve the grade that they wanted, speaks to the strengths of this method for retaining students who may fall to the wayside in a traditional course, whether because of pressures caused by the COVID-19 pandemic or because of the greater barriers they may face in a traditional university setting that was built for white, middle-class students financially able to devote all of their time to their studies. This approach is also valuable for teaching students to sit with the negative feelings that might come with perceived failures and to turn those into opportunities for further learning rather than dead ends to be ignored and avoided. However, I do plan to revisit my grade categories to see if I have been too exacting in the standards for a B range grade, particularly in first- and second-year classes in response to student feedback such as that mentioned earlier by Nardos.

While there is no doubt in my mind that I will continue with some form of ungrading in my future classes, this type of assessment is time-intensive. It requires a lot of organization to keep track of revisions being done and assignments that are only being done by part of the class. The assessment process itself is time-consuming, as are the revision assessments; however, this was offset for me by the decrease in stress and frustration that traditional grading often entails. When writing comments, I knew that they would be read at the very least, and I quickly saw from experience that they were being used by students to improve their writing and the depth of their engagement with their chosen subject. In my fourteen years of teaching, I have never seen the type of improvement within and between assignments that I saw in these classes. That alone makes the extra work worthwhile for me, but I recognize that, as a tenured professor with a two-two workload, I am lucky to be able to make that choice. However, if there is access to TA or marking support, I do think that this is feasible at higher workloads as well.

Hee-Jung S. Joo

To echo the concerns of my co-writers, my students were also initially skeptical about how an ungraded class would run. That many seemed to think it was a trick or a setup attests to the disciplinary power of schools and schooling. Their skepticism toward ungrading paralleled, in many ways, their concerns over imagining a world without police or prisons.

Above all, the type of intensive, engaged, and swift feedback on assignments required to run an ungraded course could not be possible without either a TA/marker or a smaller class size.[6] As my colleague suggests, returning the first one or two assignments quickly, so students can see what ungraded comments and feedback look like, is key to setting the tone of the class. Considering we were struggling through a pandemic, I chose to make due dates more flexible for students. Due dates were emphasized as the ideal time for them to submit their work so that their work would not start to pile up. A few days late was never a problem. If students knew they would be more than a week late, I asked them to check in with me, so that we could agree on a schedule, and I could know when to expect their work. Because there were so many assignments for the class, students more or less stuck to due dates to better manage their own workloads.

What was most striking to me was that the final grade distribution was similar to a traditionally graded course, with a variety of grades across the entire board. This had been my initial worry: that every student would obtain an A+. I have since had time to reconsider that I need to refute this capitalist logic of scarcity. In fact, isn't the ideal outcome of any course that all students achieve full credit on all assignments? However, as it turned out, not all students are craving A+ grades. Putting my own problematic overachieving tendencies in their rightful place, students taught me that for some of them, high grades were not the goal of a class. For some, if the course was not stimulating, a B or a C was enough. For others, they had never really trusted grades to reflect what they were learning to begin with, and thus an A+ was never the goal. And for others, there were more important things going on in their complicated lives, particularly during a global pandemic, that passing the class was enough. Ungrading liberated me from the constructed value of grades as much as it did many of my students.

My initial reservations about ungrading concerned students who are used to receiving high letter grades on their assignments, and those who are well-equipped in a system by being positively motivated externally. Despite the research, evidence, and direct feedback I've received from students, that traditionally high achievers also often suffer from severe anxiety around grades (Blum, 2020), I worried that they would lose motivation without the potential "reward" of getting a good grade. One thing I learned from this course is that students who receive high grades in graded courses do not really know how to submit "average" work. They have mastered the five-paragraph formal academic essay (and been richly rewarded for it) to the point that they can pump these out with relative ease, across a variety of topics they may or may not care about. Instead, I tried to encourage these students to experiment with different forms of writing, to give them opportunities to practice other ways of expressing their arguments and ideas.[7] Students noted they were happily surprised with the opportunity to be more creative in their writing, as their academic writing was often quite detached and flavourless in tone.

The last point of concern was my own self-doubt that I was teaching an "easy" class. I have been in school long enough to recognize that I have internalized the conflation of real learning with difficulty, anxiety, and sacrifice. This type of thinking is particularly harmful to marginalized students—BIPOC students on white-majority campuses, first-generation college students, 2SLGBTQQIA+ students, neurodiverse students, and others—whose very presence at the university can already in and of itself be an anxious and challenging situation. I continue to deprogram myself from the idea that a dense and heavy workload automatically equals meaningful learning, and instead embrace the fact that expressing complicated or difficult ideas can look a lot of different ways that do not (and should not) rely on punishments and penalizations as motivators. Meaningful learning, research, and writing can be—brace yourselves—pleasurable (brown, 2019).

Conclusion

To be clear, ungrading is not a perfect solution to the many problems of the letter grading system, despite the utopian tone of some of the Twitter threads and blogs about it that multiplied exponentially during the pandemic as academics struggled to deal with unfamiliar learning environments and inequalities exacerbated by COVID-19. We assume some students crossed academic integrity lines, as in any class; there were students who managed to do the bare minimum required for assignments and walked away with a high grade, as in any class. However, we propose that ungrading can be seen as a harm-reduction tactic—a way for more (but not necessarily all) students to be supported and encouraged to bring what they want and can to their own education than is possible in a traditionally graded class. In this sense, ungrading is not a solution at all, as teaching is not a problem to be solved. Rather, ungrading is one alternative method of teaching that can be more equitable, just, and inclusive for more students. It can be used to support more creative types of class and assignment design that allow students and professors to imagine different ways of learning beyond the transactional. Such alternative ways of understanding learning and assessment can help exceed the restrictive modes of objective, depersonalized writing and criticism that still dominate university classrooms.

With this more modest understanding of ungrading in mind, we suggest that it is not necessary to make a complete switch to ungrading if that is not compatible with one's teaching situation or subject.[8] Trying one or two ungraded assignments in a class can be beneficial in opening up discussions about grades and their meanings and in demonstrating to students alternative forms of formative assessment. The cliche that "the perfect is the enemy of the good" is helpful here in giving us, and hopefully others, the courage to experiment with some of these methods in their own classrooms.

Appendix 1

Dr. Joo's Grade Scale
These are the *minimum* amounts of full-credit assignments required to obtain each letter grade. Full letter grades will fall in between these.

A+: 9 discussion posts, 3 group annotations, 3 critical responses, final exam
B+: 8 discussion posts, 2 group annotations, 3 critical responses, final exam
C+: 7 discussion posts, 1 group annotation, 3 critical responses, final exam
D+: 6 discussion posts, 1 group annotation, 1 critical response, final exam
F+: Anything less than a "D"

Appendix 2

Dr. Keating's Grade Categories

A

- Minimum 90% participation and punctual course attendance (attend or listen to 13 out of 15 Zoom sessions and recorded lectures, write/speak at least two posts/comments for each prompt/exercise 11 out of 12 weeks—this can be on UM Learn and/or in the Zoom session)
- Complete all of the required assignments to a Satisfactory level (and revise if necessary)[9]

B

- Minimum 80% participation and punctual course attendance (attend or listen to 12 out of 15 class Zoom sessions and recorded lectures, write/speak at least two posts/comments for each prompt/exercise 10 out of 12 weeks—this can be on UM Learn and/or in the Zoom session)
- Complete all of the required assignments to a Satisfactory level (and revise if necessary)

C

- Minimum 70% participation and punctual course attendance (attend or listen to 10 out of 15 class Zoom sessions and recorded lectures, write/speak at least one post/comment for each prompt/exercise 9 out of 12 weeks—this can be on UM Learn and/or in the Zoom session)
- Complete 3 out of 4 of the required assignments to a Satisfactory level (and revise if necessary)[10]

D

- Minimum 60% participation and punctual course attendance (attend or listen to 8 out of 15 class Zoom sessions and recorded lectures, write/speak at least one post/comment for each prompt/exercise 7 out of 12 weeks—this can be on UM Learn and/or in the Zoom session)

- Complete 3 out of 4 of the required assignments to a Satisfactory level (and revise if necessary)

F
- Fail to meet the course requirements outlined above.

In the event that a student's performance falls between two categories, I will use my discretion to award the final grade, taking into account factors such as additional class participation within a week and assignment performance. The difference between a grade and a "+" grade in each category will also be decided based upon these factors.

Authors' Note

This project on experimenting with ungrading pedagogy, including research-assistant and teaching-assistant support, was funded by the University of Manitoba Faculty of Arts Teaching and Learning Enhancement Fund, as well as the Department of English, Theatre, Film & Media. We are particularly thankful to our talented TAs Nichole Burns, Alexander Watson, and Camilla "G.G." Dascal, who jumped on board these unconventionally taught classes with enthusiasm and aplomb.

Notes

1. We join a growing contemporary movement of ungrading teachers prompted by the tumult of remote learning during the COVID-19 pandemic, and we would be remiss if we did not mention the plethora of hands-on ungrading resources and tips that were shared over Twitter during this time, many of which have since been deleted as academics left Twitter after its purchase and rebranding as X.
2. There were some students who voiced that they preferred the remote learning environment (especially asynchronous classes) because it enabled them to better juggle their work and school schedules. When asked if perhaps a better situation than working full-time and taking remote classes would be for university tuition to be free, they resolutely agreed.
3. Research shows that students tend to not read comments on papers when accompanied by a letter grade (Schinske & Tanner, 2014, p. 161).
4. For an early take on the big business of student data mining, see Watters, 2013.
5. There were seventeen out of nineteen possible respondents for English 3620, and twenty-one out of thirty-nine possible respondents for English 2190.
6. Sieber (2005) suggests twelve as the ideal number of students in an online class being taught by someone new to online teaching.
7. For more on the limits of the five-paragraph essay, see John Warner's *Why They Can't Write: Killing the Five-Paragraph and Other Necessities* (2018).
8. See Blum (2020) for examples of ungrading in non-humanities classrooms.

9. Each assignment and activity will have a checklist outlining the requirements. You will receive detailed feedback on every assignment and a notation of "Satisfactory," "Revise," or "Edit." An assignment will not be considered complete until it receives a "Satisfactory," which means that it fulfils all of the assignment criteria and is written to a second-year university "B-level" standard. I will be available for revising advice and guidance. Because of this structure, it is important to adhere to the deadlines for assignments as much as is possible. You will get a week to revise an assignment after it has been returned.
10. This does not mean that you can drop one assignment. You are still required to turn all four assignments in; however, you are able to accept a revise or edit grade on one of those assignments.

References

Blum, S.D. (Ed.). (2020). *Ungrading: Why rating students undermines learning (and what to do instead)*. West Virginia University Press.

brown, a.m. (2019). *Pleasure activism: The politics of feeling good*. AK Press.

Crooks, A.D. (1933). Marks and marking systems: A digest. *Journal of Educational Research, 27*(4), 259–272.

de Zouche, D. (1945). "The wound is mortal": Marks, honors, unsound activities. *The Clearing House, 19*(6), 339–344.

Freire, P. (2000). *Pedagogy of the opppressed: 30th anniversary edition*. Continuum.

Gibbs, L. (2020). Let's talk about grading. In S.D. Blum (Ed.), *Ungrading: Why rating students undermines learning (and what to do instead)* (pp. 91–104). West Virginia University Press.

hooks, bell. (2003). *Teaching community: A pedagogy of hope*. Routledge.

Kohn, A. (2018). The case against grades. *Educational Leadership, 69*(3), 28–33.

McGowan, J. (2021, April 23). Decolonize the classroom: Abolish grades. *Medium*. https://medium.com/age-of-awareness/decolonize-the-classroom-abolish-grades-eec327398860

paperson, la. (2017). Land: And the university is settler colonial. In *A third university is possible*. University of Minnesota Press. https://manifold.umn.edu/read/a-third-university-is-possible/section/ba50806d-ff18-4100-9998-784aecb42ae4

Potts, G. (2010). A simple alternative to grading. *Inquiry: The Journal of the Virginia Community Colleges, 15*(1), article 4. https://commons.vccs.edu/inquiry/vol15/iss1/4

Pulfrey, C., Buchs, C., & Butera, F. (2011). Why grades engender performance-avoidance goals: The mediating role of autonomous motivation. *Journal of Educational Psychology, 103*, 683–700. https://doi.org/10.1037/a0023911

Roy, A. (2020, April 3). The pandemic is a portal. *Financial Times*. https://www.ft.com/content/10d8f5e8-74eb-11ea-95fe-fcd274e920ca

Schinske, J., & Tanner, K. (2014). Teaching more by grading less (or differently). *CBE—Life Sciences Education, 13*(2), 159–166. https://doi.org/10.1187/cbe.cbe-14-03-0054

Sieber, J.E. (2005). Misconceptions and realities about teaching online. *Science and Engineering Ethics, 11*(3), 329–340. https://doi.org/10.1007/s11948-005-0002-7

Singh, V. (2021, March 26). On grading. *Dialogues*. https://amsj.blog/2021/03/26/on-grading-2/

Spivak, G. (1988). Can the subaltern speak? In C. Nelson & L. Grossberg (Eds.), *Marxism and the interpretation of culture* (pp. 271–313). University of Illinois Press.

Stommel, J. (2020). How to ungrade. In S.D. Blum (Ed.), *Ungrading: Why rating students undermines learning (and what to do instead)* (pp. 25–41). West Virginia University Press.

Tuck, E., & Yang, K.W. (2012). Decolonization is not a metaphor. *Decolonization: Indigenity, Education & Society, 1*(1), 1–40. https://jps.library.utoronto.ca/index.php/des/article/view/18630

Warner, J. (2018). *Why they can't write: Killing the five-paragraph essay and other necessities*. John Hopkins University Press. https://doi.org/10.1353/book.61976

Watters, A. (2013, October 17). *Student data is the new oil: MOOCs, metaphor, and money*. Hack Education. http://hackeducation.com/2013/10/17/student-data-is-the-new-oil

Exposed and Exacerbated

The Social and Institutional Conditions Underlying the Years of the Pandemic

ENAKSHI DUA

> What the COVID-19 pandemic has done is expose even further the endoskeleton of the world.
> —DIONNE BRAND, "On Narrative, Reckoning and the Calculus of Living and Dying"

AS I REFLECT ON THE PANDEMIC, many dimensions come to my mind. First, my own personal privilege. Being a university professor, I was able to quickly move to "working at home," a place that had space for its household. My teenager, who was in high school, was able to study in their room. My 85-year-old mother lived with me—relatively safe from the horrors that were unfolding in nursing homes—though as the burden of keeping her protected was privatized, it fell onerously on my teenager and me. I was hyper-aware of how this privilege was not extended to many others, both within academia and in other workplaces. For some of my colleagues, staff, and students, particularly those who were racialized and had young children, working at home was difficult—as they did not have space for a quiet home office. And for folks working in so-called essential services such as health care, factories, warehouses, and grocery stores, many of whom were poorly remunerated and lacked access to private transportation, paid work involved being at greater risk for infection. Many of these workers had their older children engage in online learning alone in empty houses while being accused of putting their communities at risk as they were unable to work remotely. It was clear that these workers and children were not offered the same protection in their workplaces and communities (Public Service Alliance of Canada, 2020). Thus, while we were all vulnerable to getting COVID-19, the characteristic of racial capitalism, which emphasizes that racial exploitation is one of the basis for capitalist exploitation and accumulation (Dua, 2023; Robinson, 1983), positioned some as more vulnerable and fungible.

The authors within *Unmasking Academia: Institutional Inequities Laid Bare During COVID-19* reflect on and analyze the inequities revealed and concretized in academia. The chapters herein illustrate the larger endoskeleton of the racial capitalist relations of health, work, social reproduction, and transnational relations, and how each is located in race, class, gender, and systems of domination. As this collection demonstrates, we are in two pandemics: a health pandemic brought on by COVID-19 and a pandemic that can be better understood as based on social characteristics of racism. As my colleague Carl E. James writes in this collection, this social "virus" of inequity has long existed and is clearly revealed by the COVID-19 pandemic. This is not to say that the COVID-19 pandemic did not have devastating social impacts, including high rates of death and illness, loss of jobs, business and income, disruption of travel and international and domestic trade, lack of access to in-person education, health crisis, and deeply felt loss of communities and relationships. Such social impacts co-existed with a seeming wave of virulent racism—the violent murders of Black and Indigenous people and people of colour, the hostility toward and targeting of BIPOC folks in public spaces; the number of infection-related deaths in BIPOC communities. Yet understanding the social impact of COVID-19 requires us to go beyond the context of the first two years of the pandemic. As Brand (2020) eloquently put it, the impact of COVID-19 exposed the endoskeleton of our social world—the social relations of health, work, social reproduction, transnational relations and how each is located in race, class, gender, and inequities. While the virus and its social impact have received a lot of attention, much less attention has been paid to the social truths it revealed and is located in.

As *Unmasking Academia: Institutional Inequities Laid Bare During COVID-19* illustrates, to understand the pandemic in the context of academic institutions, we need to document and analyze the outlines of the endoskeleton that the pandemic painfully reveals. Educational institutions exist within the societal structures and social dynamics that shape inequitable schools and workplaces. Therefore, to understand how the pandemic unfolds in relation to educational institutions in Canada means understanding how these educational institutions—from kindergarten through high school to university—are deeply entangled with colonialism, capitalism, neoliberalism, and concomitantly entangled with systemic forms of inequities such as classism, racism, sexism, homophobia, transphobia, and ableism, with their intersectionalities. At the same time, universities as institutions of higher learning, along with university teachers and their professional unions, are sites of struggle and resistance. Given the mandate to carry out research, teaching, and informing social policy, academic institutions shape how educational institutions attempt to resist these forces and participate in social struggles for justice. In this book, Irene Shankar and Corinne L. Mason, and all of the contributors, bring to us a significant and timely collection that allows us to trace and reflect on the pandemic's influence on academia and to offer routes forward. Thus, importantly, the collection makes visible the ways in which the endoskeleton of our social world shaped experiences with the pandemic, it offers a rare opportunity to reflect on the lessons of the pandemic for those outside of academia.

The Endoskeleton of Health: Race, Class, and Work

The COVID-19 pandemic starkly exposed that our health and social well-being are impacted not only by state structures and their concomitant policies but as importantly by racial capitalism. It had long been clear for those in marginalized communities that private health was located in public health. The years of COVID-19 exposed that, when it comes to BIPOC communities, our public-health policies were not simply inadequate but riddled with racist stereotypes and discourses. For example, in Calgary, Filipino migrants' living conditions were blamed for the spread of disease (Green, 2020). Such instances point to Canada's long history of blaming racialized peoples for the spread of diseases by problematizing the household structures, which included extended family members and others, in racialized communities (Marwani, 2003).

Reproduced in the context of the pandemic, explanations of household composition leave untouched the question of how COVID-19 enters the household in the first place. Similarly, the association of income with the likelihood of greater underlying health issues, while certainly a factor in infections, overlooked the complex ways in which income may be interacting with other factors of transmission. Overlooking the substantial research that pointed to environmental factors associated with COVID-19 transmissions (see, e.g., Gunn et al., n.d.; Mahabir et al., 2021; Nestel, 2012) public discourse perpetuated the underlying assumption that those with low income make "poor" health choices in diet and exercise, and concomitantly greater incidences of health conditions such as asthma, obesity, and hypertension. As Strings (2020) asked, how does obesity, which is associated with the higher rates of infection and death of Black Americans, really explain higher mortality rates? According to Strings (2020), "42.2 percent of white Americans and 49.6 percent of African-Americans are obese," and yet "researchers have yet to clarify how a 7 percentage-point disparity in obesity prevalence translates to a 240 percent–700 percent disparity in fatalities." McPhail and Orsini (2021) maintain that the link between obesity and poor health outcomes during COVID-19 may have been more closely connected to racism and anti-fat bias in care rather than fatness itself being a predictor of poor outcomes.

We were all vulnerable to getting COVID-19, but, as is characteristic of racial capitalism, some were less vulnerable and others fungible. The failure to offer all workers the same protection in their workplaces and communities starkly illustrates the endoskeletons of racial capitalism. Workers in factories and warehouses, nursing homes, health care, trucking, grocery stores, cleaners of offices and buildings, garbage collectors, and those who hereto are underpaid, undervalued, and overlooked, were quickly defined by governments as "essential." While many people across Canada banged on pots to recognize these workers at the beginning of the pandemic, we have quickly forgotten which work is essential to our lives. For instance, at the time of writing, we still do not have a living wage for many of these workers. The move to remote work—for those whose work allowed it—faced an intensification of work produced by neoliberal restructuring. The neoliberal privatized organization of social reproduction was starkly clear as daycares and schools closed, and nursing homes moved to prevent visitors; the centrality of the privatized and feminized care of children, the elderly, and those who are differently abled was disrupted. Our approach to elder care, which centred on either underfunded corporate-owned nursing homes or atomistic private households, highlighted that these bodies were long considered fungible.

The move to teaching online highlighted the importance of the social aspects of schooling as well as how schooling is embedded in how social reproduction is organized. As women were tasked with caring for children, parents, and communities while coordinating their children's online learning, some were forced to leave paid work. Furthermore, the differential rates of illness, mortality, and vaccine access exposed that public health-care access is structured by race and class. The news media reported incidents of "virulent" racism daily. As discussed by authors in this collection, this reporting brought into stark view anti-Black racism, anti-Indigenous racism, colonization, and white settler nationalism. Our occupations were a major component of our risk of infection, and as such the relations of work were highlighted. Importantly, as this collection illustrates, these pandemic years also made visible the multifaceted forms of resistance—from communities organizing care such as grocery shopping to providing food baskets for those who lost income, to organized protests and to the imaginative discussions of how to revise our worlds.

One month into the advent of COVID-19 it quickly became clear to me that BIPOC folks were at much higher risk for contracting COVID-19 and had higher rates of mortality. From my reading of newspapers and blogs, this was true not only in Canada but also in the United States, England, France, and Sweden. Unfortunately, when the pandemic began, public-health offices in Canada did not collect race-based data, making invisible what those in racialized communities, particularly Indigenous communities, had long known—the consequences of racism and environmental racism had long impacted health, from premature births, infant mortality, rates of illness such as cancer, and life expectancy (Gunn et al., n.d.). Also well-known and documented is racial discrimination perpetuated by health providers (Mahabir et al., 2021). Yet, when the greater risk of exposure and mortality from COVID-19 became exposed, governments reacted with surprise, raising questions about whether such surprise was a performance allowing governments to position themselves as innocent of the outcomes. Fuelled by pressure from anti-racist activists, governments began to finally collect race-based data, especially for those who tested positive for COVID-19, and for mortality. For example, on June 29, 2020, in Ontario regulatory changes came into effect that allow for the collection of data on race, income, household size, and language from people who test positive for COVID-19 or were considered a probable case (Public Health Ontario, 2020). Notably missing was data on occupation and workplace.

This move to collect race-based data was widely recognized in newspapers and public forums as addressing the intersections of race and COVID-19 infections, but a closer analysis suggests that it failed to capture the full picture. The collection of data on race, income, household size, and language seemed to illustrate that Black and racialized groups experience higher rates of infection due to lower income that, in turn, leads to greater underlying health issues, living in higher-density communities, and the tendency to live in larger households, including multigenerational households, and due to the lack the language skills to access information of infection prevention. The assumption that lower average income along with language and cultural barriers are the main determinants of racialized differences in health has long been held within Canadian health policy (Halwani, 2004). However, a closer look at how these factors were associated with COVID-19 infection not only seems to dispute each of these popular explanations but, as importantly, point to salient characteristics of racial capitalism.

Two of the factors that were consistently overlooked in the collection of race-based data on infections and mortality were occupation and workplace. From the beginning of COVID-19, it has been clear that racialized people are more likely to be in occupations that have greater exposure. As Ethel Tungohan discusses in chapter 7, those who worked in warehouses, meat factories, bakeries, retail stores, and farms were at increased risk of contracting this disease. In trying to identify the ways in which the workplace was a site of infection, I made a crude calculation based on publicly available data on rates of mortality by occupation.[1] These calculations suggest that in the first and second waves (March 2020 to June 2021), 30 percent of all cases outside of the elderly in nursing homes were tied to workplaces in which Black and racialized people are concentrated, such as nursing homes, factories, warehouses, retail, and farms. This data suggests that racialized folks were infected through their workplace. Significantly, without the ability to make such links, we lacked, and still lack, effective public-health measures to protect these racialized and other workers, such as effective ventilation, good quality masks, and the required physical distance between workers. There were other reports that the workplace and/or occupation were key sites of transmission. Indeed, by the second year of the pandemic, public-health offices in Canada pointed to the importance of occupation for the transmission of COVID-19 (Smith et al., 2021). Despite this evidence that the way in which occupation, and therefore class and race, were crucial factors for health, there were few targeted health measures to ensure that these workers were protected. The costs of safety measures, such as effective ventilation, redesigning production so that workers were not shoulder-to-shoulder on factory lines, providing safe lunch facilities, and ensuring more public transportation to out-of-the-way workplaces, were deemed prohibitive. The use of quality masks was often the responsibility of individual workers, rather than ensuring employers provided these to all workers. Thus, despite public declarations of these "heroic" workers, a rhetoric that clearly constructed heroism as a willingness to be exposed to COVID-19, there was a glaring lack of government, corporate, and public commitment to ensuring that these "essential" workers were protected. While these workers became hyper-visible, and we collectively and publicly acknowledged that this work was what made our lives possible, the pandemic did not lead to a revisioning/restructuring of racial capitalism, of how we value work and bodies who are ignored and thus fungible.

Gender, Race, and the Intensification of Work

Another characteristic of the endoskeleton of our social world that was exposed and exacerbated by COVID-19 was how employment and social reproduction are socially organized. As newspapers reported, especially for those working off-site, "work-life balance" was decimated (McQueen, 2022) as the restructuring of work led to its intensification, and importantly, the intensification of work for those working on-site was overlooked. Moreover, Venz and Boettcher (2021) report that this intensification has not ended with the so-called end of the pandemic. For office workers, this intensification led to an acceleration of a digital transformation of work, particularly through an intensification of email usage and the surveillance of workers (Venz & Boettcher, 2021).

As the chair of the Race Equity Caucus (REC) at my university, a caucus of racialized faculty who are committed to anti-racism, I was able to see how these changes unfolded. As *Unmasking Academia* illustrates, a focus on academic work can provide key insights into the broader characteristics of employment and social reproduction. Often overlooked, the intensification of work or the labour process is an inherent characteristic of racial capitalism, and so it needs to be placed within its long history. With the closure of campuses and schools, the workload of all faculty intensified overnight. We worked quickly to move our courses online, learned how to use Zoom, and juggled research and service work with workshops on how to revamp our courses so we could be as effective as possible while undertaking online teaching.[2] The demands of supporting our students included not only assisting students in navigating new learning platforms but also the crises associated with the pandemic. The fear and uncertainty among students were palpable in my Zoom classrooms. I had students regularly share with the class about their family members' illnesses and deaths, and their profound grief about the loss in their respective communities. Still, academic and other educational institutions asked more and more from us, with vacuous recognition that lacked substantial effort to change the toll. Meetings seemed to mushroom. Our research agendas became precarious, as conferences, workshops, and keynotes were cancelled. Crucially, our ability to do research became prohibited, as we were unable to access our labs and offices, and for those whose research was based on travel or in-person interviews, the ability to conduct research was lost. Moreover, faculty with full and busy households found it difficult to carry out their work in their homes, and in many universities requests for access to office space were denied. The impact took a physical toll. Many colleagues reported that their concentration and memory were challenged. I know of at least one colleague who was hospitalized for exhaustion. Others left academia. Again, as characteristic of racial capitalism, some BIPOC faculty navigated the intensification of work and other demands by our institutions while we experienced, as I describe in the next section, a simultaneous "virulent" wave of racism.

As part II of this collection reveals, we are all embedded in communities of care. We also navigated the intensification of our care work, as explored by many authors in this collection, including Ayesha Mian Akram, Ethel Tungohan, and Gabrielle Ellen Weasel Head. The COVID-19 pandemic, including the explosion of our caregiving and domestic work, brought on uncertainty and fear. This was/is especially acute for those with children, the elderly, and differently abled and "vulnerable" family and chosen family members. Many faculty—especially untenured—reported to REC that they were unable to integrate the increased care work with their paid work, feeling it was impossible to meet expectations. For faculty members whose parents lived in congregate care, the worry was overwhelming. Many were panic-stricken as they were denied access to their relatives in care and did not know how to protect their parents from infection or worse. If their parents lived independently, they were also unable to visit or help them. Getting groceries, medicines, routine medical care, and assistance with daily living tasks became fraught, and navigating these demands was time-consuming. For those with family in another place, especially in another country, the inability to assist in caregiving became translated into numerous phone and WhatsApp calls due to closed borders and restricted travel. With time differences for those with family and community in another country, these faculty spent endless nights calling their loved ones. And if any relatives fell ill—or when there was a "wave" of infections where loved ones lived—the helplessness was debilitating.

As members of REC reported on their working conditions, we began to advocate for more effective policies, for both work and as importantly for recognition of the impacts of the public-health mitigation efforts on caregiving. At the beginning of the pandemic, the administration at my university had assured faculty they would be able to receive work accommodations. In an email, the administration stated:

> For those with caregiving challenges, the University's policy on Accommodating Family commits to ensuring that all York community members receive equal treatment without discrimination on the basis of family status, and allow for a degree of flexibility to be

exercised to alleviate disadvantages a caregiver may face. The nature of any accommodation will depend on the particular circumstances of individuals and the requirements of their job. Faculty members or instructors should contact their Dean's/Principal's Office to discuss options for accommodating caregiving responsibilities.

However, the stated policy was limited, as faculty were told if they were unable to teach they could postpone their teaching for a subsequent year—where they would "owe" courses to the university. This policy is indicative of what was taking place in many workplaces. Without committing to more resources, employers privatized and individualized the cost of the pandemic for those who had health concerns, household members who were immunocompromised, or onerous caregiving responsibilities.

Frustratingly, with the clause "depending on personal circumstances," there have been multiple reports of faculty, who attempted to access this policy to alter their teaching load, being denied. Faculty with young children and those with immunocompromised household members were told that they were not eligible as the policy only applied to immunocompromised employees. However, immunocompromised faculty were also told that they were not eligible to teach online. As one faculty in a private communication stated, "I literally feel like I was thrown into the bureaucracy...meeting after meeting explaining my situation in detail to a relentless, disrespectful and cruel bureaucracy." As in other workplaces, faculty knew that refusing to accept the lack of accommodation could lead to a violation of employment contracts. These faculty filed grievances that were time-consuming and often so drawn out that there were no resolutions as the beginning of the semester approached. Many of these faculty had to frantically come up with a backup plan for caregiving, and, if immunocompromised, for exposure. As the York University Faculty Association wrote in an email to its members: "You may know that YUFA staff, our Chief Stewards, our rep on the Joint Committee and the COVID table have devoted much time and energy trying to deal with the frustrating complications of this process." Concerns of loss of research time, especially for untenured faculty, were only vaguely addressed by the university while concerns about the impact of online teaching evaluations were overlooked.

Like other workers, especially those in pandemic unionized workplaces, faculty challenged these structures, particularly the privatizing of caregiving responsibilities. Faculty published powerful articles that documented the particular challenges they faced, including by "international" faculty and junior faculty (see, e.g., Chatterjee, 2021). Our faculty associations, such as the Canadian Association of University Teachers and the Ontario Confederation of University Faculty Associations raised awareness of these issues (Canadian Association of University Teachers, 2020). REC and YUFA continued to ask for institutional support, pointing to the stress and consequences for faculty members' mental health. At REC we wrote about these conditions to the administration and we met with senior administration. We asked that access to office space be made possible during shutdowns. We suggested concrete ways this could be done with the intent of preventing infections, such as getting portables so that each faculty who needed office space could have their own private workspace. There was no take-up of our suggestions by the university. We asked for meetings to collectively think of innovative ways that child care could be provided for faculty, students, and staff. For example, we suggested that the university use the closed campus daycare facilities designed for large numbers to be repurposed for a small number of children, with access prioritized based on need. Notably, the province of Ontario provided similar child care to healthcare workers. Again, there was no take-up of our suggestions by our university.

To more fully engage the administration, we organized a forum and invited senior administration to attend. In the forum, we described the working conditions and put forward several concrete measures, including a policy where those with onerous caregiving would be provided course releases, implementation of bereavement leave, allocation of increased TA hours for all faculty, relaxing of institutional research criteria, reduced service obligations for those with care responsibilities, and the inclusion of emotional labour as service. We also asked the employer to allow for the reimbursement for child-care and elder-care expenses as part of our professional reimbursement funds, permitting junior faculty to take a pre-tenure sabbatical, to offer more resources for junior faculty members to access guest lecturers, to reconsider teaching and professorship expectations, and allow postponements of tenure applications where postponements were backdated so as not to impact career paths.

Sadly, after over a year, we had limited success. We received funds allocated for guest lectures and marking support. However, the conditions to access these funds were both onerous and restrictive, so few faculty members were able to access them. Discussion of service was deferred to department chairs—it was reported that few chairs initiated such a discussion. Actions for concerns around tenure were deferred to forthcoming announcements. As we waited for a response from the administration, we tried to implement faculty-based support measures. Through our departments and faculty association we organized a mutual care roster—a temporary measure while we asked for more effective policies—where colleagues who found themselves in a situation of stress and overwork, especially those with small and school-age children, single-parent responsibilities, other care-work obligations, and health concerns, could access a roster of colleagues who were willing to volunteer by giving guest lectures, entertaining kids, and providing other forms of logistical assistance. We also attempted to raise funds for faculty to hire guest lecturers. But as with many volunteer initiatives that lacked the labour, this initiative was difficult to access and thus failed to get taken up by all who needed it.

The unresponsiveness of employers and governments to the intensification of work and the concomitant crisis in caregiving reveals the endoskeleton of both public education as well as social reproduction. Prior to COVID-19, public education had been criticized for being inefficient (Connell, 2013, p. 102), subject to decreases in funding, as well as to calls to make it a site for profits (Canadian Centre for Policy Alternatives, 2006, p. 4; Farhadi, 2019). Educational technology, or "ed-tech," particularly online learning, was promoted as a "cost-effective" solution to rationalize education. COVID-19 created a sellers' market in ed-tech, especially commercial digital learning platform providers. During the years of the pandemic, governments drew on powerful networks of big tech companies such as Google, Microsoft, and Facebook, as well the global education industry of edu-businesses, consultancies, investors, and technology, to define how education systems should respond to the crisis—an opportunity to further restructure public education (Williamson, 2020). In other words, the pandemic facilitated conditions for private technology companies to "quietly push for long-held goals in the frantic political and economic environment created by the outbreak" (McCabe, 2020, para. 4).

As important as employing ed-tech was to rationalizing the tasks of education workers, Kuehn and colleagues (2018) illustrate that online courses are viewed as an opportunity to circumvent unions and further contract out services. Especially, as Brabazon (2021, n.p.) has pointed out, the conditions of work during the pandemic further placed "education workers in market conditions…that emphasized competitive individualism, commodification, and existing inequitable hierarchies." As she points out, the lack of institutional support positioned faculty as "commodities that need to be 'work-ready,'" further intensifying academic work, especially through ed-tech. Thus, while administrations presented the intensification of academic work as a new and temporary measure brought on by the economic crises associated with the virus, as Naomi Klein's concept of "disaster capitalism"[3] suggests, it brought an opportunity to further restructure public education.

The struggles faculty experienced with caregiving during the pandemic also illustrate the endoskeletons of not only the gendered, classed, and racialized dimensions of social reproduction but also how social reproduction is a structural aspect of racial capitalism. Feminist scholars have pointed to the white, patriarchal, and normative family, underpinned by ideologies of white femininity and mothering, where white women carried out unpaid domestic labour as the basis of reproducing workers for a capitalist system (Luxton, 2018). Notably, Black and racialized women's relationship to social reproduction has been mediated by a white settler and nationalist project, where they have been compelled to participate in paid labour (Dua, 1999). In the period of neoliberalism, as an increasing proportion of women in heteronormative families engage in paid labour, social reproduction has become more complex.[4] The state response to the increased labour force participation of women has been to supplement unpaid reproductive work— that has continued to be carried out mainly by women in heterosexual households—by commodifying many aspects of caregiving through privately organized child care, elder care, care for those who are differently abled, cleaning of households, and food preparation (Green & Lawson, 2011). Much of the commodified work is performed by racialized and migrant workers; work that is underpaid, precarious, and until the pandemic, undervalued and invisible.

The almost universal lack of response by employers and the state to the crisis in social reproduction is exemplified by the disregard for support for employees, and the disregard for researchers who pointed out that privatized nursing homes had higher rates of infection than public ones. Furthermore, the intelligibility of parents to qualify for the Canadian Emergency Response Benefit makes clear the government's unwillingness to put financial resources into social reproduction. This lack of response makes visible the ways in which social reproduction is imbricated with the ideologies of autonomous liberal personhood, whereby the economically self-sufficient individual is placed at the site of the crisis in social reproduction (Gordon-Bouvier, 2021). As the commoditized aspects of caregiving, as well as the ways in which households relied on communities of care collapsed, the fragile infrastructure that enabled people to perform domestic labour collapsed, making its importance for social reproduction starkly exposed. As Salzinger (2022) powerfully stated during the pandemic, "capitalist exploitation is a parasite; social reproduction is its host, and right now the host is not thriving" (p. 502).

In many ways academia is a microcosm of neoliberal racial capitalism—workers are commodities and disposable in the search to secure and increase profits. The neoliberal restructuring brought in just-in-time production, the casualization of work, and a gig economy that made workers disposable—a workforce that can be hired and fired as needed to secure profits, partial commodification of social reproduction. As *Unmasking Academia* traces the lack of effective response by employers and governments to the crisis, caregiving perpetuated both privatization and commoditization of social reproduction, exposing the salient relations between unpaid labour, the paid labour of racialized workers in caregiving, and racial capitalism. The intensification of academic work through the undermining of unions, employing ed-tech, and opening up public education for private profits, exposed the salient character of racial capitalism—the requirement that workers ask not what employers can do for them but rather what they can do for their employers.

Historic and Ongoing Pandemic of Racism in Academia

From the beginning of the pandemic, a number of racist incidents were reported in newspapers and social media, seemingly on a daily basis, of violence toward and murders of Black, Muslim, Indigenous, Asian and South Asian people—with the police murder of George Floyd capturing international attention. For many BIPOC folks, neither the sheer quantity nor the violence of these incidents was surprising. As Brand (2020) powerfully pointed out, "I know, as many do, that I've been living a pandemic all my life; it is structured rather than viral; it is the global state of emergency of anti-Blackness" (para. 1). Yet the heightened response to this onslaught of racism did feel different, and certainly in my community of BIPOC folks the impact was heightened. As I read newspapers, Twitter and Instagram feeds, and engaged in conversations within my community, many BIPOC folks were deeply affected by these incidents, and, as they have done historically, are once again reorganizing to challenge racism.

Moreover, after the police murder of George Floyd, social institutions such as newspapers, universities, governments, corporations, and non-governmental organizations were suddenly publicly committing to challenging anti-Black racism. As anti-Black racism, racism, and colonization have been normative in our social world, I wondered what led the mainstream media, corporations, and others to this affective turn. Was the reporting of such events different in mainstream media? Was it something in the ways folks were isolated and fragmented? Was it our tether to social media at the time? Was it our heightened sense of vulnerability that made folks more open to racism and racialized violence? And what would be the outcome?

When universities responded to the murder of George Floyd by claiming to renew their focus on EDI, my cynical self—careful of placing too much hope in institutions—was cautious. Yet I, and some of my colleagues, felt we had little choice but to walk through the crack that had opened in the door, all the while despairing at our presentient cynicism. In a retrospective of these years, we can see that these commitments have led to limited structural changes. Indeed, a closer tracing of these responses suggests that rather than a deep commitment to challenging anti-Black racism and racism, the outpouring of academic responses was shaped by other dimensions.

As explored by the authors in this collection, for many BIPOC faculty, the ongoing violence against Black and racialized folks was difficult to witness and to bear, as many felt powerless due to our social isolation combined with the intensification of our work. The universities' public statements on the police murder of George Floyd marked a very different institutional response than earlier responses to racism.

Many BIPOC faculty had been working on challenging racism and anti-black racism in universities. At my own university, for over twenty years we had organized forums and workshops, met with administrators, advocated for representative (fair) hirings, raised issues of chilly climate, and attempted to change the curriculum. We spoke about the experiences of racism among undergraduate students, graduate students, staff, and faculty. We pointed to the specificities of anti-Indigenous and anti-Black racism. We challenged our colleagues when we witnessed a reluctance to change practices and unfair hiring decisions, most often resulting in placing ourselves as the target of increased racism, including ostracization. We promoted and participated in the collection of race-based data. As members of REC, we had developed collective language to eliminate the barriers toward hiring, suggesting revised language for affirmative action, and targets for Black and Indigenous hires. In doing this we were often called on to present "proof" of systemic discrimination, and to this request, written reports.

University administrations at my institution, like many other universities, responded to the murder of George Floyd within days. There was a flurry of statements and pledges of a new commitment to addressing anti-Black racism. The statements came from all levels of the university, senior administrators, deans' offices, and academic departments. The content of the statements is noteworthy. Many statements claimed to stand in solidarity with those protesting anti-Blackness and colonialism. Some statements condemned police violence but often did not mention George Floyd. When Floyd was mentioned, his murder was sometimes referred to as "the death." Some statements dedicated white folks to working to dismantle "white supremacy," individually, and collectively. Some statements committed to educating "ourselves" and included links to resources. The irony was not lost on me that the referred links were often to the writings of BIPOC colleagues as well as the material included in these BIPOC colleagues' courses, yet these contributions had rarely been acknowledged prior to these statements. A few departments at my university claimed a commitment to organize workshops, change the curriculum, and hire more Black and Indigenous faculty.

During this flurry of statements, members of REC met again with senior administration, outlining in detail the ways anti-Blackness is experienced on campus, as did folks in many other universities. Our "asks" were not new. We articulated what we had documented and had long advocated for: policies that address anti-Black racism, addressing the ways in which campus security impacts BIPOC folks, pointing to the lack of Black colleagues in senior administration and mentoring programs, financial assistance for Black undergraduate and graduate students, a special post-doctorate program for Black PHD students, support for a Black studies program, and support for research centres where work on anti-Black racism is carried out. Moreover, we pointed out that in 2018, REC had proposed a targeted Black hire program, which had been negotiated in our collective agreement in 2019 but had not been implemented by July 2020, despite repeated requests by the faculty association.

The consequences of these "asks" have been mixed. In the next six months, three special advisors in equity and anti-Blackness were appointed. New committees were formed. A review of how the campus experiences safety and security was implemented. Many faculties implemented new programs, ranging from developing strategies to recruit Black students, financial assistance for Black undergraduate students, mentoring programs, a special post-doctorate program for Black students, support for a Black studies program, and one-time financial support for research centres where work on anti-Black racism is carried out. A review of campus security was undertaken. Within two months the university announced they would have sixteen targeted Black hires, in addition to the six Indigenous targeted hires that were already in place.

As there was a heightened urgency to carry out all of these initiatives, members of REC worried about the implications for workload, especially as we were still in the first year of the pandemic. As both Mian Akram and Tungohan explore in this collection, anti-racism initiatives are important, but the labour of such initiatives falls largely on BIPOC faculty. In my experience, BIPOC faculty were called on to serve on hiring committees for sixteen hires—often in other departments as affirmative action officers or dean's representatives. Some members served on multiple hiring committees. BIPOC faculty were appointed to the new committees on anti-Black racism—while they continued their work on existing committees. As some of the chapters in this collection illustrate, the workload for BIPOC faculty mushroomed, and the level of exhaustion heightened at the intersection of COVID-19 and EDI. We asked that BIPOC faculty who carried out additional labour in the burgeoning equity apparatus be compensated with course releases. This proposal underwent tense and difficult negotiations. It was only through collective bargaining in 2022 that a half-course release program for those carrying out "extraordinary" equity-related service was initiated. BIPOC faculty have reported that the conditions for applying for this program have been restricted such that the equity work they undertake is not considered sufficient to access the program.

Importantly, while new policies and programs were implemented, the financial resources to allow these programs to be successful were rarely committed. The equity advisors who were appointed rarely came with resources. Instead, the appointments were often solitary faculty without support staff or resources to develop and implement policies. Moreover, despite the seemingly public commitment by university administrators and colleagues to challenging anti-Black racism, we found resistance—unsurprisingly—to implementing deep structural changes. As new policies were developed, they were worded carefully. For example, in one committee that was developing a university-wide equity plan, members were reluctant to add the words anti-Black racism and racism (as well as other isms) as some members argued that a list of targeted inequities would exclude unseen forms of marginalization. Rather what was proposed was wording about "ecosystems." The reluctance to name inequities, especially racism and colonialism, concomitantly re-centred whiteness, and this supposedly utopian vision of inclusivity displaced well-known inequities, which seem to include everyone (and the environment) except white heterosexual affluent able-bodied men.

While the targeted hires increased the numbers of Black and Indigenous faculty, these hires did not address why these groups were historically underrepresented, despite an affirmative action program. Members of REC pointed out that the need for targeted hire programs illustrated the existence of practices that have led to unrepresentative hiring decisions in the university. We suggested that addressing the historical and ongoing unrepresentative hiring decisions (as we had been for many years) would involve a broad analysis, starting with looking at how areas for hires are decided and defined, how recruitment takes place, how units evaluate candidates, how our affirmative action program employed a category of racialized faculty which erased Blackness and Indigeneity, and how the university's institutional investments in equity training did not result in anti-racism, or for that matter equity.

As we moved through the first year, the commitment to challenging anti-Black racism was almost forgotten, as public articulations of commitment to challenging racism when incidents took place waned. For example, the deaths of Delaina Ashley Yuan, Xiaojie Tan, Daoyou Feng, Soon Chung Park, Hyun Grant, Suncha Kim, and Yong Ae Yue were part of a long year (centuries) of horrific incidents of violence against Asian Canadians, yet evoked only a handful of statements. Requests to union leaders were met with a note that they were busy and perhaps I could write one for them (overlooking that REC did send out a statement). Requests to senior administration were met with the reply that it was on the list of to-dos, but as the statement never was made it suggests that it never made it to the top of the list. In the third year, after the seemingly "virulent" wave of racism, the gains have been small—which in itself is telling.

Given that in 2020 we witnessed so many seemingly heartfelt articulations addressing anti-Black racism and racism, why were deep changes so difficult to implement? Does the affective character of such statements suggest that the race to action after George Floyd's death was deeply embedded in the affective resonance of watching a human being die before our eyes? Yet, this was not the first time we had seen stark violence being recorded. Perhaps this resonance was located in living in a period where most felt vulnerable to infection. Or perhaps all of the commitments that were articulated to address anti-Black racism were commitments to address the fragility that white subjects felt in witnessing the horrific death of an African-American man?

While these questions warrant more analysis than can be dealt with in this afterword, several chapters in *Unmasking Academia* provide vital insights. Shankar and Mason point out EDI mandates and policies within the university should not be understood as transformational projects but rather as tools to contain and control more radical, decolonial, and insurgent knowledge and activism on campuses. Citing Thobani (2021, p. 4), they suggest that EDI mandates are caught in the "configurations of power" within the university. The response to racism during the pandemic does ask us to evaluate what kinds of configurations of power these responses are embedded in.

Conclusion

On May 5, 2023, Tedros Adhanom Ghebreyesus, the director-general of the World Health Organization, cautiously declared "with great hope" an end to COVID-19 as a public-health emergency ("WHO Chief," 2023). Yet, the social crises we experience are ones that we cannot easily declare an end to. As Brand (2020) pointed out six months after the pandemic began, the public narratives that these social relations would "end" when we return to "normal" were not only misleading but worked politically, economically, and psychically to hide the fabrics of our societies:

> I have never used [the word *normal*] with any confidence in the first place; now, I find it noxious. The repetition of "when things return to normal" as if that normal, was not in contention. Was the violence against women normal? Was the anti-Black and anti-Indigenous racism normal? Was white supremacy normal? Was the homelessness growing on the streets normal? Were homophobia and transphobia normal? Were pervasive surveillance and policing of Black and Indigenous and people of colour normal? Yes, I suppose all of that was normal. But, I and many other people hate that normal...that awful normal that is narrativized as minor injustices, or social ills that would get better if some of us waited, if we had the patience to bear it, if we had noticed and were grateful for the minuscule "progress." (para. 2)

Indeed, the years of the pandemic brought into stark visibility that the forces that both structured and exacerbated the normal were located in the logic of racial capitalism. The difficulties we experienced were not simply located in the unanticipated crisis posed by COVID-19 but due to the salient characteristics of our social world. The consequences of the pandemic on our academic work were embedded in the logic of neoliberal restructuring of academic work—a logic that was based on the erosion of funding to public education and that allowed for opportunities for ed-tech. The response to the pandemic of racism made visible the ways in which responses to racism within neoliberal universities are contradictory. The ways in which public-health offices responded to the risk of infection exposed not only the way in which racialized discourses shaped public health but as importantly the lack of resources to ensure workplaces were safe, exposing the ways in which "essential" workers are fungible.

The authors in *Unmasking Academia* offer crucial insights into the ways in which racial capitalism shaped experiences with the pandemic. Importantly, this collection exposes both the endoskeletons of the normal, as well as the ways the normal was exacerbated. Moreover, as Shankar and Mason point out, "returning to normal" is not possible—not simply because the normal is characteristic of racial capitalism. As they eloquently remind us, for those who experience long COVID, the normal is not possible. And as importantly, academia continues to face neoliberal restructuring, as the pressures to increase our productivity, in research, service, and through teaching larger classes, have been intensified. In Ontario, a crisis in funding to higher education has led to the elimination of much of the work carried out by part-time instructors, as underpaid and precarious as they were. Many of the part-time instructors are now unemployed. And, with the continued rise of the alt-right, and the genocide in Palestine, the normalization of racism and colonialism is clearly exacerbated.

Importantly, this collection also offers crucial insights into the ways we have resisted racial capitalism—insights that allow us to think through how to continue to challenge it. As Shankar and Mason eloquently argue, the pandemic offered a moment of reckoning for both academia and our social world. The contributors document the ways scholars and students resisted racial capitalism—through their survival tactics, rethinking ways of teaching, service and research, by establishing new social relations with each other, with students, and with communities. In doing so, these contributions offer vital re-imaginings of our social world. Such visions, in the words of Shankar and Mason, provide a blueprint for decolonizing the institution of the university, and indeed a portal into transforming our social world. Thus, *Unmasking Academia* not only provides a rare analysis of the ways the pandemic impacted academia but also crucial insights into the impacts and legacies of the pandemic on our social world.

Notes

1. These calculations employed mortality data reported in Canadian newspapers and public-health reports between 2020 and 2022. Sporadically these sources would report the numbers of deaths for those working in nursing homes, health care, sometimes factories, meatpacking plants, and warehouses. These numbers were aggregated and then compared to overall mortality figures for the same period. These calculations underrepresented the role of the workplace. Notably, public-health reports contained more accurate figures of death for those who resided in nursing homes—and as these clearly did not refer to essential workers these numbers were taken out of the overall mortality figures.
2. The normal support for developing an online course includes one to two course releases, twelve to eighteen months of preparation time, and the help of three staff members—one of whom is an online learning consultant, and each of whom supports only about two other courses. Instead, at universities across Canada, the move online under COVID-19 is not called "online teaching" but "remote teaching," which universities seem to think absolves them of the responsibility to give faculty sufficient technological training, pedagogical consultation, and preparation time (Brabazon, 2021).
3. Klein (2007) points to how evoking "crises" allows for states and corporations to entrench neoliberal reforms—including suspending normative decision-making processes.
4. Not only has the proportion of both racialized and white women in the paid workforce grown sharply, dual-parent households have become a small proportion of households, as single-parent households and the percentage of adults living alone have grown (Salzinger, 2022).

References

Alcoff, L.M. (2024). The roots (and routes) of the epistemology of ignorance. *Critical Review of International Social and Political Philosophy*, 27(1), 9–28. https://philpapers.org/rec/ALCTRA

Brabazon, H. (2021, April 29). The academy's neoliberal response to COVID-19: Why faculty should be wary and how we can push back. *Academic Matters*. https://academicmatters.ca/the-academys-neoliberal-response-to-covid-19-why-faculty-should-be-wary-and-how-we-can-push-back/

Brand, D. (2020, July 4). On narrative, reckoning and the calculus of living and dying. *Toronto Star*. https://www.thestar.com/entertainment/books/2020/07/04/dionne-brand-on-narrative-reckoning-and-the-calculus-of-living-and-dying.html

Canadian Association of University Teachers (CAUT). (2020). *COVID-19 and the academic workplace—Resources for members*. https://www.caut.ca/content/covid-19-and-academic-workplace-resources-members

Canadian Centre for Policy Alternatives (CCPA). (2006). *Commercialism in Canadian schools: Who's calling the shots?* https://policyalternatives.ca/publications/reports/commercialism-canadian-schools

Chatterjee, S. (2021, April 29). Care work during COVID: A letter from home about privilege, resilience, and capitalism in the academy. *Academic Matters*. https://

academicmatters.ca/care-work-during-covid-a-letter-from-home-about-privilege-resilience-and-capitalism-in-the-academy-2/

Connell, R. (2013). The neoliberal cascade and education: An essay on the market agenda and its consequences. *Critical Studies in Education, 54*(2), 99–112.

Dua, E. (1999). Beyond diversity: Exploring the ways in which the discourse of race has shaped the institution of the nuclear family. In E. Dua & A. Robertson (Eds.), *Scratching the surface: Canadian anti-racist feminist thought* (pp. 237–260). Women's Press.

Dua, E. (2023). Colonialism: Interrogating the sociological understanding of the emergence of capitalism. In J. Jean-Pierre, V. Watts, C.E. James, P. Albanese, X. Chen, & M. Graydon (Eds.), *Reading sociology: Decolonizing Canada*. Oxford University Press.

Editorial board. (2020, May 31). America's willful ignorance about Black lives. *Boston Globe*. https://www.bostonglobe.com/2020/05/31/opinion/americas-willful-ignorance-about-black-lives/

Farhadi, B. (2019). *The sky's the limit: On the impossible promise of e-learning in the Toronto District School Board*. [Doctoral dissertation, University of Toronto]. https://tspace.library.utoronto.ca/handle/1807/9744

Gordon-Bouvier, E. (2021). Vulnerable bodies and invisible work: The Covid-19 pandemic and social reproduction. *International Journal of Discrimination and the Law, 21*(3), 212–229. https://doi.org/10.1177/13582291211031371

Green, K. (2020, April 27). *"This virus was not made by us": Filipino employees say they face discrimination after Cargill COVID-19 outbreak*. CTV News. https://calgary.ctvnews.ca/this-virus-was-not-made-by-us-filipino-employees-say-they-face-discrimination-after-cargill-covid-19-outbreak-1.4914137

Green, M., & Lawson, V. (2011). Recentring care: Interrogating the commodification of care. *Social & Cultural Geography, 12*(6), 639–654. https://doi.org/10.1080/14649365.2011.601262

Gunn, B.L., University of Manitoba, Stuber, J., Meyer, I.H., & Link, B. (n.d.). Ignored to death: Systemic racism in the Canadian healthcare system. In EMRIP the Study on Health, *EMRIP the Study on Health* [Journal-article]. https://www.ohchr.org/sites/default/files/Documents/Issues/IPeoples/EMRIP/Health/UniversityManitoba.pdf

Halwani, S. (2004). Racial inequality in access to health care services. Ontario Human Rights Commission.https://www.ohrc.on.ca/en/race-policy-dialogue-papers/racial-inequality-access-health-care-services

Kirkwood, I. (2020, May 12). Ontario to deploy Kitchener startup's remote learning platform across school districts. *BetaKit*. https://betakit.com/ontario-to-deploy-kitchener-startupsremote-learning-platform-across-school-districts/

Klein, N. (2007). *The shock doctrine: The rise of disaster capitalism*. Knopf Canada.

Kuehn, L., Mathison, S., & Ross, E.W. (2018, June 5). The many faces of privatization. Institute for Public Education, British Columbia. https://instituteforpubliceducation.org/wpcontent/Uploads/2018/06/Many-Faces-of-Privatization-IPEBC-Occasional-Paper-1.pdf

Luxton, M. (2018). The production of life itself: Gender, social reproduction and IPE. In J. Elias and A. Roberts (Eds.), *Handbook on the international political economy of gender* (pp. 37–49). Edward Elgar.

Mahabir, D.F., O'Campo, P., Lofters, A., Shankardass, K., Salmon, C., & Muntaner, C. (2021). Experiences of everyday racism in Toronto's health care system: A concept mapping study. *International Journal for Equity in Health, 20*(article no. 74). https://doi.org/10.1186/s12939-021-01410-9

Marwani, R. (2003). "The island of the unclean": Race, colonialism and "Chinese leprosy" in British Columbia, 1891–1924. *Law, Social Justice & Global Development, 1.* https://warwick.ac.uk/fac/soc/law/elj/lgd/2003_1/mawani/

McCabe, D. (2020, April 3). How tech's lobbyists are using the pandemic to make gains. *The New York Times.* https://www.nytimes.com/2020/04/03/technology/virus-tech-lobbyists-gains.html

McPhail, D., & Orsini, M. (2021). Fat acceptance as social justice. *Canadian Medical Association Journal (CMAJ), 193*(35), E1398–E1399. https://doi.org/10.1503/cmaj.210772

McQueen, C. (2022, August 24). Work-life balance has been decimated during the pandemic—can we get it back? *The Globe and Mail.* https://www.theglobeandmail.com/business/article-work-life-balance-has-been-decimated-during-the-pandemic-can-we-get-it/

Michigan Department of Human Rights. (2020, June 3). *Michigan Civil Rights Commission issues statement on killing of George Floyd and protests against police brutality.* https://www.michigan.gov/mdcr/news/releases/2020/06/03/statement-george-floyd

Miller, M. (2020). Ontario school boards aren't getting new money to purchase free iPads for students. *BlogTO.* https://www.blogto.com/city/2020/04/ontario-government-wont-begiving-new-free-ipads-students-after-all/

Mills, C.W. (1997). *The racial contract.* Cornell University Press. http://www.jstor.org/stable/10.7591/j.ctt5hh1wj

Mills, C.W. (1998). *Blackness visible: Essays on philosophy and race.* Cornell University Press.

Minor, M. (2020, June 8). Enough is enough: Stop the ignorance. *Forbes.* https://www.forbes.com/sites/mariaminor/2020/06/08/enough-is-enough-stop-the-ignorance/

Moore, S.D.M., Jayme, B.D.O., & Black, J. (2021). Disaster capitalism, rampant edtech opportunism, and the advancement of online learning in the era of COVID19. *Critical Education, 12*(2), 1–21.

Neal, D. (2022). *An empirical analysis of white racial ignorance in the wake of George Floyd.* [Master's thesis, University of Florida].

Nestel, S. (2012). Colour coded health care: The impact of race and racism on Canadians' health. The Wellesley Institute. https://www.wellesleyinstitute.com/wp-content/uploads/2012/02/Colour-Coded-Health-Care-Sheryl-Nestel.pdf

Public Health Ontario. (June 2020). *Collecting race, income, household size and language data.* https://www.publichealthontario.ca/-/media/documents/ncov/main/2020/06/introducing-race-income-household-size-language-data-collection.pdf?la=en [site discontinued]

Public Service Alliance of Canada. (2020, April 27). Resources on the pandemic: Analysis and action. https://psacunion.ca/resources-pandemic-analysis-and-action

Robinson, C. (1983). *Black Marxism: The making of the black radical tradition.* University of North Carolina Press.

Salzinger, L. (2022). Seeing with the pandemic: Social reproduction in the spotlight. *Feminist Studies*, *47*(3), 492–502. https://escholarship.org/uc/item/32v5r66b

Simpson, N. (2020, June 2). Canada has race-based police violence too: We don't know how much. *The Tyee*. https://thetyee.ca/Analysis/2020/06/02/Canada-Race-Based-Violence/

Smith, P.M., Smith, B.T., Warren, C., Shahidi, F.V., Buchan, S., & Mustard, C. (2021). The prevalence and correlates of workplace infection control practices in Canada between July and September 2020. *Health Reports*, *32*(11), 16–27. https://doi.org/10.25318/82-003-x202101000002-eng

Strings, S. (2020, May 25). It's not obesity. It is slavery. *The New York Times*. https://www.nytimes.com/2020/05/25/opinion/coronavirus-race-obesity.html

Sullivan, S., & Tuana, N. (2007). Introduction. In S. Sullivan & N. Tuana (Eds.), *Race and epistemologies of ignorance* (pp. 1–10). State University of New York Press.

Tate, A.A., & Page, D. (2018). Whiteliness and institutional racism: Hiding behind (un)conscious bias. *Ethics and Education*, *13*(1), 1–15. https://doi.org/10.1080/17449642.2018.1428718

Thobani, S. (Ed). (2021). *Coloniality and racial (in)justice in the university: Counting for nothing?* University of Toronto Press.

Venz, L., & Boettcher, K. (2021). Leading in times of crisis: How perceived COVID-19-related work intensification links to daily e-mail demands and leader outcomes. *Applied Psychology*, *71*(3), 912–934 https://doi.org/10.1111/apps.12357

Williamson, B. (2020, April 1). *New pandemic edtech power networks*. Code Acts in Education. https://codeactsineducation.wordpress.com/2020/04/01/new-pandemic-edtech-powernetworks/

Wooten, M.E., & Branch, E.H. (2012). Defining appropriate labor: Race, gender, and idealization of Black women in domestic service. *Race, Gender & Class*, *19*(3–4), 292–308. http://www.jstor.org/stable/43497500.

WHO chief declares end to COVID-19 as a global health emergency. (2023, May 6). UN News. https://news.un.org/en/story/2023/05/1136367

Contributors

Pallavi Banerjee is Associate Professor in the Department of Sociology at the University of Calgary and a UCalgary Research Excellence Chair. Her research is situated at the intersections of immigration, gender, families, unpaid and paid labour, intersectionality, and transnationalism. She is the author of the award-winning book *The Opportunity Trap: High-Skilled Workers, Indian Families and the Failures of Dependent-Visa Policy* (New York University Press, 2022). She directs the Critical Gender, Intersectionality and Migration Research Group at the University of Calgary, and her research is supported by SSHRC and Immigration, Refugees and Citizenship Canada (IRCC).

Sepideh Borzoo is a postdoctoral fellow at Toronto Metropolitan University. Her research is motivated by her understanding of gender and race as organizing structures of work experience that act in conjunction with class and immigration status. Her research spans the areas of immigrant labour, institutional inequality, work and organization, intersectional feminism, racialization, and embodiment.

Enakshi Dua is Full Professor in the School of Gender, Sexuality, and Women's Studies at York University. She has published extensively on theorizing racism and anti-racism, racism in Canadian universities, equity policies and anti-racism policies, the racialized and gendered histories of immigration processes, and the racialization of masculinity and femininity. Her notable publications include "Decolonising

Anti-Racism" in *Social Justice; The Equity Myth: Racialization and Indigeneity at Canadian Universities*; "Our Canadian Culture Has Been Squeamish About Gathering Race-Based Statistics" in *Coloniality and Racial (In)Justice in the University*; "'When You Hear or See Something Wrong It's Up to Everyone to Let People Know': Homonationalism and the Reconstitution of 'White' Heteronormative Masculinity" in *The Palgrave Handbook of Critical Race and Gender*; and "When Home and Harem Collide: The 'Hindu Women's Question': A Mass Spectacle of the Canadian Nation, Family, and Modernity" in *Unmooring the Komagata Maru*. She has more than thirty years of experience in feminist, anti-racist, and equity work. She has held a number of administrative positions.

Isabel Fandino is an international student support advisor with International Student Services at the University of Calgary. She directly assists international students and their families in their transition to Canadian higher education and supports students with immigration matters. Isabel received a master's degree in Sociology from the University of Calgary and is a Regulated International Student Immigration Adviser (RISIA). Her research interests are international students, immigration, gender, and qualitative methods.

Leah K. Hamilton is Vice Dean, Research and Community Relations, and Professor of Organizational Behaviour in the Faculty of Business, Communication Studies, and Aviation at Mount Royal University. She is a community-engaged scholar who works with newcomer communities and 2SLGBTQIA+ communities to better understand the impacts of policies and programs. She also researches public attitudes toward immigrants, 2SLGBTQIA+ communities, and other equity-deserving groups. Her research is funded by SSHRC.

Carl E. James holds the Jean Augustine Chair in Education, Community, and Diaspora in the Faculty of Education at York University. He studies how institutional policies, programs, and practices structure the social, economic, cultural, judicial, political, and health conditions in which race—intersecting with ethnicity, gender, class, generational status, etc.—and racialization operate in shaping the educational opportunities, academic performance, and social achievement of students and Canadians generally. His most recent publications include: *Colour Matters: Essays on the Experiences, Education, and Pursuits of Black Youth*; and with Leanne Taylor, *First-Generation Student Experiences in Higher Education*.

Hee-Jung S. Joo is Professor in the Department of English, Theatre, Film, and Media at the University of Manitoba. Her research and teaching interests include speculative fiction by writers of colour, critical race theory, and queer theory. Locally, she is a member of Prairie Asian Organizers! (PAO!) and the Prison Libraries Committee (PLC).

Erin Keating is Associate Professor and Graduate Chair in the Department of English, Theatre, Film, and Media at the University of Manitoba and Associate Editor of the journal *Restoration: Studies in Literature and Culture*. Her areas of research are Restoration secret history, theatre and affect, celebrity, and contemporary fantasy fiction and comics. Her commitment to accessible and engaged pedagogy has been recognized with the Olive Beatrice Stanton Award for Excellence in Teaching (2020), the Merit Award for Teaching (2020), and the Arts Award for Excellence on Teaching—New Faculty (2018).

Corinne L. Mason is Professor of Women's and Gender Studies at Mount Royal University. Their current research program is inspired by two central curiosities: i) the institutionalization of feminist and queer logics in higher education and ii) queer kinship and parenting. They are currently writing a book entitled *Reproduction in Crisis* and are the author of *Manufacturing Urgency: Violence Against Women and the Development Industry* (University of Regina Press, 2017) and the editor of *Routledge Handbook of Queer Development Studies* (Routledge, 2018). Corinne serves on the Editorial Board for *Atlantis: Critical Studies in Gender, Culture & Social Justice* and is the co-chair of the association for Women's, Gender and Social Justice.

Ayesha Mian Akram (she/her) is Assistant Professor (teaching) in the Department of Sociology at the University of Calgary. She is an educator and community-based researcher whose work is rooted in the intersections of critical Muslim studies, sociology of racialization, transnational feminist theories, and emergent qualitative research methodologies. She obtained her PHD in Sociology/Social Justice from the University of Windsor where her SSHRC-funded doctoral research explored Muslim women's community-building and the politics of resistance through wellness and care.

Nardos Omer is a Grade 7 teacher in the River East Transcona School Division and an alumna of the University of Manitoba. Her professional interests include assessment practices, classroom management strategies, and early literacy education. Her teaching philosophy centres on fostering a positive and inclusive learning environment.

Fawziah Rabiah-Mohammed is a faculty member in the Community Nursing & Healthcare, Nursing College, Umm Al-Qura University, Makkah, Saudi Arabia. Fawziah is a registered nurse in Saudi Arabia. Her primary research interest is in the area of health-system and social inequalities in disadvantaged populations, with an emphasis on mental health and well-being.

Irene Shankar is Professor in the Department of Sociology and Anthropology at Mount Royal University. Dr. Shankar's scholarship and teaching are centred on examining the complex intersections of marginalization and inequality within society. Her areas of research and teaching include feminist theories, sociology of gender, critical race theory, qualitative methodology, and the sociology of health and illness. Dr. Shankar's utilization of her critical scholarship to inspire activism and change has resulted in numerous commendations for her leadership in both teaching and research, such as the MRU Distinguished Faculty Award and the Faculty of Arts Outstanding Researcher Award. She has published widely on issues of gendered violence, medical sociology, and inequity within post-secondary institutions.

Carieta Thomas is Assistant Professor in the Department of Sociology and Anthropology at Carleton University. Her areas of research include intersectionality, race, care work, immigration, and technologies of surveillance. Her doctoral research connected her immigration-law background and Pan-African critical perspective with the sociology of care work. It used intersectionality theory to compare how surveillance in the form of pre-employment screening impacts the lives and employment choices of undocumented Caribbean women care workers in Canada and the United States. Within a context of increased nativism, her research centres Black immigrants, who are underrepresented in immigration scholarship and policy.

Ethel Tungohan is Associate Professor of Politics at York University and a Canada Research Chair in Canadian Migration Policy, Impacts, and Activism. Her work looks at immigration policy and social movements, frequently using socially engaged research methods. Her collaborative projects with grassroots migrant communities explore the effects of policies on migrants' lived experiences. In her free time, Ethel, along with Dr. Nisha Nath and Wayne Chu, produces *Academic Aunties*, a podcast that demystifies academic norms for racialized communities and other underrepresented groups in the academy.

Gabrielle Ellen Weasel Head, Tsapinaaki, is a member of Kainai, part of the Blackfoot Confederacy. An Associate Professor in Indigenous Studies with Mount Royal University, her teaching background includes instructing on topics around Indigenous history and current issues, Indigenous Studies (Canadian and International perspectives), and Indigenous research methods and ethics. Research interests include meaningful assessment in higher education, Indigenous homelessness, intercultural parallels in teaching and learning research, Indigenous lived experience of resilience, Indigenous community-based research, parenting assessment tools, reform in child welfare, anti-colonial theory, and anti-racist pedagogy.

www.ingramcontent.com/pod-product-compliance
Ingram Content Group UK Ltd.
Pitfield, Milton Keynes, MK11 3LW, UK
UKHW012207031225
465679UK00004B/227